Charles Woodruff Shields

The United Church of the United States

Charles Woodruff Shields

The United Church of the United States

ISBN/EAN: 9783337261870

Printed in Europe, USA, Canada, Australia, Japan

Cover: Foto ©Lupo / pixelio.de

More available books at **www.hansebooks.com**

THE UNITED CHURCH
OF THE
UNITED STATES

THE UNITED CHURCH

OF THE

UNITED STATES

BY

CHARLES WOODRUFF SHIELDS
PROFESSOR IN PRINCETON UNIVERSITY

NEW YORK
CHARLES SCRIBNER'S SONS
1895

TO THE

CATHOLIC UNITY CIRCLE

COMPRISING THE REVEREND DOCTORS

EDWARD ABBOTT
DAVID NELSON BEACH
GEORGE DANA BOARDMAN
AMORY H. BRADFORD
CHARLES AUGUSTUS BRIGGS

EDWARD B. COE
CHARLES CUTHBERT HALL
WILLIAM REED HUNTINGTON
WM. CHAUNCY LANGDON
HENRY Y. SATTERLEE

THESE COLLECTED ESSAYS ARE INSCRIBED

WITH THE BROTHERLY LOVE OF

THE AUTHOR.

PREFACE.

It has been becoming evident to many thoughtful observers that the chief Christian problem of our age is the Reunion of Christendom, and that the most favorable conditions for its solution are found in this New World, where the churches and denominations of the Old World have become compacted together within a new political environment, yet with perfect freedom of action and intercourse. The growth of public interest in the question during the past ten years has been surprising. If the present volume have no higher value, it may serve to mark the course of opinion in this new direction, and to afford some outlook for the future. It contains the results not only of private study, but of conference with representative thinkers holding all the possible views in respect to the problem of American Church Unity.

The interest of the writer in the subject dates as far back as the year 1862, when he published a Manual of Worship in the United States Army and Navy, compiled from ancient liturgies and modern formularies, and jointly recommended by eminent clergymen of all denominations. This was followed in 1864 by his edition of the Book of Common Prayer, as amended by the Presbyterian Divines in the Royal Commission of 1661, and as designed, with other more special objects, "to increase the spirit of catholicity and fraternity among such Churches of the Reformation as originally contributed to the formation of the Prayer-book, by restoring to more general use those liturgical formulas which are their several production or common inheritance and, next to the Holy Scriptures, the closest visible bonds of their unity." Some results of his studies at that time were embodied in an essay which, after awaiting a ripened state of public interest for twenty years, at length appeared in the *Century Magazine* of 1885, under the title of "The United Churches of the United States," and at once drew forth a wide discussion from leading divines in different denominations. Together with that discussion, it forms the first part of this collection of papers. As belonging to the early history of the question it is presented without amendment, although some expressions and suggestions have already been made obsolete by the rapid progress of opinion.

In the following year the House of Bishops of the Protestant Episcopal Church at Chicago issued the proposals, afterward amended by the Lambeth Conference of 1888, and now known as the Quadrilateral or Four Articles of Church Unity. The author has advocated these articles in a paper read before various circles of representative divines in New York, Boston, Philadelphia, Baltimore, and Washington, and before several public assemblies, after introductory addresses by President Seth Low, of Columbia College; by President Daniel Gilman, of the Johns Hopkins University, and by the Hon. Justice William Strong, of the United States Supreme Court. It is here reproduced, with a review of some of the valuable opinions to which it gave expression.

The other essays refer to different practical aspects of the question as still under discussion; and two essays have been added, which are designed to illustrate the unifying value of the English liturgy among the Christian denominations, and the momentous importance of church unity as a Sociological Question.

The periodical press has been furnishing us with various symposia, which at times make church unity look like a bubble or a dream. For some minds even the iridescence is gone. But other minds only see more plainly that the great problem is not to be solved by the denominational opinions of more or less interested leaders, but rather by a long educational process requiring many years, perhaps successive generations, ere it will come to full effect. To such minds there is not only the promise of Holy Scripture but the logic of Providence in the movement. If there be such a thing as historic cause and effect, the chief historic Churches are already recoiling from their rash extremes toward substantial agreement and re-union. The growth of Church unity in the coming century would be no more marvelous than that of State unity in the past century. In the ecclesiastical as well as political sphere our country seems destined to become the wonder of Christendom, not by renewing its time-worn issues and fighting them over again, but by burying them out of sight forever in one United Church of the United States.

CONTENTS.

I.

THE UNITED CHURCHES OF THE UNITED STATES, ... 1–32
    Organic Unity of Churches.
    Germs of Organic Unity.
    Agreements in Doctrine.
    Agreements in Polity.
    Agreements in Worship.
    Revivalism and Ritualism.
    The Claims of Æstheticism.
    New-made Liturgies.
    Excellence of the English Liturgy.
    Catholicity of the English Liturgy.
    Reaction Toward the English Liturgy.

II.

DENOMINATIONAL VIEWS OF CHURCH UNITY, ... 33–63
    Episcopalian Opinions.
    Presbyterian Opinions.
    Congregationalist Opinions.
    Consensus of these Opinions.
    Signs of Church Unity.
    Proposals of the House of Bishops.
    Historic Relations of Presbytery and Episcopacy.
    Reunion of Presbytery and Episcopacy.
    Advantages of Historic Episcopacy.

III.

THE FOUR ARTICLES OF CHURCH UNITY, ... 65–109
    Church Unity Defined.
    Federation of Churches.
    Assimilation of Denominations.
    False Ecclesiasticism.
    False Denominationalism.
    Feasibility of Church Unity.
    The New Promise of Church Unity.
    The Claim of the Historic Churches.
    The Claim of the Reformed Churches.
    The Need of a Practical Consensus.
    The Chicago and Lambeth Proposals.
    Catholicity of the Four Articles.

x   *Contents.*

Catholicity of the Historic Episcopate.
Adaptability of the Historic Episcopate.
Unifying Power of the Historic Episcopate.
Unification by Confederation.
Unification by Consolidation.
Unification by Organic Growth.
Organic Reunion of Presbytery and Episcopacy.
Ideal Fulfilment of Church Unity.
Slow Growth of Church Unity.
Logical Tendencies to Church Unity.
Decline of the Denominational Spirit.
Revival of the Ecclesiastical Spirit.
Popular Tendencies to Church Unity.
The Coming Campaign of Education.

IV.

PAGE

DENOMINATIONAL VIEWS OF THE QUADRILATERAL, ... 111–13!

Congregational Opinions.
Presbyterial Opinions.
Episcopal Opinions.
Review of the Ecclesiastical Situation.
Favorable Signs.
Unfavorable Signs.

V.

THE QUADRILATERAL STANDARD AMONG THE DENOMINATIONS, . . 135–165

Congregational Denominations.
Presbyterial Denominations.
Episcopal Denominations.
Church Unity Societies.
Catholic Unity Circles.
Studies in the Quadrilateral.
The League of Catholic Unity.

VI.

THE HISTORIC EPISCOPATE AND THE THREE CHURCH POLITIES, . . 167–178

Preliminary Principles.
The Scriptural Episcopate.
The Apostolic Episcopate.
The New Made Episcopate.
Comprehensiveness of the Historic Episcopate.
Its Alleged Hierarchism.
Its Alleged Sacerdotalism.
Studies in the Historic Episcopate.

VII.

THE HISTORIC PRESBYTERATE AND THE HISTORIC EPISCOPATE, . . 179–214

Appeal to Presbyterians and Episcopalians.
Apostolic Succession.
Practical Union by Ignoring the Question.

Gradual Unification.
Pulpit Exchanges.
Presbyterian Orders.
Mutual Recognition.
Hypothetical Ordination.
Concurrent Ordination.
The Hope of Reunion.

VIII.

THE HISTORIC LITURGY AND THE HISTORIC CHURCHES, ... 215-256

Analysis of Prayer Book.
Composition of Daily Offices.
Composition of Communion Office.
Composition of Baptismal Offices.
Composition of the Occasional Offices.
Catholic Formularies.
Protestant Formularies.

IX.

THE SOCIOLOGICAL QUESTION OF CHURCH UNITY, ... 257-285

Early Christian Socialism.
Anti-Christian Socialism.
Spurious Christian Socialism.
Christian Doctrine of Social Distinctions.
Christian Doctrine of Poverty.
Christian Doctrine of Stewardship.
Non-Christian Socialism.
Church and State Socialism.
The Masses and the Classes.
Capitalistic Laborers.
Derangement of Social Classes.
Social Need of Church Unity.
The Church the Great Social Teacher.
The Church the Social Conservator.
The Church the Social Regenerator.
Urgent Need of Church Unity.

I.
THE UNITED CHURCHES OF THE UNITED STATES.

I.

THE UNITED CHURCHES OF THE UNITED STATES.

The associative tendency of the Christian masses has shown itself wherever they could act freely together. In our own country for more than a hundred years there has been a steady effort after religious unity, following the political movement through the successive stages of the colonization, the confederation, the constitution, and the recent consolidation of the United States. During the colonial period the few mission churches scattered along the Atlantic coast were temporarily fused together by the evangelistic labors of Whitefield and Wesley. In the revolutionary war they were simply massed and compacted in the common struggle for civil as well as religious freedom. Since the declaration of Independence we have seen them at first separately organizing themselves, and then spontaneously combining in great common causes, such as the American Bible Society, the American Tract Society, the American Sunday School Union, the American Boards of Domestic and Foreign Missions, as well as the various moral reforms in which they became leagued against vice and infidelity on the platform of their common Christianity. In the late civil war they appeared as one holy phalanx of charity and mercy in the Sanitary and Christian commissions; and at the present time they are interlaced by a network of Young Men's Christian Associations, Inter-Denominational Alliances and Church Congresses, designed to combine them practically in Christian work and intercourse, to say nothing of inter-ecclesiastical councils, based upon organic bonds of unity between kindred churches.

It is true that all such compacts, being temporary expedients, as fast as they serve their purposes must decay and disappear; and it is also true that in some cases the dissolution of a league of churches has been followed by their seeming recoil and reassertion of sectarian peculiarities in more pronounced form than ever, as may now be seen in the various boards of charity and missions maintained by the different denominations. But it will be found, at the same time, that another set of causes has been tending, if not to bring them together again in closer bonds and on a more enduring basis, yet at least to reveal to them, more and more clearly, the ultimate grounds of a true organic unity.

Organic Unity of Churches.

By the organic unity of churches is here meant such unity as inheres in their internal organization, and is traceable in their forms of doctrine, government, and worship, as well as in their whole historic life and development; and is not, therefore, due to any mere artificial arrangement or conscious effort. Institutions are not made, but grow; and sometimes they grow so slowly that one generation rejects as irrational and visionary what the next generation accepts as the logic of events. Whole churches, as well as states, have thus been reasoned out of the divine right of English monarchy and American slavery; and it is safe to assume that any scheme of ecclesiastical union which could now be devised, even though the true one, would be repudiated, perhaps by all existing denominations, as involving the suppression of some essential truth or the sacrifice of some valuable principle. We are not yet ready for such schemes, and it would only be a waste of time to discuss them. The first lesson to be learned is, that the unification of the American churches, if it is ever to come at all, cannot be precipitated by platforms, coalitions, compromises, in short by any mere external association of the different denominations, which leaves them still without internal modification and vital connection, as true and living branches of the Vine of Christ.

How then is such organic unity or union ever to be reached? Perhaps we can trace a rough likeness between the case of the American churches at the present time and that of the American states at the close of the revolution. The articles of confederation had proved a rope of sand. The colonies, in becoming independent of the British crown, had also become independent of one another, and with their diverse creeds, institutions, races, and climates seemed on the verge of anarchy. It was not until they had surrendered some of their sovereign attributes and readjusted their whole domestic polity, that they could come into the more perfect union of the constitution; and ever since then they have been racked with internal conflicts, until at last welded together by the fiery blows of civil war. In like manner the different denominations, after having been loosely confederated in various compacts and alliances, are falling apart in fresh estrangement, wasting their resources in mere propagandism, and often wrangling over time-worn theological issues in the face of their common foes. And now, it is thought by some, they can only be driven together again by the rod of persecution. The peace of Westphalia, they will tell us, was but a truce, and the warfare once waged between the Catholic and Protestant powers of Europe is yet to be decided by some terrible intestine struggle within our own borders, fulfilling the great Armageddon of the Apocalypse. With the sects thus cast into the furnace of affliction, to be purged of their errors, and melted and molded to one likeness, the church militant is at length to come forth from the ordeal united and triumphant.

GERMS OF ORGANIC UNITY.

We need not, however, push a mere political analogy so far. Rather may we hope that the age of religious wars is past, and that any remaining issues between religious parties are to be fought out, not with carnal weapons, but with spiritual. Certainly, the American churches have at least gained all the freedom that they need. Free of the state and free of one another, they may now peacefully work out their respective missions without let or hindrance. But while thus left to the combined action of Providential events and spiritual causes, it is inevitable that in the long future they will undergo much modification, perhaps gradual assimilation to each other, or to some one divine model toward which they are tending. Despite their present divided and distracted appearance, if we will survey them from a high outside point of view, in a Christian philosophical mood, we shall discern amongst them vast unifying tendencies which have been operating quietly through successive generations, and which can only be measured by comparing one period of their history with another. We can no more control such tendencies than we can control the winds of heaven. It is the part of wisdom to recognize them and shape our course by means of them. We need not forsake our respective positions; we cannot force an immediate harmony of views; but at least we may profitably engage in a study of the existing germs or grounds of organic unity in the American churches.

In entering upon this study, whatever theories of the church we may severally hold, we should lay aside even just prejudices, so far as to take into view impartially the various Christian bodies claiming an ecclesiastical title and jurisdiction, which are co-extensive with the nation, or which may be otherwise due them in courtesy. Such are the "Evangelical Lutheran Church in North America," (Northern and Southern); the "Presbyterian Church in the United States" (Northern and Southern); the "Protestant Episcopal Church in the United States;" the "Reformed Church in America" (Dutch), the "Reformed Church in the United States" (German); the "Roman Catholic Church," the "United Brethren" (German and Moravian), the "United Presbyterian Church of America," the "Universalist Church in the United States," the "Baptist Churches" (Calvinistic and Arminian), the "Congregational Churches" (Trinitarian), the "Disciples of Christ" (Campbellite), the "Society of Friends," the "Unitarian Churches." Some of these bodies, and others which might have been named, are inconsiderable in numbers and influence, and not likely to play any chief part in the development of American Christianity. Confining our attention to the great Christian denominations of the country, we may fairly concede to them the possession of ecclesiastical elements more or less perfectly organized; and our task will be to look into their respective forms of doctrine, of polity, and of worship, in search of the three corresponding grounds of unity which are afforded by their dogmatic agreement, their ecclesiastical or political likeness, and their liturgical culture.

AGREEMENTS IN DOCTRINE.

The first of these three grounds of unity is the least hopeful. Perfect consent in theological views, were it attained between the different denominations, might indeed issue in their perfect union, if not in their homogeneous organization, since among other doctrines it would include the same doctrine of church polity; but it may be doubted if such consent is in the nature of the case attainable. Doctrinal distinctions are largely due to the paradoxical relations of essential truths which are alike derived from Holy Scripture, as well as to original diversities in human nature which are alike legitimate. Accordingly, they appeared among the Apostles themselves in the two schools of St. Paul and St. Peter; they were renewed among the church-fathers by Augustine and Pelagius; they were reaffirmed among the schoolmen by Thomas Aquinas and Dun Scotus; they were emphasized among the reformers by Calvin and Arminius; they were early transferred to our own churches by Whitefield and Wesley, and have since spread with enormous growth over the whole continent; and they are likely to continue in some form until the end of the world.

If history teaches anything plainly, it shows that the attempt to organize churches on the basis of mere dogmatic distinctions will always tend to schism rather than unity. They often exclude more true Christians than they include, and sooner or later go to pieces in some fresh dissension. And even more difficult would it be to connect together conflicting churches on such a basis. It is certain that none of the leading Protestant confessions, not the Augsburg, not the Belgic or Heidelberg, not the Westminster, not the Thirty-nine Articles would now be generally accepted by the American churches. It is doubtful if any of the great Catholic creeds, the Athanasian, the Nicene, or even the Apostles' Creed, would afford a platform broad enough to embrace all the denominations calling themselves Christian. And still less could they be marshaled together by any of the new-made creeds of our own time and country.

Nor can it be said that such attempts as have hitherto been made at a dogmatic confederation of churches have been very successful or promising. The Evangelical Alliance of Protestant churches, though based upon a partial consent in doctrine, took a polemical attitude by its very name against the Roman Catholic Church. The proposed league of the Protestant Episcopal and Russian Greek churches would have excluded all the other Protestant churches, besides covertly involving the gravest doctrinal differences. Even the Presbyterian churches in their late general council could not reach a consensus of their own kindred standards. The Congregational churches, discarding all the old creeds, are engaged in framing a new one. And other large family groups of churches, such as the Baptist and the Methodist, show but few signs of either agreeing among themselves or seeking agreement with the rest of the American churches.

To see how complex is the problem before us, we should need only to bring together the various creeds and confessions for comparison and contrast, and arrange them in their degrees of difference between the extremes of Catholicism and Protestantism. It would be found, at the first view, that the points of variance are simply endless, embracing a variety of opinions upon numerous questions in every department of sacred science, theology, anthropology, christology, soteriology, ecclesiology, eschatology. On closer examination we would see that the two extremes of Unitarianism and Romanism, in their latest outcome, would utterly refuse to coalesce, consenting in nothing but the few articles of natural religion which Christianity has in common with Judaism and Paganism. Next, we would find that between these extremes the chief evangelical confessions, whilst agreeing with the Roman Catholic creeds in some essential doctrines, such as the trinity, the incarnation, the atonement, disagree with them in others no less essential, and still further disagree among themselves by all the differences known to Lutheranism, Calvinism, Arminianism. Then, we would discover that the Lutheran, Calvinistic, and Arminian confessions, though largely consentient as to the chief essential doctrines termed evangelical, are most widely dissentient as to some relatively non-essential doctrines, such as are held by Episcopalians, Presbyterians, and Congregationalists. And, lastly we would see that it is precisely some one of these non-essential doctrines which each denomination puts in the front as its standard, claims as the source of its life and the only reason for its existence, and often cherishes as an inherited faith, hallowed by the blood of martyrs and endeared by all the associations of home and kindred. In a word, the concords of American creeds would be so drowned and lost in their discords as to leave us hopeless of anything like a true doctrinal harmony.

From this showing of the case, it is plain that the utmost

we can hope for is some ultimate consensus which cannot now be formulated into a common creed of the churches, but must be largely matter of surmise and speculation. We may assume, not unreasonably, that it will exhibit the essential faith in distinction from the non-essential, and exalt the great things in which Christians agree above the small things in which they differ; and we may expect, on good grounds, that in the course of its evolution some dogmas will be sloughed off as erroneous, others reduced to a relative importance, and still others left indifferent. But we cannot hope to see it start forth at one blow as a feat of logic by some ambitious peacemaker, or even carefully wrought out as a piece of legislative wisdom by some advanced body of divines met to adjust the disputes of Christendom. Rather must we look forward to it as to a coming survival of truth over error, to be slowly evolved from the present conflict of opinion, in the general progress of Christian knowledge, and through a growing spirit of Christian freedom, charity, tolerance, and catholicity.

It is a cheering remark of Dr. Schaff, at the close of his survey of the creeds of Christendom, "That the age of separation and division is passing away, and the age of the reunion of a divided Christendom is beginning to dawn." Glance at some of the grounds of this inspiring hope here in our country. In the first place, we should not overlook the doctrinal agreement already known and expressed, such as the consent of the Roman Catholic and some Protestant churches in the Athanasian, Nicene, and Apostles' creeds; the consent of the Lutheran and Moravian churches in the Augsburg confession; the consent of the various Episcopal churches, the Protestant, the Methodist, the Reformed, in the Thirty-Nine Articles; the consent of the Congregational, the Baptist, and the various Presbyterian churches in the Westminster Standards, together with the indorsement by the reunited Presbyterian Church of the Heidelberg catechism of the Dutch and German Reformed churches. In the second place we may find some tendencies to a doctrinal agreement between these different groups of churches,—in their American revisions of these various standards which show, now and then, a slight though unsought mutual approximation; in their fraternal intercourse, which always brings into view a large latent consent in the great evangelical doctrines of our common Christianity; in their very controversies, which often serve only to show how trifling is their dissensus as compared with their fundamental consensus; and even in their heretical departures, which sometimes express that consensus with a primitive simplicity free from the scholastic technicality of the old creeds, whilst their pulpit expositions of it are ever setting it forth with scriptural freedom, freshness and power. And lastly, we may everywhere discern the signs of a waning interest in the mere dogmatic distinctions, which have long hindered the growth and assertion of a true doctrinal agreement,—such as the decline of theological controversy in the New England churches, the disappearance of the old and new schools in the reunited Presbyterian Church; the comprehension of doctrinal differences within the Episcopal church, and the rise of Broad Church parties in other churches; the spread of open communion in the Baptist churches; the liberty of preaching in the Methodist church; the allowance of heretical departures in many churches up to the point of scandal; the searching revision of creeds in the light of modern thought and science; the disuse of the old scholastic catechisms, the decay of polemic preaching, and the growing preference for evangelical themes of a moral and practical purport. Through the silent action of such causes, it may yet happen in some distant future, not indeed that all dogmas shall be obliterated, but subordinated and graduated in harmony with the one universal faith. Even now, could the American churches, leaving their existing standards unchanged, be simply confederated in a formal profession of the Nicene or Apostles' Creed,[1] in which most of them might

---

[1] This suggestion was published two years before the Episcopal Declarations at Chicago and Lambeth, proposing these two creeds as doctrinal bases of Church Unity.

readily join, their denominational dogmas would at once sink toward a proper relative value, their essential consensus would begin to emerge into view, and so far forth they would appear to the world as the United Churches of the United States.

Agreements in Polity.

The second and more hopeful ground of unity is that of ecclesiastical likeness or affinity in church government. The problem is no longer to produce agreement as to the whole mass of dogmas, but only a single doctrine or set of doctrines of minor importance except when made by some extreme view to involve other more essential doctrines. And it would seem easier to secure external attachment to an ecclesiastical polity than internal unanimity in all the endless points of theological science. Experience has shown that Christians who agree in scarcely anything else may hold the same views of church government and even dwell together in the same organization. The church has often included different schools of theology, but no school of theology ever yet included the whole church. Indeed it is a common reproach of Protestantism that in its grand effort for freedom and progress, it has given birth to a medley of jarring sects, by exaggerating doctrinal differences which had been allowed and adjusted within the pale of the church from the Apostles' time until the Reformation. And that such outward ecclesiastical unity may be more than the mere enforced uniformity or feigned conformity, so often charged against State churches, might be proved by examples in free churches where no political restraints have been imposed. Even conflicting churches, the most unlike in their dogmatic standards, Lutheran, Calvinistic, Arminian, Socinian, may be found substantially alike in their ecclesiastical organization.

In order to bring into view these latent affinities of the American churches, we may conveniently group them in three great classes according to their structural likeness: First, Congregational, those which make each local congregation self-governed and independent, such as the Baptist, the

Unitarian, and the Orthodox churches; Second, Presbyterial, those which unite congregations under presbyteries composed of representative clergymen and laymen, such as the Lutheran, the Dutch and German Reformed, and the various Presbyterian churches; Third, Episcopal, those which subordinate both congregations and presbyteries to bishops as a higher order of clergymen, such as the Methodist, the Protestant, and the Reformed Episcopal, the Moravian, and the Roman Catholic churches. It will be seen at a glance that these three classes when viewed together, present a scale rising from the simplest to the most complex forms of polity, and on closer inspection it would be found that each higher class includes the lower with more or less modification, Presbyterian churches being not without Congregational elements and Episcopal churches being not without Presbyterial elements.

Nor can it be said that some organic union of these more or less kindred organizations would be wholly beyond analogy and precedent. In less than two hundred years the world has seen a medley of incongruous polities, theocratic, monarchic, democratic, aristocratic, grow up into that cluster of homogeneous republics known as the United States, by a series of transforming events,—first by the ascendancy of the Protestant over the Catholic powers in North America, then by the revolutionary destruction of the royal and proprietary charters in the colonies, and at last by a vindicated constitution forever guaranteeing the freedom of states, classes, and races. And so complete a political metamorphosis could not but affect the religious bodies which have been more or less involved in it. Freed thereby from the papal supremacy, from a foreign establishment, and from all connection with our own government, they were at the same time freed from the causes which once drove them asunder, and brought under the causes which have since drawn them together. Not only has each group of kindred churches been fraternizing and coalescing; Congregational with Congregational; Presbyterial with Presbyterial; Episcopal with Episcopal; but the different groups have been growing like each other, in their structure as well as in their aim and spirit. Congregational churches, no longer in conflict with a Presbyterian parliament and monarchy, have themselves been becoming Presbyterial, with their series of representative associations, consociations, conferences, and councils, and their facile combination with Presbyterian bodies in fit emergencies. Presbyterial churches, delivered from a prelatical peerage as well as from state patronage, have been allowing Congregational freedom in their parishes and adopting Episcopal elements in their overseeing boards, agencies, and secretaryships, as well as becoming pervaded with churchly tendencies. Episcopal churches, freed from royal control and left wholly self-dependent, have been admitting Presbyterial deputies, clerical and lay, into their diocesan conventions and standing committees, and otherwise curtailing the extraneous powers of the episcopate; whilst some churchmen have almost stript it of doctrinal significance and left it with a mere expediential or political value, as a sort of Episcopal Presbyterianism or so-called Congregationalism tinctured with Episcopacy. Reformed Episcopalians interpret the Ordinal in the sense of the early Presbyterian school of Archbishop Usher. Methodist Episcopalians also hold to an Episcopacy without apostolic succession, and have adopted lay-representation as well as lay-preaching in their administrative policy. The Moravians practically tend to a kind of Presbyterian Episcopacy. Even the Roman Catholics, at the late Plenary Council, seem to have taken the first step toward bringing their Episcopal system into formative contact with republican institutions. At the same time the average American lay-man has a growing dislike of hierarchical orders and exclusive pretensions. With the exception of the Anglican and Roman Catholic churchmen who claim a divine right and special grace in their own ministry, the chief Christian bodies have been fast becoming congruous in polity as well as consentient in doctrine.

It is conceivable that these assimilative changes may go on, together with lessening dogmatic differences, until all existing ecclesiastical distinctions shall have become more superficial than fundamental, more nominal than real, if not themselves be merged in some comprehensive polity which shall be at once Congregational, Presbyterial, and Episcopal, and wherein Protestant freedom and intelligence shall appear reconciled with Catholic order and authority. Already, indeed, were it possible for the leading denominations to give visible expression to their own hidden structural unity by acts of mutual recognition, organic connection, and coöperative charity, like the scattered bones which Ezekiel saw coming together into a great army, they would at once start into new life and activity as the United Churches of the United States.

Hitherto we may seem to have been investigating grounds of unity which are obscure and only lead out into a visionary future; but the one still to be considered—liturgical culture—belongs to our own time, and calls for practical thought and action.

AGREEMENTS IN WORSHIP.

It would seem that the first step toward true church unity must be liturgical rather than doctrinal or strictly ecclesiastical. Christians who differ cannot begin to agree until they come together in the region of devout feeling and are thus predisposed to brotherly concord. Hence it was amid the Pentecostal fervors in the early church that all divisions of race, language, lineage, sect and party became for the time effaced, and ever since then it has been found that in the fire of true devotion the sternest sectarian feuds melt away and are forgotten. People of all creeds, Calvinists, Arminians, Episcopalians, Presbyterians, Baptists, Methodists, can and do unite in performing the same acts of worship, in observing the same sacraments, and in commemorating the same religious events. And such devotions are not confined to times and scenes of revival excitement. When they have become expressed liturgically in time-hallowed hymns and prayers which breathe the common Christian heart of all ages, in significant rites and emblems which set forth the essential Christian faith in all churches, and in annual festivals which thrill the whole Christian world with the consciousness of great Christian facts and doctrines, there is then afforded a permanent practical communion of saints between different denominations.

It is such a liturgical fusion that has long been going on amongst us, hidden and unnoticed. The great historical churches, whose doctrinal standards have remained fixed for generations and whose ecclesiastical bounds are still jealously guarded, have meanwhile been so modifying their service-books and insensibly so interchanging their modes of worship that now, with scarce a thought of any incongruity, Catholic creeds are recited in Protestant assemblies, Anglican rites are couched in Lutheran forms, Presbyterian prayers are intoned by Episcopalian priests, Wesleyan hymns are sung after Calvinistic sermons, portions of High Mass are chanted by Covenanter choirs, and Puritan meeting-houses are decked with Christmas evergreens and Easter flowers. It is in fact no longer possible to ignore a deep and wide-spread liturgical movement pervading the leading denominations like a groundswell and threatening some day to upheave and bury out of sight the sectarian differences in which the popular mind has ceased to take interest. The general demand, as we are often told by the secular press, is for more of Christian life and worship and less of a mere metaphysical theology. The people, not content with having the choicest literature and oratory in the sermon, are calling for the aids of music and architecture in the service and secretly revolting from a mode of worship in which a theological lecture is the one all-absorbing feature and by which feeling has been divorced from expression, devotion from art, and doctrine from every day life. In some denominations, as in the Lutheran, the Dutch and German Reformed, the Presbyterian and the Methodist, their own defunct liturgies have been restored or republished and brought into discussion, whilst in others attempts are made to construct new formularies, without regard to antiquity, catholicity or authority. At the same time, the Protestant Episcopal Church has been reaping a harvest of conversions not likely to have been made upon strictly dogmatic grounds, and is itself already engaged in the timely work of enriching the prayer-book and adapting it to American life and institutions.

It would be a great mistake to think this whole movement due to the clergy alone, or even confined to the educated and fashionable classes. In some churches the people have been acquiring the liturgical culture which once belonged only to the priest and choir, and can say or sing in English the Gloria, Te Deum, etc., whose Latin titles show their origin. Where such culture is not found, the plainest and rudest, gathered in slums or in the backwoods, seem glad to become active worshipers instead of mere passive listeners, and to have their devotion enkindled through the senses as well as the intellect and conscience. And as if to insure such a culture in the future, the whole rising generation in our Sunday-schools is being trained into a liturgical habit by a crude lectionary, responsive psalter, recited prayers, and often all the appliances of a dramatic ritual.

Even those who do not sympathize with the movement have ceased to deride it, and exchanging indifference for grave astonishment at its portentous bearing, are casting about for means of explanation and resistance. By many of them it will no doubt be summarily set down to the account of our original depravity, as due to a general decline of vital religion, or to the increase of wealth, luxury, and fashion, or to the demoralizing influences of a civil war, or to some merely temporary excess or aberration of modern civilization. After duly allowing for such causes, however, we may still accept the new development as a necessary, and in the main a sound reaction of the Protestant mind from an extreme into which it was driven under the impulse of the Reformation,—

an extreme which was unavoidable in so great a religious revolution, and which was needed at the time for the purification of European Christianity and for the colonization of the American churches, but which, now that those great ends have been attained, may well give place to some more moderate and reasonable course. In other words, it would seem the true policy neither to ignore nor to oppose this reactionary tendency, but to candidly recognize what is true and valuable in it, to indicate its needed checks and safeguards, and to provide for its legitimate gratification. We need not renounce existing Protestantism as a failure; we cannot accept existing Catholicism as a success; but surely we may look somewhere between these extremes for the path of wisdom and safety.

REVIVALISM AND RITUALISM.

On surveying the present state of religious culture we shall find two conflicting theories of worship, in neither of which exclusively is the great body of Christian people likely to abide. The one, for want of a better word, has been called revivalism; the other is known as ritualism. The one would take exalted religious sentiment amounting to rapture as the normal state of every worshiping congregation; the other aims at the outward expression of religious sentiment in a ceremonial and artistic form, with the view of impressing the mind through the imagination and the senses. The most perfect example of revivalism, that to which it constantly appeals for its warrant, was the rapt assembly at Pentecost, with its many-tongued psalmists and inspired prophets, its transports and fervors and miraculous conversions. The typical illustration of ritualism, and that to which it naturally reverts for its model, was the mediæval cathedral, with its supposed re-enactment of the great tragedy of the Cross, amid all the æsthetical influences of architecture, sculpture, painting, music, and eloquence. Whilst the affinities of revivalism are with new and rude populations, which have neither the means nor the taste for literary and artistic modes of worship, the tendencies to ritualism are found in older and richer communities, whose culture and art must sooner or later permeate their religious as well as domestic and social life.

Now, it is enough thus to fairly state the two theories in order to see that neither can hope to exterminate its opposite, or arrogate to itself the whole truth in respect to the vital matter of Christian worship. Too often their respective advocates have proceeded upon such assumption, until they have simply become incapable of appreciating each other. The mere revivalist has ended in decrying all artistic culture as essentially irreligious, and conceiving it to be impossible for refined and fashionable people to be as good Christians as himself, whilst the mere ritualist has at length reduced his whole religion to a fine art, and learned to look upon all other manifestations of religious feeling as vulgar rant and hypocrisy. But the history of Christianity shows that neither tendency can be safely pushed to an extreme. Even in the primitive church the revival spirit, with all the advantage of miraculous gifts, gave rise to so shocking abuses that the Apostles enjoined a more decorous and formal mode of worship, and often since then, when not wisely checked and guided, it has fostered a spasmodic type of piety, consisting of nervous exaltations, followed by dreary collapses, destructive of all normal church growth and healthy Christian activity. In like manner the ritualistic spirit very soon began to harden the simple usages of primitive worship into an elaborate ceremonial to which all the arts contributed, until the church became a temple of the Christian Muses; and in our day even that earnest expression of a once living belief has sometimes given place to a mere scenic symbolism akin in effect to the spectacular drama.

At the same time notwithstanding these extremes, the essential good that is in each tendency is still apparent. It would be folly to treat as mere morbid excitement such a great religious awakening as that which attended the preaching of

Whitefield and Wesley, when like new apostles they traversed the American colonies, kindling them into a flame of devotion; and on the other hand it would be almost an insult to argue that liturgies foster a low type of Christian faith and practice, in view of so illustrious examples as Bernard, Herbert, Taylor, and Keble. In our own time much of the earnest working Christianity of the Church of England has gone into the ritualistic party, and in our own country a high order of liturgical service may be found associated not only with faithful pulpits, but with city charities and frontier missions. Even the evangelists, Moody and Sankey, resort to a kind of crude ritualism in their revival meetings, whilst the ritualist Fathers Maturin and Knox-Little tincture their ritual with a kind of mild revivalism. The simple truth is that both tendencies are legitimate and valuable within the limits which they impose upon each other. There are churches, especially those still doing pioneer work, in which revival methods must long prevail; and there may be times in the history of all churches when such methods will be needed to refresh their languid faith, and quicken them into new life; but for the ordinary sound states of feeling in churches becoming replenished with learning and culture, the need of a more or less literary and artistic form of worship presents itself as a foregone conclusion for which due provision should be made.

The Claims of Æstheticism.

It will be easy at this point to sneer at literary and artistic tastes as weak and trivial compared with religious interests. That is not the question: that may be granted. Nevertheless the faculties used in the cultivation of letters and the fine arts, small as they may be, are an original part of human nature and essential to a fully developed manhood. Unless they be simply obliterated, they must somehow share in the regenerative power of the Christian faith, and find their due place in any symmetrical scheme of Christian nurture. Neglect them or train them apart from religious ideas and influences, and

The Claims of Æstheticism.

sooner or later they will ally themselves with vice and superstition, and at length appear in some terrible Nemesis of faith like that which avenged the Puritan rigor with the licentious reign of Charles II. Moreover, it has become a practical question how to deal with them. The culture which has invaded our homes cannot be kept out of our churches. In fact it has already come into them, and come to stay. If we will not go back to the Puritan meeting-house, the Covenanter psalm-singing, the Methodist camp-meeting, the Quaker silence, we must go forward to some new adjustment of the advanced civilization and Christianity of our day.

Precisely what that adjustment should be, how far the contemporaneous literature and art of a community can be wisely admitted within the sphere of Christian worship, it might not be easy to decide as an abstract question. Practically, however, as we have seen, it is being settled for us by the course of providential events, by the spontaneous working and interaction of the two interests. The much-dreaded corruption of religion by science, of piety by art, of devotion by taste, has not come to pass. Allowing for exceptions we may fearlessly claim just the opposite result. Pulpits as orthodox and steadfast as any of the last generation are to-day reinforced with all the stores of modern literature, and applying Scripture doctrine, as never before, to current questions in trade, morals, politics, and philosophy. Congregations as devout and earnest as any once gathered in the barn-like chapel or imitated Greek temple, are now worshipping in Christian buildings, amid Christian emblems and legends, and with the aid of choir and organ offering up the glorias and canticles of a Christian ritual. In short, churches which have been longest on the soil and most fairly express our national life and social growth, without any loss of their early purity and zeal, and without the least compromise of their distinctive orthodoxy, are adopting all the elements of liturgical worship.

NEW-MADE LITURGIES.

Leaving it to appear hereafter, how much of this movement is crude and rash and likely to pass away, we come at once to the practical questions—How is it to be met and satisfied? Whereto does it tend? And to the former question the answer is plain, that it cannot be met and satisfied by new-made liturgies or patchwork services. Such expedients proceed upon a misconception of the true liturgic ideal as an historical growth and flower of the piety of the whole church in all lands and ages. In distinction from extemporaneous worship, a liturgy is a system, for both minister and people, of fixed forms of prayer and praise, of administering rites and ceremonies, of methodically reading the Holy Scriptures, of commemorating events and doctrines, together with any literary and artistic aids which may be afforded by the existing state of religious culture. Such a system cannot be made by one man, in a day. To attempt it would be to set at nought the wisdom of eighteen centuries of Christian worship. It would be the absurdity of composing new hymns as well as prayers, of framing new creeds, of celebrating the Lord's Supper, baptism, matrimony and burial with new ceremonies, of constructing tables of Scripture lessons, which have never been tested, and of instituting Christian festivals of which the church has never heard. It is something like this absurdity which is perpetrated whenever a liturgy-maker sits down in his study to write out an original and complete formulary for the use of his people or of his denomination, in ignorance and sometimes in contempt of the devotional treasures which have been accumulating for ages.

And scarcely any better is the incongruous mixture sometimes made of liturgical with extemporaneous worship. Each is good in its own place, and either in place is better than the other out of place. In social prayer-meetings, especially during times of revival, the prayers, hymns, and exhortations will be free and spontaneous, and anything like a liturgy would be felt as an intolerable bondage, but in large assemblies on public occasions there must be more of method and formality. It would seem a strange impropriety, when we think of it, to improvise stated, ordinary acts of divine service, to extemporize the administration of solemn rites, to express the moods and wants of but one individual out of a thousand people and often leave their most essential devotions to his chance impulse. And yet something very much like this will be endured by intelligent congregations who have taken steps to formulize their worship in some respects but not in others; who will come together for impromptu services in a cathedral-like structure adapted to ritual uses; who will insist upon a carefully written sermon, but sit listless through long desultory prayers; who will let their children read the same appointed Scripture lesson with all the Sunday-schools in Christendom, but have their own public reading of God's word arranged, if arranged at all, on some occult principle known to the minister alone; who will grope after him through a service supposed to be introductory to the unknown theme of his sermon; who will only join him intelligently in saying a Psalter which was meant to be sung, or have his unpremeditated effusions mixed with a few liturgical forms, such as the Lord's Prayer, the Apostles' Creed, the Commandments, the Glorias, torn piecemeal from their only proper liturgical connection; who will keep anniversary days and weeks of prayer by human appointment, but discard the observance of Lent as without divine warrant, or perhaps celebrate Christmas, Good Friday, and Easter as mere public or social incidents, without regard to the Christian year in which they find their true significance; in a word, who will seek to blend fragments of the ancient liturgy with an otherwise informal service. The wonder is that the two can live together, and it would seem certain that sooner or later one or the other will have to be abandoned.

This brings us to the other practical question as to the issue of the liturgical movement, and the answer is already at hand:—it must have its logical conclusion in the English prayer-book as the only Christian liturgy worthy of the name. I do not forget the Lutheran, Dutch and German Reformed and early Presbyterian formularies, each admirable in its own day and for its own purpose; and were it at all likely that any of them could now come into general use among our churches it might be well to pause and estimate their claims. But on their face it will be seen that, being of foreign origin and modern translation, they are wanting in the quaint classical English of the age of Shakespeare, as well as in that solemn Scriptural style which is so desirable in order to separate the phrase of public worship from that of ordinary literature and conversation. Moreover, in their structure it will be found that they break more entirely with Christian antiquity than would now be deemed desirable, whilst their own contents, as we shall see, have been largely included in the prayer-book compilation, together with other forms of still greater liturgical value.

Let it be here premised that by the English prayer-book in this essay is meant the liturgy of the Church of England as it has existed substantially for more than three hundred years, long before any other American churches had come into being; and that liturgy chiefly in distinction from the Articles and the Ordinal, with neither of which is it indissolubly connected, as is shown, not only by their separate origin and use, but also by the existence of other versions representing other views of doctrine and polity, Calvinistic, Arminian, Socinian, Presbyterian, Methodist, and Congregational. For the main purpose of this argument the Protestant Episcopal edition, with which we are happily so familiar, need not be taken specially into account, but our attention simply fixed upon that ancient service, whose structure and contents have remained essentially the same through all the revisions to which it has been subjected and amid all the varieties in which it is still extant.

Excellence of the English Liturgy.

The English liturgy, next to the English Bible, is the most wonderful product of the Reformation. The very fortunes of the book are the romance of history. As we trace its development, its rubrics seem dyed in the blood of martyrs; its offices echo with polemic phrases; its canticles mingle with the battle-cries of armed sects and factions; and its successive revisions mark the career of dynasties, states, and churches. Cavalier, covenanter, and puritan have crossed their swords over it; scholars and soldiers, statesmen and churchmen, kings and commoners, have united in defending it. England, Germany, Geneva, Scotland, America, have by turns been the scene of its conflicts. Far beyond the little island which was its birthplace, its influence has been silently spreading in connection with great political and religious changes, generation after generation, from land to land, even where its name was never heard.

At first sight, indeed, the importance which this book has acquired may seem quite beyond its merits, as the Bible itself might appear to a superficial observer a mere idol of bigotry and prejudice. But the explanation is in both cases somewhat the same. It is to be found in the fact that the prayer-book, like the sacred canon, is no merely individual production, nor even purely human work, but an accumulation of choice writings, partly divine, partly human, expressing the religious mind of the whole ancient and modern world, as enunciated by prophets and apostles, saints and martyrs, and formulated by councils, synods, and conferences, all seeking heavenly light and guidance. Judaism has given to it its lessons and psalter; Christianity has added its epistles and gospels; Catholicism has followed with its canticles, creeds, and collects; and Protestantism has completed it with its exhortations, confessions, and thanksgivings. At the same time each leading phase of the reformation has been impressed upon its composite materials. Lutheranism has molded its ritual; Calvinism has framed its doctrine; Episcopalianism has dominated both ritual and doctrine; whilst Presbyterianism has subjected each to thorough revision. And the whole has been rendered into the pure English and with the sacred fervor peculiar to the earnest age in which it arose; has been wrought into a system adapted to all classes of men through all the vicissitudes of life; and has been tested and hallowed by three centuries of trial in every quarter of the globe.

CATHOLICITY OF THE ENGLISH LITURGY.

It would be strange if a work which thus has its roots in the whole church of the past should not be sending forth its branches into the whole church of the future; and any one who will take the pains to study its present adaptations, whatever may have been his prejudices, must admit that there is no other extant formulary which is so well fitted to become the rallying-point and standard of modern Christendom. In it are to be found the means, possibly the germs, of a just reorganization of Protestantism as well as an ultimate reconciliation with true Catholicism, such a catholicism as shall have shed everything sectarian and national, and retained only what is common to the whole Church of Christ in all ages and countries. Whilst to the true Protestant it offers evangelical doctrine, worship, and unity on the terms of the Reformation, it still preserves for the true Catholic the choicest formulas of antiquity, and to all Christians of every name opens a liturgical system at once Scriptural and reasonable, doctrinal and devotional, learned and vernacular, artistic and spiritual. It is not too much to say that were the problem given, to frame out of the imperfectly organized and sectarian Christianity of our times a liturgical model for the communion of saints in the one universal church, the result might be expressed in some such compilation as the English Book of Common Prayer.

This ideal fitness of the work to serve as the nucleus of a reunited Christianity will especially appear in the American churches, if we view it in connection with their historical origin and their present condition. In the first place, it sustains historical relations to those churches, which though forgotten or obscured, are vital and enduring. Owing to the mode of its compilation from other liturgies, the very materials out of which it was at first formed have an organic affinity for the various ecclesiastical elements which now lie around it in this country as disjecta membra, as yet unassimilated and discordant. Whilst its Catholic or ancient portions, derived from the Greek and Latin churches, may be regarded as the common heritage of all Christians, its Protestant portions can be traced back to their sources in those Reformed churches of Germany, Geneva, Holland, Scotland, and England in which the American churches have severally originated; and were they now disposed to any formal correspondence or union, they would only have to come together in the light of their common history in order to see that the English prayer-book, next to the Holy Scriptures, affords the closest visible bonds between them. The Evangelical Lutheran Church, besides recognizing in it some of the ancient Catholic formulas which she has also retained, could find in the offices of baptism, matrimony, and burial large portions of the liturgies of Luther, Melancthon, and Bucer. The Reformed churches (Dutch and German) could refer important parts of the daily prayer and communion service to a common origin with their own liturgies in the formularies of Calvin, Lasco, and Pollanus. The Presbyterian church, whose standards were framed mainly by presbyters of the Church of England in the Westminster Assembly, could not only discern in the articles of religion the original skeleton of her confession of faith, but trace through the entire liturgy her revising hand, and might regain a living embodiment of her directory of worship in that amended prayer-book which some of her own founders strove to establish two centuries ago. The Protestant Episcopal church, the only church that has faithfully kept and honored the whole book among us, after guarding her connection with the Anglican, Latin, and Greek churches, might also acknowledge her large indebtedness to other Protestant churches, now in a position, as never before, to recognize and respect their mutual relationship. The Methodist Episcopal church, which herself originated in an Oxford movement, besides deriving the model of her polity from the Ordinal, still retains the prayer-book as edited and authorized by Wesley. Even the Congregational churches (Trinitarian, Unitarian, Baptist), though without the same historical continuity, might look for broken links in the Westminster catechisms and King's Chapel prayer-book, as well as in the early Puritan revisions before the rise of Independency. In fact, nearly all the leading denominations, were they to retrace their history, would come back to the English liturgy as a work which their ecclesiastical forefathers did not so much aim to destroy as to amend; which they finally abandoned only in the larger interests of civil and religious freedom; and which they might now, in the changed circumstances of another age and country, easily resume and modify without the least sacrifice of denominational pride or logical consistency.

REACTION TOWARD THE ENGLISH LITURGY.

If this picture seem strange and visionary, let it be observed in the second place, that the American churches for some time past have been steadily, though unconsciously, drifting back toward the midway position held by the English prayer-book between the extremes of Catholic and Protestant Christianity. Whilst the European churches, Roman, Anglican, Scotch, Dutch, German, have for several centuries remained fixed in their original seats as state religions, with but little intercourse and mutual modification, the American churches meanwhile, escaping from these narrow confines, have migrated to another hemisphere, become compacted together under a republican form of government, made free and equal before the law, and left to their own spontaneous development. The result is that they have been slowly rebounding from the rash extremes into which they were driven by sectarian warfare in the Old World, and no longer held apart by political restraints, are now under common impulses tending toward substantial unity in the midst of trivial diversity. In matters of order and worship here and there, they have actually exchanged positions in their recoil, and come nearer to each other than to their respective mother churches on the other side of the Atlantic. Presbyterians have been adopting the liturgical usages which once kindled the wrath of Jenny Geddes into a revolution of the three kingdoms, whilst Episcopalians have been admitting the lay elements which brought Archbishop Laud to the scaffold. Congregationalists are reproducing the church buildings which their ancestors defaced as Popish chapels, whilst American churchmen are proposing to make the old Puritan Thanksgiving a holy day in the Church year. Baptist ministers have begun to borrow from a prayer-book which John Bunyan renounced for the Elstow jail, whilst neighboring rectors have engaged in prayer-meetings which the bishops of that day would have legally suppressed as a crime. Methodist congregations, founded by John Wesley, have costly churches, service-books, and written sermons, whilst the Oxford reformers of to-day have surpliced lay-readers, clerical exhorters, and ritual missions. Not long since an association of city ministers devised a "non-Episcopal observance of Lent," whilst Lenten revivals were being conducted by a Protestant order of priests. The whole Christian world is alive with such changes, and becoming visibly marshaled for the issue. On the one side are the various Protestant churches, already beginning to resume those portions of the prayer-book which were once falsely associated with tyranny and superstition, and in spite of inherited prejudices, exploring anew the whole field of Catholic antiquity; and it would be strange indeed, if these enlightened Christian bodies, thus moving in the line of great historical causes, should pause in the midst of so inevitable reactions. On the other side are the Roman and Anglican churches, no longer able to bind up the Catholic portions of the prayer-book with hierarchy and social caste, but themselves permeated as never before with the influences of Protestant freedom and culture ; and it remains to be seen whether even these least pliable types of organized Christianity must not yet yield to the pressure of democratic institutions and the plastic force of American society. Be that as it may, so long as the religious, political, and social influences by which the different denominations are being sifted and fused together continue to operate amongst them, they will in various degrees unitedly approximate a Catholicism which shall be truly Protestant, as well as a Protestantism which shall be truly Catholic. In a word, if we are ever to have anything answering to the grand conception of the United Churches of the United States, it must come through that spirit of Protestant Catholicism of which the English liturgy properly amended and enriched, would be the best conceivable expression.

And now the very process of such a liturgical concretion of different denominations about the nucleus of the prayer-book has reached a point where it only awaits accomplishment. Bring together the fragments of that ancient liturgy as preserved by some churches, or coming into use in others, and recombine them as they may be found in its various offices ; restore more fully the links of the Christian year, which are already socially and legally recognized among us, and let them be illustrated by the epistles and gospels which have marked their circuit for centuries past; arrange the present random lessons so that the whole Scriptures may be publicly read in their inspired connection ; reduce the rambling " long prayer" to the lucid order and fullness of the Litany, and add a few well-chosen collects from the best liturgies; purge existing hymnals of their copious doggerel and enrich them only with hymns which have become classical, and at the same time scrupulously retain a learned pulpit and the liberty of extemporaneous worship for fit times and occasions ; and the result would be an American liturgy expressing the essential common faith of Catholic and Protestant Christianity.

The general conclusion of our study is now before us: a doctrinal compact of the American churches can only be looked for in the distant future; their ecclesiastical confederation may be nearer at hand; but their liturgical fusion is passing before our eyes toward its only logical issue in the prayer-book. How such a fusion is likely to affect the relations existing between the Protestant Episcopal Church and other American churches; whether it will leave those relations unchanged or at length lead to mutual recognition and organic connection—are interesting questions which may here force themselves into some minds; but they are not the most urgent questions growing out of the investigation; they belong, as we have seen, to the future rather than to the present; and they are quite aside from the main object of this essay. I have simply aimed to present certain facts and truths to those who are deeply interested in knowing them.

II.
DENOMINATIONAL VIEWS OF CHURCH UNITY.

II.

DENOMINATIONAL VIEWS OF CHURCH UNITY.

The reader will have observed that the preceding essay was in no sense representative of denominational views, as held in any church or party, but was simply an independent survey of all Christian denominations with their existing grounds of organic unity in doctrine, polity, and worship. The paper was written with no thought whatever of the criticism which has been converged upon it by champions of the different churches. It has been under discussion for many months, until nearly all the interested parties have been fully heard. In offering a brief reply, I might regret the seeming odds of a battle with so many giants at once, did I not hope to stay out of the battle as much as possible, and keep to the main question, in which alone the public can be interested. A mere controversy on Christian unity would indeed be but a sorry absurdity.

As it has been strangely assumed that the essay put forth some new-made scheme of denominational union, in particular a formal coalition on the basis of the Anglican prayer-book, I beg to recall with emphasis my introductory statement:—

"We are not yet ready for such schemes, and it would only be a waste of time to discuss them. The first lesson to be learned is that the unification of the American Churches, if it is ever to come at all, cannot be precipitated by platforms, coalitions, compromises, in short by any mere external association of the different denominations, which leaves them still without internal modifications and vital connections, as true and living branches of the Vine of Christ."

In pursuance of this statement, the former paper was a mere historical sketch of the unconscious growth of leading American Churches toward organic likeness and oneness, as seen especially in their liturgical communion. The plain facts presented in that sketch have not been denied by any of the distinguished respondents, and all the objections to some supposed liturgical scheme of union have, therefore, been but so many formidable javelins hurled into the air. The position taken was briefly this: Our chief historical churches have long been reacting toward the Protestant Catholicism expressed in the English prayer-book. That position has not even been assailed or questioned. Here the case might rest, if the aim had been to succeed in an argument rather than to arrive at the truth.

But while the critics of the essay have seemed somewhat to differ from it, they have much more largely agreed with it, and with one another, and have thus revealed a remarkable consensus of opinions, upon which we may now build up a constructive argument for the continued growth of church unity in the future along the lines revealed by the discussion. To this task the present paper is mainly devoted. If it shall be performed even imperfectly, the protracted discussion will not have been in vain.

We have seen that the various ecclesiastical and quasi-ecclesiastical or pseudo-ecclesiastical bodies of which our American Christianity is composed may be studied in three general groups or classes, according to the principles prevailing in their structure: The EPISCOPAL, including the Roman Catholic, Methodist, and Protestant Episcopal Churches; the PRESBYTERIAL, including the Lutheran, Reformed, and Presbyterian Churches; the CONGREGATIONAL, including the Baptist, Orthodox and Unitarian churches. Representative divines in each group have spoken on the question of Christian union or church unity, and thus furnished the materials for a full comparison of views. Let us take them in the order which we have adopted.

EPISCOPALIAN OPINIONS.

The Right Rev. Bishop Dudley and the Rev. Dr. J. H. Hopkins of the Protestant Episcopal Church, have treated the essay with great kindness, justice, and clearness. They both admit substantially its general conclusions—that full dogmatic agreement is still a long way off, and that the liturgical fusion, which has begun, is but a desirable first step towards true church unity. But as to the matter of polity, they consistently hold that Episcopacy affords the only basis or form of organic oneness.[1] Against this opinion their opponents will urge several considerations:—

First. That forms of doctrine and worship, or creeds and sacraments, as well as polity, are ecclesiastical elements affording grounds or germs of organic unity, and are much more important than any mere polity, though it were imagined to be of the most perfect Episcopal form.

Second. That as a matter of fact the Episcopal polity, though common to the Greek, Roman, and Anglican churches, is but little known in the Protestant churches of Europe and America.

Third. That Presbytery, rather than Episcopacy, is the one polity which by common consent has continued historically, from the Apostles' time until the present day, in all the chief churches of Christendom, both Catholic and Protestant.

Fourth. That the claim to an Apostolate, as maintained in these letters, is not allowed by other Protestant churches nor by the Roman Catholic Church, and is practically viewed by both as involving organized schism rather than organic unity.

Fifth. That instead of seeking a remote alliance with the

---

[1] "Leaving out of view entirely the question of a scriptural revelation, and granting that there is no definite ecclesiastical polity laid down in Scripture, yet none other than a threefold Ministry of Apostolic succession can by any possibility be made satisfactory to the great and ancient Churches of the East and of the West, even could the Anglican Communion be induced for the sake of unity to accept another."—*Bishop Dudley*.

Greek and Latin Churches, it were better to begin with some organic connection of the kindred English-speaking Protestant churches, Congregational, Presbyterial, and Episcopal, and on the basis of their common Anglo-Saxon Christianity to aim at the more general unity of Christendom.

Whether these views be right or wrong, they are existing matters of opinion which must enter into the present discussion, as may appear hereafter. It is a very pleasing feature of both of these letters that they breathe an earnest Christian desire and hope of ultimate church unity.

The Rev. Dr. George R. Crooks, of the Methodist Episcopal Church, also writes in a union spirit and is in accord with the essay on some essential points, with differences which seem mainly verbal. Mistaking the word "organic," as hitherto defined and used, he applies it to that figurative organism or spiritual body of Christ in which all true Christians are joined as members, rather than to those ecclesiastical organizations or organized churches which are not one, but many, and more or less hostile to each other.[1] Organic oneness, in the former sense of one Christian body, is indeed an established fact, and happily a fact that goes without the saying in these papers, since they would scarcely be possible but for its tacit assumption; but organic oneness, in the common sense of one church organization, is unhappily not a fact; and though such unity be not deemed vital or fundamental, yet it may be important, if not indispensable, as will hereafter be shown. Dr. Crooks also mistakes the term Catholic for "Roman Catholic," and is thereby led into a view of the relations of Protestantism and Catholicism which may be modified by one or two suggestions.

First. True Catholicism, if defined to be historic Christianity as freed from Roman errors, is not inconsistent with " New

---

[1] "The unity of the Churches is an established, a divine fact, and that unity is necessarily organic. The Church is already one by virtue of the life which pertains to all its members as members of Christ."

Testament Christianity," but is the choicest fruit of its own divine development in history. The Protestants themselves, as their name implies, did not wholly renounce it; nor can we renounce it, unless we are ready for the frightful theory that during fifteen centuries from the Apostles' time until the reformation there was no Church or providence, but only one long reign of sin and Satan.

Second. Such Catholic Christianity is in fact more or less fully retained by Protestant churches in their forms of doctrine, polity, and worship, which are not to be found clearly set forth in the New Testament, but are very largely an outgrowth from it in Church history under divine Providence. The Methodist Church, for example, has a modified episcopate, liturgy, and articles, which it inherited directly from the Church of England, remotely from the Church of Rome, though without other accompanying dogmas held in those churches.

Third. The Protestant body in its recoil from Romanism may have gone too far away from Catholicism, into such extremes as sectarianism, rationalism and revivalism; but a healthy reaction has already begun, as we have shown, in regard to the historic liturgy, and it may yet extend to the other diseases or abuses of Protestantism, until a true church unity shall have taken the place of our sectarianism, and our latest rationalism at length give way to the vindicated Catholic faith.

Fourth. The Roman Church and the chief Protestant churches, notwithstanding their wide differences, rest primarily upon the same Holy Scriptures and share largely the same Catholic Christianity; and it is at least conceivable that in the lapse of time, by the transmuting force of American institutions, and under the pressure of common dangers, they may be brought slowly together from their present extremes, having shed their respective errors until at last they join in the one essential faith of Protestant Catholicism as the full flower of New Testament Christianity. Professor Crooks himself argues very forcibly that the chief Roman dogma of sacerdotal supremacy is doomed to die out, both in Church and State, in the wake of political causes; and he may thus refute his own imaginary picture of an immediate crude coalition of "Romanists and Protestants in one ecclesiastical government."

Fifth. The English liturgy, as we have seen, affords the grounds and germs of such a gradual coalescence of Protestant with Catholic Christianity in the American churches; and when the Methodist Episcopal Church completes its reaction with the rest, the Wesleyan prayer-book, instead of lying a nullity, will serve to bring it into more visible communion and organic connection with the other great historic churches of Christendom.

Dr. Crooks, as a representative of episcopacy without apostolical succession, finds no organic bond between the Greek, Latin, and Anglican churches, but hopes for some closer union of the Protestant churches, to be reached by recognizing their essential spiritual unity as a divine fact; by acknowledging one another's churchly standing in their intercourse; and by coming into more organic coöperation for the great ends of their common Christianity.

PRESBYTERIAN OPINIONS.

The two representatives of the Presbyterian church have reviewed the essay from different standpoints. The late Dr. Archibald Alexander Hodge, as if with a prophetic utterance, and in an elevated Christian tone befitting the theme, discussed the doctrine of the invisible Catholic Church, and set forth in glowing terms its unbroken unity, as including not merely all true believers on earth, but the whole company of the redeemed in heaven.

The surviving disputants may well recognize such doctrine as common ground, while still taking to themselves the reproach that the visible church as yet so little reflects the oneness of the Church invisible. Unhappily, our existing denominations cannot be viewed merely as so many harmonious groups of organized churches, or legitimate varieties of church organization, dwelling together in manifest unity. Having been largely produced by warring sects and factions, excommunicating and unchurching one another, they exhibit an apparent dismemberment of the very body of Christ, which has become the great flagrant scandal of our age and country, and has made it the plain duty as well as impulse of all Christian people to seek for more outward organic unity, as well as to hail the providential signs of its inward growth and expression. In any other view, we could only adjourn our questions of doctrine to the millennium, and wait until we may all join in the perfect liturgy of heaven. Practically, indeed, this is the course taken by some extremists who would consecrate mere denominationalism, extenuate sectarianism, and make schism itself chronic, in the face of their own false dormant ideal of an invisible Catholic Church.

In contrast with such errors, Dr. Hodge has impressively shown that the various church organizations, through the indwelling Spirit, will yet grow together toward a true organic unity consistent with due variety, as but so many members in the one mystical body of Christ. And the latter part of his letter refers to such unity in the three organic spheres of doctrine, polity, and worship. As to the first, his hopeful view of the dogmatic consensus of Protestant Trinitarian churches is a most valuable and timely contribution to the general argument for church unity, and would be only more complete could it include on the basis of a common American Christianity, those Unitarian churches which express the flower of Puritan culture, as well as the great Roman Catholic Church which is already in the lead on such social questions as marriage, temperance, education, and property. As to the second opinion, that unity in polity would be more difficult than unity in dogma, I have nothing to add to the former paper, except what may be found in the sequel. As to the third, it may be said that the argument from numbers against the growth of liturgical communion, like most statistical arguments, can be used on both sides of the question, and will probably be met from the other side by such answers as the following :—

First. That the liturgical churches of Christendom outnumber in membership the non-liturgical churches as three or four to one.

Second. That in this country it is the least ecclesiastical denominations, the evanescent sects, that are without liturgical tendencies, as they are crude in their doctrine and polity; while only the historical churches, of European origin, can yield the proper data of the church problem, and these are vitally connected with the contents of the English liturgy in a ratio of forty or fifty to one. Moreover, as we have seen, they are already, knowingly or unknowingly, resuming elements and portions of that liturgy in their worship, and logically tend to it as the best devotional formulary of Catholic and Protestant Christianity.

This starts the only question in the other letter demanding attention. In meeting it, I must reluctantly forsake, for the moment, an independent position, and come down to the denominational ground which the critic has taken. The Rev. Dr. Howard Crosby, declaring himself an out-and-out Presbyterian, offers seven objections to the prayer-book as received opinions in the Presbyterian Church.[1] With due respect, I am obliged to say that not one of them has any foundation in the recognized standards of that body. My replies must be brief.

First. The Directory for Public Worship (ch. v.) does not

---

[1] 1. " They object to the breaking up of prayer into little fragments, each beginning with an invocation and ending with a formal peroration. They consider this style of prayer too artificial and leading to a mechanical worship.

2. They object to the open-eyed reading of prayer, as tending to withdraw the mind from the unseen.

3. They object to the stereotyped prayer, however excellent.

4. They object to the Litany *in toto*, as putting the believer far off from God, calling on him to *spare* him as a miserable sinner. . . . The Litany has no

"object to the stereotyped prayer, however excellent," but does object to " mean, irregular, or extravagant effusions, as a disgrace of divine service." Such effusions, becoming themselves stereotyped, are worse than any " open-eyed reading of prayer," and in fact sometimes open the eyes of the unhappy listeners.

Second. The Larger Catechism (Q. 186–188) does not object to the invocation, peroration, and well ordered brief petitions which it finds in the Lord's Prayer as being " too artificial and tending to a mechanical mode of worship ;" but it does prescribe the right use of that liturgical form and didactic model of common prayer. To repeat it, at least once in each public office is not treating it " as a mere magical formula," but is keeping strictly within the scriptural rubric, " When ye pray, say Our Father."

Third. The Shorter Catechism (Q. 99) enjoins the whole word of God as a rule of prayer; and if therefore any " Presbyterians object to the Litany in toto as putting the believer far off from God and calling on him to spare him as a miserable sinner," they simply object with the Pharisee to the very words of the contrite Publican, as well as to the penitential prayers of priest and people weeping between the porch and the altar. If they object to its devout repetitions as " unmeaning," they must object to the like repetitions in Holy Scripture. If they could object to its solemn pleadings and tender entreaties and manifold intercessions as " having no feature suited to the child of God or joint heir with Christ,"

---

feature suited to the "heir of God or joint-heir with Christ." Many of the features of the Litany (like the prayer against sudden death) are but relics of Romanism, and its repetitions are unmeaning.

5. They object to the absolution *declaration*, which is only a toning down of the Roman absolution *bestowal*.

6. They object to the repetitions of the Lord's Prayer, as if it were a magical formula, which was made effective by frequent repetition.

7. They object to the clear remnants of transubstantiation in the Communion Service and of baptismal regeneration in the Baptismal Service—two doctrines which Presbyterians abhor."

they would object to the supplications of the prophets and apostles themselves. But before they object to its scriptural petition against sudden death as "a relic of Romanism," they should consult the Roman original (a subitanea et improvisa morte) or the Anglo-Saxon version (a subita et eterna morte). They might also profitably consider the beams in their own extempore litanies, the "irreverent," the "sarcastic," the "tedious prayers," etc., of which that accomplished Presbyterian divine, Dr. Samuel Miller, speaks in his useful treatise.

Fourth. The Form of Government (ch. iii. v.) does not "hold that all believers are priests" in the sense of being Ministers, or that "a minister is only an ordained ruler and leader of the people, with no more authority to pronounce absolution upon the penitent than any one who is not a minister;" but it does most plainly distinguish him from the mere representatives of the people as a minister of Christ and ambassador from God, declaring pardon in Christ's stead. The Confession also (ch. xxx.) names among his high functions, "power to open the kingdom of heaven unto penitent sinners by the ministry of the Gospel, and by absolution from censures, as occasion shall require." Consistently with such teaching, the declarative Absolution, prefixed to the English daily service is simply an authoritative proclamation of the Gospel, made solemn and direct by a special act of worship on the part both of minister and people. If any Presbyterians are thoughtless enough to object to that formula as "a remnant of the Roman Absolution," they should be informed that its very motive was as Protestant as its meaning; that it was first suggested by Calvin himself; that it was taken very largely from a Calvinistic liturgy; and that it was alternatively called the Absolution or Remission of sins, in deference to Puritan scruples against a word of Popish sound.

Fifth. The Confession of Faith (ch. xxviii.) does not "abhor the doctrine of baptismal regeneration" as rightly stated, but does declare it a "great sin to contemn this ordinance," guards carefully against the abuse of it, and defines it as a "sign and seal of regeneration even unto infants" (Q. 177). And the Baptismal Offices merely express the substantial sense of this definition in strong liturgical terms. Any Presbyterians who abhor such doctrine may find it discreetly maintained by that saintly man, the late Dr. Archibald Alexander, in the second chapter of his work on religious experience. As to the Holy Supper, the Confession takes some higher views of the Real Presence than can anywhere be found in the English Communion office. In fact, the only "remnant of transubstantiation" that appears in that office is a solemn ordinance against it as "idolatry to be abhorred of all faithful Christians." Presbyterians who are horrified at such a rag of popery will have their horror increased on learning that the stringent rubric was first procured by that uncompromising reformer, John Knox, in 1552, and fully confirmed at the last revision in 1661, according to Mr. Procter's history of the prayer-book, "in compliance with the wishes of the Presbyterians."

Sixth. The chief framers of the above named standards, though certainly "not in love with the Episcopal liturgy" as it was imposed upon them by the Act of Uniformity two centuries ago, protested that they had "not the least thought of depraving or reproaching the Book of Common Prayer," but wished only to "avoid both the extreme that would have no forms and the contrary extreme that would have nothing but forms;"[1] and their exceptions to the prayer-book, in matters of mere usage and taste as well as principle, like some of the objections before us, have long since been fully met by the changed conditions of American Presbyterianism which now neither enjoins nor forbids the use of a liturgy.

Seventh. The Presbyterian Book of Common Prayer affords a summary refutation to Dr. Crosby's objections, all and each of them. Among the legal revisers of the English Liturgy in 1661 were the very authors of the Presbyterian formularies,

---

[1] Documents of Revision, 1661.

such as Anthony Tuckney, Regius Professor of Divinity at Cambridge, who had written nearly the whole of the larger Catechism; John Wallis, Savilian Professor of Geometry at Oxford, who had been secretary to the Westminster divines, and had himself prepared the Shorter Catechism; Edward Reynolds, afterwards Bishop of Norwich and author of the general Thanksgiving, who had composed the most important parts of the Confession of Faith; Edmund Calamy, the very leader of the Presbyterian clergy, who with Spurstow, Newcomen, and Arrowsmith had been in the Assembly's committee that framed the Directory of Worship and Church Government; to say nothing of the learned Lightfoot, the silver-tongued Bates, the saintly Baxter, and other great Presbyterian scholars whose praise is in all the churches. The emendations and exceptions of such men, duly modified by American authorities, precedents, and usages, yield an edition of the prayer-book[1] to which no Presbyterian can bring any objections whatever without taking the ground from under his feet. On such ground an out-and-out Presbyterian, could only become a valiant champion, not merely of the prayer-book, but of that church unity which is an essential principle of Presbyterian polity as well as the flower of Christian charity.

Resuming now our task, we may sum up Presbyterian opinion, according to the teachings of Dr. Hodge, as based upon the inward spiritual oneness of the churches, yet looking forward to their outward organic oneness, still to be attained through the slow ripening of their knowledge, love, and zeal, and other graces of the Holy Spirit.

---

[1] The Book of Common Prayer, as amended by the Presbyterian Divines in the Royal Commission of 1661, and in agreement with the Directory for Public Worship of the Presbyterian Church in the United States. With a supplementary treatise by the author of these essays.

CONGREGATIONALIST OPINIONS.

The letters of the two learned divines representing the Orthodox Congregational churches, though making no allusion to the essay, admit of a logical connection with it as affording valuable opinions needed to complete this survey. President Seelye, of Amherst College, gives a profoundly spiritual view of the fellowship of saints and of churches, and likens the universal church to a universal state, as being one in its essence, though manifold in its forms, Congregational, Presbyterial, Episcopal, and as tending finally to a Christian theocracy, in which the autonomy of the particular church shall be consistent with the autocracy of the universal church. The analogy, however, fails at the essential point, since there is no invisible universal State corresponding to the invisible catholic Church of which Christ is the head.

Professor Fisher, of Yale College, in his more practical and very suggestive letter, maintains that, since the decree of Papal infallibility, Christian union is practicable only among Protestant denominations; and he finds three obstacles to such union—one, in the reigning dogmatic intolerance; another, in the prevalent ritual diversity, especially as to the rite of baptism, and a third, in the divine-right theory of church government as held by Episcopalians, Presbyterians, and some Congregationalists. At the same time, he admits that a mere governmental, as distinguished from a sacerdotal Episcopacy, would not be repugnant to other Protestants, and that an optional liturgy, used alternatively with spontaneous worship, might in some cases prove an advantage. Professor Fisher clearly discerns the rising spirit of church unity, when he says: " The centrifugal age of Protestantism is closed. The centripetal action has begun."

Although both of these writers say but little of any organization beyond the limits of the local church or parish, yet it is well known that such organization exists, more or less ecclesiastical in its tendencies and without destroying the self-government of congregations, as is seen in their voluntary association for some church purposes, as well as in that practical congregationalism which prevails under presbyterial and episcopal systems.

Two eloquent divines have spoken for the Unitarian Congregational churches. We can all agree with the Rev. Dr. Edward Everett Hale, when he asserts that Christian Unity exists in America now, in the sense in which he understands it.[1] But church unity, the fusion of Christian sects into the one church, does not exist, nor can "people who want it find it by going out of doors," by simply mingling together in humane recreations, however good and healthful. The civilized Christain of this epoch does not always live out-of-doors. Church organizations, with creed and ritual rooted far back in history, have earned their right to be; and just now they are reasserting that right. Dr. Hale very aptly likens them to the independent colonies before they had become compacted in the national union; and denies that "the work of the church is better done by its several sections when they keep a strict organization among themselves, and each lets the other sections severely alone." That was once the war cry, we remember, of a large section of the United States; and now and then we hear something like it among the united churches. But if ever we get a good working constitution for them, it will harmonize the local with the general church in all forms of Christian well-doing, and, unlike that lost formula of church polity which our accomplished critic describes, it can neither be mislaid nor burned in a Boston fire. More forlorn even than the "Man without a Country," whom he has depicted, would be a Christian without the Church.

With a generous largeness of view, Professor A. P. Peabody,

---

[1] "The simple truth seems to be that Christian unity exists in America now for any one who wants it. Those people have it, who were born out-of-doors, in the open air freedom of the Christian Church. . . . He has only to walk out of his own house and go to work with other men in some good enterprise, which the good God wishes to have carried through."

of Harvard University, reveals the ground common to Unitarianism and Orthodoxy in the divine humanity of Christ, though he maintains, like other correspondents, that full agreement in the realm of metaphysical divinity is not attainable, nor desirable. His practical conclusion is that Christians should unite in recognizing heartily their common Christlikeness, in promoting Christian righteousness, and in maintaining Christian worship so far as the common faith will allow. These are not only important grounds of Christian union, but may also be ranked among the conditions precedent to church unity.

As an able representative of the Baptist Congregational churches, the Rev. Dr. R. S. MacArthur, of New York City, dwells upon the growth of union in worship by means of liturgies as well as revivals, and upon the large amount of essential unity in doctrine which already exists in default of anything like organic union. But when Dr. MacArthur so intrepidly maintains that "organic union can only be reached at the baptistery," because many scholars have admitted that immersion is a scriptural mode of baptism, he forgets what an insignificant minority have held that it is the only scriptural mode, and how prevalent infant baptism has been in the universal church.[1] The spread of open communion in his own denomination is one of the most cheering signs of the times, and affords practical ground for the hope that pedobaptist and anabaptist congregations might yet be embraced within the same denominational or ecclesiastical system. The need of the hour is not concession, but toleration.

Of all the congregationalist letters, Orthodox, Unitarian, Baptist, it may now be summarily remarked, that not one of them has exhibited congregationalism as hostile to church unity or as wholly inconsistent with some ecclesiastical or-

---

[1] "The point I make is this: All are agreed on immersion as baptism; all cannot agree on anything else. . . . The plain teaching of the Bible to the unlearned, is in harmony with the conclusions of the highest scholarship."

ganization of congregations, which did not trench upon their local rights and privileges.

Such are the three chief sets of opinions now before us for comparison. At first sight the differences might seem to be very great; but it will be found that some of them are greater within the same denomination than between different denominations, or greater within the same group than between different groups of churches. And it will also be found that all the differences are much less vital and important than the agreements.

Consensus of Opinions.

In the first place, there is a consensus of Congregationalist, Presbyterian, and Episcopalian opinions in regard to the spiritual oneness of all true Christians, however variously they may be organized in their different churches and denominations. This unity has been described with more or less clearness as a communion of saints, a universal fellowship of believers, a spiritual unity of churches, an invisible Catholic Church; but however expressed, it is a note of essential harmony amid the apparent discord. It enables the strictest churchman, whether he be an Episcopalian, a Presbyterian, or a Congregationalist, to recognize heartily the Christian character of multitudes, now attached to organized forms of Christianity, which he believes to be false and pernicious, and cannot by any official act recognize as regular or valid; and it affords a broad platform on which our churches may combine more or less consciously and formally, in the confession of the same Catholic creed, and largely in the use of the same historic liturgy. Underneath all existing structures of church polity ever remains this common Christianity, this united faith in Christ, as their one divine foundation.

In the second place, even as to the remaining differences in polity, the writers are agreed that such barriers are not fixed and final, but shall yet, somehow, disappear in the church of the future. The Episcopalian may hope to see the episcopate supersede all other systems or become their unifying bond and center. The Presbyterian may look forward to some further extension of the Presbyterial principle through existing church organizations. The Congregationalist may anticipate self-governing congregations even under presbytery or episcopacy, as stripped of hierarchical claims. Each may project his ideal church into a millenium, more or less distant; may behold in that church a unity consistent with more or less diversity; and may see that church unity at length attained through causes more or less divine or human. But all will consent to view the present sectarian condition of Christianity, especially of Protestant Christianity, as abnormal and transient, and stand ready to welcome any hopeful means of promoting greater oneness and harmony.

In the third place, the remaining differences in mere church polity admit, even now, of a theoretical adjustment. Without wandering off into a vague future, we can fancy an ecclesiastical system in which Congregationalism, Presbyterianism, and Episcopalianism, as we know them in this country, might so limit and modify each other as to exist without conflict, each in its own beneficent sphere of action. In such a complete polity presbytery would keep the equipoise between the centrifugal tendencies of congregationalism and the centripetal tendencies of episcopacy, ever preserving particular congregations in their due autonomy, and at the same time combining them in a true cathedral system of schools, missions, and charities. It may be the destiny of the American church thus to bring into normal connection and organic life three ecclesiastical elements, which, in the Anglican establishment were forced together in false relations or driven out of it into hurtful extremes, but which in this new world have had full scope and development until now they are ready for a just coalescence. In this manner might be reached what was described in the former essay as "some comprehensive polity, which shall be at once Congregational, Presbyterial, and Episcopal, and wherein Protestant freedom and intelligence shall appear reconciled with Catholic authority and order." By this means the very terms Presbyterial, Congregational, Episcopal would lose their polemic sense, and all sectarian titles vanish in an organization which would be in fact, even if not in name, the American Catholic Church.

In the fourth place, such an ideal adjustment of differences in church polity has long been becoming actual in the history of the American churches. As we have seen, the old issues between them are all but dead, if not ready for honorable burial. The Cavalier, the Covenanter, the Huguenot, and the Puritan now live only in history and romance. Their hot blood has become peacefully blended in their American descendants, and we now dwell upon their virtues rather than upon their faults. He must simply fight against himself who would fight against any one of them. In other words, the unconscious assimilation of churches, after a hundred years of intermarriage and social fusion, has reached a point where they differ more in names than in things. Congregationalists have now and then an extemporized presbytery called an Association, and here and there a truly episcopal divine without the title of Bishop. Presbyterians in emergencies practice the most independent congregationalism, and love to speak of their pastors as parochial bishops, lacking only the excellent rite of confirmation. Episcopalians, after having been also without that rite during the two hundred years of their colonial history, may now boast of presbyterian elements in their polity and a congregationalist freedom in their ritual. And all three are not only professing the same essential doctrines, but singing the same hymns and beginning to say the same prayers. Let such changes go on, and after awhile we may wake out of our useless strifes to find that we have only been viewing the same shield from different standpoints, the same church under different phases; becoming Presbyterians, Congregationalists, Episcopalians, by turns without knowing it.

In the fifth place, this gradual fusion of such ecclesiastical differences has at length come into public consciousness as an avowed aim for concerted action. Christian people all over the land are trying to find how much they agree, rather than how much they differ. Leading minds in the various churches, from their several points of view, are approaching the great problem of compacting our American Christianity against the gathering foes which menace it. Union in church as well as in state is looming high and large as the question of questions before which all others must sink into insignificance. Not union for the mere sake of union—that is but a sectarian sneer;—but union as the very heart in the body of Christ and crown of all the graces; union as a duty no less than as a sentiment; union for the maintenance of truth and religion and virtue; union to prevent so immense a waste and friction in our charities and missions; union for the preservation of Christianity itself amid dangers hitherto unknown; union against the materialism that is corrupting the life of the nation; against the socialism that is assailing property, marriage, government, law, and order; against the agnosticism that is undermining all creeds, codes, and manners; against the sectarianism that is parleying and wrangling in full view of such enemies; union, if need be, against the very disunion that would keep the churches, as it would have kept the States, discordant and dismembered, in the supreme hour of peril.

SIGNS OF CHURCH UNITY.

Never were the signs, as well as the needs, of such union more apparent. Never was the feeling so deep and growing that the divisions in the Christian church must somehow come to an end. It will not be quenched by such adjectives as "sentimental," "romantic," "utopian." Sectarian interests may throw obstacles in the way, a false conservatism may raise alarms, and veteran divines draw the sword to fight their battles over again,—but in vain. In this movement the people are more determined than their rulers, and the church universal will prove stronger than any sect or party. Look at the progress made since the question was opened a few months ago. The chief denominations of the country have been taking practical steps toward church unity in distinction from mere Christian union. The Congregational churches of New England have been removing the walls which separate Baptists from Pedobaptist communions. The Presbyterian churches of the Middle States have been settling the vexed question of their psalmody, while those of the South and the North are adjusting their political differences, and those of the East are in conference with the Reformed churches, Dutch and German. The Cumberland Presbyterian and Methodist churches of the West are blending Calvinism with Arminianism. The great Lutheran churches give signs of becoming more homogeneous and American. The Baptist churches have declared for union of denominations. The Episcopal church has been inwardly moved as never before towards other Protestant churches. The Evangelical Alliance is taking the form of a national league. And as a visible presage of the new era, we have already had what might be called a provisional Congress of the "United Churches of the United States."

PROPOSALS OF THE AMERICAN BISHOPS.

In the midst of these remarkable movements, the assembled Bishops of the Protestant Episcopal Church have sent forth a noble and far-reaching declaration seeking to embrace all branches of Christendom in the bonds of a true church unity. The four terms proposed are so large and fair that they will almost carry consent in their statement.

First. The Holy Scriptures are already the accepted basis of all Christian churches, besides affording the consensus of Christianity with Judaism, and with heathenism in the work of missions.

Second. The Nicene Creed was simply the faith of the undivided early church, and still expresses the most essential consensus of nearly all modern churches, with room for their later creeds, such as the Thirty-nine Articles, the Westminster, Augsburg, and Heidelberg confessions.

Third. The Gospel Sacraments, whenever and wherever rightly administered, cannot but exhibit the communion of that visible Catholic Church which includes all baptized Christians and their children.

Fourth. The Historic Episcopate might become an added bond among existing church systems, if viewed according to the meaning of the phrase, as a fact rather than as a doctrine, without raising the question whether it has been a development of the apostolate or of the presbyterate of the early church.

It is this last proposal which is likely to stir the keenest debate, and all eyes are now turned toward this one point as the focus of the discussion. If the unifying movement is to go forward, it is plain that it should be led and guided by those churches or systems which are historically and logically most nearly allied in doctrine, polity, and worship, as well as providentially fitted to represent the Protestant and Catholic wings of Christendom. Now these conditions are met by Presbytery and Episcopacy; by Presbytery as included in the Lutheran, Reformed, Congregational, Presbyterian, and Methodist churches; and by Episcopacy as found in the Greek, Latin, Anglican, and Protestant Episcopal churches, —not Presbytery and Episcopacy, viewed merely as complemental institutions in an ideal polity, but also as kindred ecclesiastical elements, with the same roots in Scripture and in History, and having a true and vital affinity for each other.

Here we touch the embers of smouldering controversies, which a breath might kindle into a flame. It would be easy enough to recall old grievances and revive dying prejudices which arose in another age and country, when Presbyterians and Episcopalians made martyrs of each other by turns, in a fierce and sectarian warfare, until, like two combatants chained apart, they were forced by the civil arm to settle down into the established churches of England and Scotland. There are those who would be in haste to import the waning castes of churchman and dissenter into a free republic, to apply the effete policy of the seventeenth century to the nineteenth, and to measure the wants of a hemisphere by those of an island. But the large hearts and noble minds on both sides will resolutely keep dead issues out of sight, will rise above sects and parties to the view of general and lasting interests, and will seek to minimize their trivial differences in order to gain the maximum amount of sincere and honorable agreement.

HISTORICAL RELATIONS OF PRESBYTERY AND EPISCOPACY.

Approaching the question in this spirit, we shall be at no loss for favorable signs and arguments. Not only do the mother-churches of England and Scotland bear an original likeness as twin daughters of the Reformation, descended from the same Catholic church, with the same historical continuity from the apostles' time, and only different lines of succession since they parted; not only may their existing standards be correlated and blended, the Book of Common Prayer as but a liturgical expression of the Directory for Public Worship, the Confession of Faith as but a logical expansion of the Articles of Religion, and the diocesan Episcopate as but a fit complement of the synodical Presbytery,—but besides all this, the two forms of polity, as transplanted to our shores, have developed new types of church life and culture, which would be especially valuable in combination, and have already become leading factors in our Anglo-American civilization, the one as expressive of the best Protestant, and the other of the most Catholic Christianity. Add still further: that for a hundred years past they have been unconsciously coming together and growing like each other. At the very outset, when they became independent of the mother-churches, the American Directory was enriched with liturgical rules and suggestions, and the American Ordinal was enlarged by an alternative form of authorization. Ever since then American Presbyterianism has been steadily reacting from the narrow views of the Puritans and Covenanters toward a larger Christian culture and more liturgical mode of worship, as well as producing a pure theology and a learned ministry unsurpassed in the country; while American Episcopacy, having escaped from the Anglican establishment with a Catholic faith and noble liturgy, has been admitting presbyterial government, lay and clerical, into its dioceses and combining extempore prayers with its liturgy, until it has surrendered the very points on which the Presbyterian party in the Church of England was defeated two centuries ago. We have lived to see Episcopalian prayer-meetings as well as Presbyterian prayer-books. The two hereditary foes have not merely met half-way, but actually crossed the lines as in friendly rivalry on the battle-fields of former generations.

REUNION OF PRESBYTERY AND EPISCOPACY.

Now it seems worth while to ask if the ancient family feud might not somehow be effaced and forgotten. Both churches, after long estrangement, have come back to ground where they may well recognize and respect their common lineage, their organic likeness, and their reciprocal interests. Both of them, in fact, have long since conceded enough, and more than enough, for a full and frank understanding. Had such concessions been made in the beginning, no separation could have occurred. Were such concessions now more generally known, a reunion might soon follow. Even that last barrier to reunion, the vexed question of orders, when fairly met and sifted, may but disclose a ground or link of organic connection in the one simple fact that Episcopal ordination could take nothing from, but only add something to Presbyterian ordination, howsoever either may be viewed by either party. Presbyterians do not differ from Episcopalians more than Episcopalians differ from one another in estimating that rite. In such a state of opinion the differences are no longer worth weighing against the agreements and accruing advantages. As it might prove a great gain to American Episcopacy to be reënforced with Presbyterian orthodoxy and churchliness, so it might prove a great gain to American Presbytery to recover the Episcopal order and liturgy. The reunion would be as organic to each as the original rupture was disorganizing to both. Indeed, it could easily be shown that the chief authors of the Presbyterian standards, if now living, would find their ideal in our Protestant Episcopacy; or, in other words, that the American Episcopacy of to-day has recovered English Presbytery of a classic type, and so fully recovered it that the two systems, at fit times and places, especially in our large cities and great missions, might wisely and well be conjoined or confederated, if not at length merged in one organization.

How far such union or fusion is now feasible need not here be discussed. Whatever changes of church law or practice might be needed, the way to them could be found as soon as there is the will to find them. Presbyterian usage already concedes the validity of episcopal ordination, and the episcopal Ordinal enjoins no polemic theory of presbyterial ordination, but is even held to involve presbyterial coördination. Why not begin at once to act upon these facts and principles? Why should there be a so-called hypothetical ordination on the one side or a covert conditional acceptance of it on the other. Let both parties openly and generously recognize each other in concurrent ordinations or reordinations, as occasion requires. By such means all question of valid ministrations would at length die out, as in a marriage of rival houses. The most extreme Episcopalian, from his own point of view, would only be sanctioning orthodox learning, churchly aims, and evangelical labors; and the most extreme Presbyterian, from his own point of view, would only be gaining more authority or grace for a larger service; and the two together would simply be honoring both episcopacy and presbytery in the one catholic and apostolic Church of Christ.

ADVANTAGES OF EPISCOPACY.

Without claiming to speak for others, but looking at the question from a strictly undenominational point of view, I venture to hope that in any union to be devised the historic episcopate can be retained, if only as one remaining bulwark against the well-meant but lawless evangelism which is running wild in our churches and bringing all the divine institutions of the Christian religion into contempt. The great revivalists, Whitefield and Wesley, were trained clergymen and ever appeared as such, even when driven from the pulpit into the field. But our lay evangelists are pressed from the field into the pulpit, and a divine success is claimed for them on the very ground that they are not clergymen but mere laymen. When earnest and gifted preachers of the Gospel, like Mr. Moody, decline to become ordained ministers of any church, while everywhere exercising ministerial functions, with learned divines and faithful pastors sitting at their feet, and the whole order of God's house set aside, can we wonder if the popular inference should be that the ministry itself is but a human convenience, if not already a failure? Is any transient good, done by them, to be weighed for one moment against the lasting evil of overthrowing the most sacred ordinances and institutions, to say nothing of feverish excitements, whose track is often that of the simoon through the fairest pastures of Christ? Our chief danger in this land and age of freedom is not hierarchy. Instead of too much ecclesiasticism, there is too little. The clergy are fast losing their normal rank and influence. The time may yet come when pure presbytery and true episcopacy shall appear not only congruous but inseparable, and together essential in maintaining that "catholic visible church unto which Christ hath given the ministry, oracles, and ordinances of God."

There is also a large and growing class of minds in all churches for whom the historic episcopate, as now associated with the prayer-book, seems practically the only guarantee of a pure scriptural worship. Time was indeed when that liturgy had been so rigorously enforced as to extinguish all other forms of devotion. No wonder Milton could then cry out against it: "To imprison and confine by force, within a pin-fold of set words, those two most unimprisonable things, our prayers and that divine spirit of utterance which moves them, is a tyranny that would want longer hands than those giants who threatened bondage to heaven." But out of that tyranny we have long since fought our way to a ruinous victory. The time has now come to distinguish liberty from license in the worship of God, and to assert order and decency against confusion in the assemblies of saints. Keep for fit times and places the free, extempore service which has been so dearly won; but keep also that historic liturgy which has come down to us from all the Christian ages. Let the people have pure English and sound doctrine at least in their devotions; let them learn the whole word of God in appointed lessons; let them offer up prayers which they can call their own; let them follow their Lord, from his cradle to his cross, through each year of his grace; let them receive holy sacraments and rites in the meet words of apostles, saints, and martyrs; let them thus worship with angels and archangels and the whole company of the redeemed on earth and in heaven. Already, indeed, some of these things have been reclaimed for them as their just heritage, and we are beginning to find that the prayer-book can co-exist with the prayer-meeting as easily as episcopacy can concur with presbytery.

Besides these advantages, the historic episcopate might also bring a valuable conservative force into our presbyterial systems of church government. Aside from the claim of apostolical succession, it is appreciated as a spiritual and ancient institution of the Christian religion as fitted to secure the choicest wisdom, learning, and piety of the Church in the direction of its affairs, and as demanded by new exigencies which have arisen in our time and country. Since it became detached from the English peerage and monarchy, it has grown into harmony with our Republican institutions, while supplying needed checks upon their radical tendencies. Moreover, it is certain that Episcopacy as well as Presbytery would have a voice in any Provisional Congress or General Council of the Lutheran, Reformed, Congregational, Presbyterian, Methodist, and Protestant Episcopal churches which could be duly called; and should the time ever come for the federation or consolidation of these bodies, it might be found that a House of Bishops and House of Presbyters, like the Senators and Representatives in our National legislature, would support and balance each other, reconciling rival claims and interests, and ever securing the new popular institutions of the American church as well as keeping it in the line of historic Christianity. He would be a bold prophet who would strike out either presbytery or episcopacy from the future Christian civilization of this continent.

The chief obstacles to a reunion of our episcopal and presbyterial systems are not so much any doctrinal differences inhering in those systems as the mere incidental influences of denominational pride, inherited prejudice and general ignorance—an ignorance largely enveloping the clergy as well as the people. Nothing would seem plainer than that both parties left their grievances behind them three thousand miles away, two hundred years ago; and yet the memory of them so rankles in our blood that we still shudder at them as if we might encounter another Laud in some good bishop of an American diocese, or provoke some Janet Geddes to hurl her tripod in response to a Presbyterian liturgy. The political, social, and religious conditions which once kindled so fierce a strife between Presbytery and Episcopacy, and drove them asunder to so rash extremes, could not be transferred to this free land and can never arise among its free churches; but we seem often to fancy that the same battle is still raging, and fill the air with the old familiar slogans and cheer on our champions to new encounters, though all the while no lordly prelates are sitting in our legislatures, and no bloody Claverhouse is abroad pursuing our peaceful worshipers; though no psalm-singing Puritans are despoiling our new cathedrals and no outlawed Covenanters are waylaying our excellent bishops. Episcopalians are ever boasting of a church lineage which they espoused but yesterday; and Presbyterians, of a line of martyrs whom they no longer follow. We forget that those honored Anglican prelates would have dispersed our Episcopal Conventions as so many rebels, schismatics, and dissenters, and those revered Scottish worthies would have made swift bonfires of our Presbyterian hymnals, organs, and service-books. And should some candid investigator expose to us, in the clear light of history, how groundless are our prejudices and how foolish our divisions, we can do nothing perhaps but accept his statements, as highly interesting but very useless, and scarcely know whether to frown or smile upon him as, by turns, he provokes admiration or indignation on both sides of the question.

The writer cannot hope to escape such influences. By some of his most respected readers this paper may be viewed as a pure speculation. It will be easy to call it the dream of a recluse, or say that the time is not ripe for it. Nevertheless, the present generation might see it becoming real, if only events move forward as fast as they have moved since the former paper was written. And no prophet is needed to tell us what would be the issue.

Let the day ever come for a general reunion of Presbytery and Episcopacy, either by formal agreement or by practical fusion, and it would mark the turning point in the problem of an American Catholic Church. It would be but the forming nucleus of a wide confederation and consolidation of churches and denominations, which are already in ministerial communion and more or less organic connection. Presbytery would include the German, Dutch, French, Scotch, and English type of Protestantism; Episcopacy would involve the

Greek, Latin, Anglican, and American germs of Catholicity; and all these varied elements acquiring fresh vigor would come into new and vital relations, correcting and molding each other. Our best American Christianity would react upon our whole American civilization against the crying evils of sectarianism, infidelity, and vice. The great vanguard churches of the land, no longer idly saying one to another in the very front of battle, " I have no need of thee," would stand compact together, and grow up in Christ the Head as his living members, and at length, it may be, lead on to·*one United Church of the United States.*

III.
THE FOUR ARTICLES OF CHURCH UNITY.

III.

THE FOUR ARTICLES OF CHURCH UNITY.

It has been said that the greatest wonder of the World's Fair was its Parliament of Religions. It put upon exhibition not merely the principal Heathen beliefs, but the various Christian denominations, with champions rehearsing their claims. Whether it shall pass away like another Babel or open a new Pentecost, depends upon the use now made of its lessons. And its chief lesson was not the supremacy of Christianity, which required no proof; but the absolute need of harmony and unity in order to establish its supremacy throughout the earth. Let that lesson go unheeded, and the Christian Religion may only have exposed its weakness in the face of its enemies. Henceforth the conquest of heathenism, as well as the maintenance of civilization, will demand more than ever the reunion of Christendom.

Let us approach this momentous question, as far as we may, with strict definitions and clear conceptions. While such preliminaries are essential to all good thinking and sound opinion, they are especially needful in dealing with so difficult a problem as Church unity, and one already so beclouded with vague terms and specious phrases. Several distinctions are to be premised and maintained throughout the inquiry.

CHURCH UNITY DEFINED.

First of all, Church unity should be distinguished from Christian unity or the oneness of believers in Christ. There is a sense in which all Christians are one already, and one simply because they are Christians. They are one in the unity of the spirit. They are spiritually united to Christ by faith and love as branches of one vine and members of one body. They thus form one holy brotherhood, one mystical fellowship, one communion of saints, the world over. This one invisible Church, as it is often called, persists in and through all visible churches and denominations, survives their mutations and destructions, and remains intact even amid their conflicts and schisms. And it cannot be too highly exalted in the present discussion. That we are all one in Christ is an admitted fact from which we proceed, and the common ground upon which we stand. Without it we could not even consider the question before us. But while Christian unity is thus to be held as the condition precedent to church unity it is not church unity itself. By a vague figure of speech it is sometimes confounded with church unity, and even miscalled organic unity in allusion to a metaphorical organism; but in a strict sense it can only be applied to the spiritual fellowship of saints or invisible church. Nevertheless this invisible church ever becomes more or less visible in organic form and strives to manifest its oneness. It can no more exist without an organism or an organization than the soul without the body. Organization, if not essential to its very being, is at least indispensable and of divine origin and warrant. The institutions of Christianity, its ministry and sacraments, are revealed in the Scriptures, no less than its doctrines. In fact, but for its institutions we should have had neither its Scriptures nor yet its doctrines. As a bare Gospel, apart from the church, it might have died out in the first century, with no more echo in history than the teachings of Socrates or the morals of Seneca. It became, however, a compact organization in the midst of pagan society, with its sacraments and its Scriptures; and it continued thus compact and undivided for some centuries afterward. In that one Catholic Apostolic Church we have an example and model of church unity, not only as consistent with Christian unity but as expressing and maintaining it. Indeed, it is only in and through such church unity that Christian unity can find due and full expression. Without such unity it must remain as a vague ideal or crude sentiment, if it be not made a mere pretext for schism and excuse for sectarianism. The most factious sectaries are sometimes loudest in their appeals to the Christian unity which they have defied and obscured, yet cannot destroy. Never let it be forgotten that Christian unity, spiritual oneness, already exists as a divine fundamental fact in the churches; and the real problem is, how to express this Christian unity in an organic church unity which shall exhibit the mystical body of Christ as no longer mutilated and distracted, but with its various members in normal exercise and conscious harmony.

FEDERATION OF CHURCHES.

Church unity should also be distinguished from Church union or the federation of denominations.[1] The different Christian bodies in our country have often become externally conjoined without internal modification or concession, somewhat as sovereign states form leagues and compacts. Under the impulse of common aims and the pressure of common dangers they have been combined in Bible and Tract Societies, in Sunday-school Unions, in Boards of Domestic and Foreign Missions, and in various associations for promoting temperance, purity, charity, peace, and other Christian virtues. Such coalitions, though purely superficial and transient, besides furthering the good ends in view, have served to demonstrate an essential agreement amid the general diversity. We have also had examples of a more organic union of denominations, based upon affinity in doctrine, polity, and worship, such as the recent federation of the different Anglican bodies in Canada. In some cases divided Churches have been reunited, as when the Old and New School

---

[1] It should be premised that, throughout this essay, the word "denomination" will be used in the legal sense (see Preface of the Prayer-book), as applicable alike to all Christian bodies, Catholic or Protestant, whatever may be their ecclesiastical claims or merits.

Presbyterian Churches again became one ecclesiastical body. The Methodist Episcopal and Protestant Methodist churches were merged together in the same manner. At first sight this would seem to be a most hopeful field in which to labor for church unity. Why should the Protestant Episcopal and Reformed Episcopal churches remain apart after the Chicago Declaration? Why do not the Dutch and German Reformed churches come together, when they are so much alike that it is hard to tell one from the other? What should hinder the great Methodist churches, Northern and Southern, or the Presbyterian churches, North and South, from reuniting as one church since we are under one government? Might not the different Lutheran Synods and Councils be colligated? Could not the large family of Baptist denominations be at least confederated? Is there anything in the claims of local autonomy to forbid a more organic union of Congregational churches? Ought not the chief denominations thus to unite in kindred groups? And then, on the basis of such special unions, why not build up a general confederation in some grand national council of denominations, a sort of Congress of the United Churches of the United States, having its Senate of Bishops as the conservative element, and its House of Presbyters as the progressive element, with its ratio of Congregational representation and its legislation restricted to domestic charities and foreign missions? What a magnificent spectacle would such an ecclesiastical confederacy present to the rest of Christendom! How it would shine like a constellation in the firmament of the Universal Church! The bare mention of it is inspiring and elevating. But the bare mention also shows it to be crude and visionary. At the first touch of analysis the nebulous splendor dissolves into the stars of which it is composed. Confederation is not unification. It is but a mechanical union of social bodies, not their chemical fusion and vital growth. It has twice proved a failure in our political history; first, when it could not hold the United States together, and afterward when it strove to tear them apart. There could be no perfect union of churches or of states, without some mutual concession of sovereignty, some submission to common authority, some agreement in essential opinions. At its best estate, on its face, denominational confederation is but masked denominationalism, and a mere temporary expedient, carrying its own dissolution with it. Often it is only a truce in mid battle, or patching of old family quarrels. If it serve as a first step toward church unity it cannot be the last one, but must advance or else recoil with fresh estrangement and harsh assertion of sectarian prejudice worse than before. First or last, whatever else it may be, it is not church unity.

ASSIMILATION OF DENOMINATIONS.

Church unity should be distinguished still further from Church uniformity or the assimilation of denominations. This is the other extreme from federation. It would efface denominational distinctions and reduce all Christian bodies to one type of doctrine, polity, and worship. It is a process which seems to have been long going on in our country. The Churches of the Old World as transferred to the New, and compacted together under one political system, have been growing like each other through social intercourse and unconscious imitation. Protestants have been reviving the Catholic sisterhood and fraternity under new names and guises; while Catholics are resorting to the Protestant platform and newspaper in their conflicts and troubles. Episcopalians have restored Presbyterian elements to their polity and extempore prayers to their liturgy; while Presbyterians are recovering Episcopal agencies of administration and liturgical modes of worship. Both Presbyterians and Episcopalians have learned something from the Methodist revival; while Methodists have learned to have choirs and divinity schools as well as campmeetings and lay preachers. Lutherans, Congregationalists, Baptists, in like manner, are taking on all the hues of the Church year and ritual. At first sight there might seem to be no limit to such assimilation. We are ready to fancy the denominations blending into a sort of composite likeness. But on closer view the superficial resemblances vanish, and the old essential differences assert themselves. Each will be found prizing more the distinction which it keeps than the differences which it has effaced. And such distinctions cannot and should not be wholly obliterated. Absolute uniformity is not possible either in the world of nature or of grace. According to the chosen metaphors of Scripture, the Church is one vine, but with different branches; one body, but with various members; one building, but of composite structure. In political society we see the greatest variety of classes, parties, and opinions; aristocratic, democratic, republican, socialist, populist; no one of them absorbing or exterminating the rest. As little in religious society may we hope to find all Christians at once becoming Baptists, or Congregationalists, or Methodists, or Presbyterians, or Episcopalians, or Romanists. Much less could they be made alike by any civil or ecclesiastical process. The experiment of enforced uniformity has been tried for several hundred years in Episcopal England and Presbyterian Scotland, with only a brood of non-conforming sects growing up around both establishments. The same lesson is taught us here by the conflict of usage with rubrics, by the disuse of directories, and by the rise of heresy under the strictest creeds and confessions. All experience shows that a rigid uniformity in doctrine and ritual could only breed dissent and schism, and issue in renewed failure. Were it attained, instead of promoting Church unity, it would destroy it.

The definition of a true Church unity is now before us. It would not ignore our common Christianity, but would more fully express and maintain it. It would not undervalue denominational confederation, but would look beyond it to a more perfect union of denominations. It would not obliterate denominational peculiarities, or sacrifice them to a cast-iron uniformity, but it would legitimate, subordinate, and readjust them in one large ecclesiastical system as different members knit together in the one living body of Christ. In a word, it would maintain unity in variety as well as variety in unity.

FALSE ECCLESIASTICISM.

At this point we shall be met by several objections which must be cleared out of the way before we can proceed. It will be said that Church unity tends to ecclesiasticism. History will be invoked to warn us against any renewed compact of denominations as involving the latent evils of churchly power and state religion. But history does not repeat itself, where the conditions are changed; nor do revolutions ever go backward. The dread of priestcraft which once had fitness in European countries has no place in modern civilization, though it may linger as an inherited prejudice in some of our popular discussions and partisan appeals. With the pope himself little more than a state prisoner at Rome, any supremacy of the papacy in international politics has become a dead issue. With the Anglican and Scottish establishments already doomed and waning, any domination of prelacy or presbytery in our political affairs is but the ghost of a dead issue. And to imagine the wrangling sects of this country combining to seize the United States Government and convert it into a theocracy is to imagine a species of ecclesiasticism which cannot be stated without showing its intrinsic absurdity. Let us not be frightened by the mere word "ecclesiasticism." The real dangers which threaten us are not in the ecclesiastical sphere, but in the political or social sphere; not in the hierarchy of the dead past, but in the anarchy of the living present. And against such dangers Church unity simply means the mustering together of our common Christianity in defence of our common civilization.

FALSE DENOMINATIONALISM.

There is a kindred objection, that Church unity would destroy the witness-bearing character of the denominations. At their origin each of them had some high mission to fulfil, some great problem to solve, some special doctrine or principle to uphold. The Lutheran and the Huguenot protested against the papacy. The Covenanter made a solemn league against prelacy. The Puritan fled away from a false ecclesiasticism into the wilderness. The Methodist broke the bonds of formalism with a pentecostal revival. These are not small achievements, to be lightly esteemed or rashly put in peril. Granting them, however, it remains to ask, whether by this time such denominational missions have not been sufficiently accomplished, and whether in this country they are any longer in place. Why continue mere Protestants in a land where Roman Catholicism is coming under American influences if not already in the ordeal of reformation; mere Covenanters, where Episcopacy has long since conceded nearly everything for which the Presbyterian party in the church of England contended; mere Puritans, where the lost ideal of the church is coming back into the Puritan consciousness; or mere revivalists, where even orthodoxy and ritualism are leavened with Methodist usages and influences. Would it not be better to bring together such denominational types as complementary traits of Christian character, and harmonize such denominational claims as rival schools or tendencies in one church system? As expressed in diverse organizations called churches, they become frightfully exaggerated; they tend to obscure or mutilate more essential truths; and they lead to immense waste, loss, and conflict in all missionary and humanitarian efforts. Whereas the same different beliefs and usages as tolerated in one organization or in one church would retire from public view; would sink into due relative insignificance; would modify and check one another; and would render both missions and charities more compact and efficient. There is, in fact, no good thing for which the denominationalist pleads, which in such a system might not be retained, while much sin and evil that he laments would be avoided. Church unity, it has been aptly said, is "not anti-denominational but super-denominational."

FEASIBILITY OF CHURCH UNITY.

The most practical objection is, that church unity, however desirable in itself, is not feasible. Often it is accepted as a "pium desiderium," a consummation devoutly to be wished, but not to be actually sought after; and sometimes its advocates are only pitied as amiable visionaries. Against such skepticism stands not merely the scriptural ideal of one church but all analogy and much experience. Take the analogy of living nature. As we ascend the organic scale, from the mollusk up to the mammal, rank above rank, species after species, we find increasing unity amid increasing variety, the more complex the more compact the structure, until at the summit in man, as naturalists tell us, all inferior organisms are recapitulated as many members in one body, and set forth as the very masterpiece of creation. And what God has wrought in the kingdom of nature, shall He not yet work out in the kingdom of grace? Take the nearer analogy of political society. In our own country, during less than two centuries, we have seen the most varied nationalities, English, French, Dutch, Spanish; in the most varied climates, Northern, Southern, Eastern, Western; with the most varied creeds, Catholic, Huguenot, Puritan, Cavalier, Covenanter; under the most varied governments, theocratic, monarchic, aristocratic, democratic, all together emerging at length as the United States with the realized motto, "E pluribus Unum." And what worldly men have done in their political relations, cannot Christian men do in their religious relations? Go back to the experience of early Christian society. In that first organization of the church we see congregational, presbyterial, episcopal institutions, but no separate Episcopalian, Presbyterian, and Congregationalist denominations with the apostles in one, the presbyters in another, and a few synagogues in the third. We find various schools of doctrine as distinct as those of Luther, Calvin, and Arminius, but no Pauline, Petrine, and Johannean churches so-called, unchurching one another for a dogma or a rite. On the contrary, we behold all our unhappy divisions dwelling together in one undivided Apostolic Church. And what the church has been once, may it not become again? Look abroad in Christian society now. Every denomination is asserting unity against diversity. The Baptists and the Congregationalists, in spite of their localism, would become national and comprehensive. The Lutherans, the Presbyterians, the Methodists would be called churches "of the United States." The Reformed would be no longer Dutch or German. The Protestant Episcopalians would drop their very name from the title of the church. The Catholics would show themselves American as well as Roman. All, in one form or another, have before them the ideal of one American Catholic Church.

THE NEW PROMISE OF CHURCH UNITY.

I do not forget the past experiments in Church unity. Has not the Western church for twelve centuries been vainly trying to make peace with the Eastern church? Did not the Eastern church refuse to make peace with the Reformed churches? Could the Reformed churches even make peace among themselves? Were popes, prelates, and presbyteries successful in securing uniformity or conformity among the churches of England, Scotland, and Ireland? Have the numerous eirenicons since devised by large-hearted ecclesiastics like Usher, Leighton, Pusey, Muhlenberg proved any more successful? Why follow in the train of these dismal failures? For a twofold reason: first, because it is only through repeated failures that we can pass to ultimate success; and also, because former causes of failure are dying out in our age and country. Geographical barriers to unity have disappeared. The Eastern and Western churches, the German, French, English, and Scottish churches, are here compacted together within one territory and fusing into one nationality. Political barriers have disappeared. The temporal power of the Pope, the civil establishment of prelacy and presbytery, have given place to free churches in a free land, conspiring under one government with one patriotic aim. Dogmatic barriers are disappearing. Lutheranism, Calvinism, Arminianism, by their own attritions, concessions, and revisions are approaching one common faith and ritual. At the same time, powerful causes of unity are working. Democratic influences are undermining the walls of mere Romanism. A papal theocracy has humbled monarchies, and subdued aristocracies, but never has it conquered a democracy; and out of such a conflict it could only emerge itself conquered. Social influences are consolidating Protestantism. The Huguenot, the Puritan, the Cavalier, the Covenanter have been intermarrying for several generations, until now he who fights unity will have war in his own household. Religious influences are working. The spirit of unity itself is seizing the Christian masses like a passion, and carrying their wrangling leaders along with them as with the might of a revolution. Never before in any Christian century, nowhere else in any Christian country, have all the conditions been so favorable for realizing the long-lost ideal of one Holy Catholic and Apostolic Church.

In order to keep this discussion within the region of facts, two principles are important, the one as to the scope, and the other as to the basis of unity. The first is that a true church unity must include all existing churches within its scope. Its horizon must be as wide as Christendom, and its point of view must be taken in the midst of the churches and not within the narrow pale of any of them. Otherwise we shall lose sight of large portions of the Christian world, or only seek to unify some portions against the others.

THE CLAIM OF THE HISTORIC CHURCHES.

First of all, we must take into our view the great historic churches which have come down to us from the Apostles' time. It is hard to believe that the devil has governed the Christian Church for twenty centuries. We shall fly in the face of universal Providence if we try to date the Christian era from the Diet of Worms, or to close it at the Council of Nice. The divine work of the Universal Church is not to be tossed aside as mere ecclesiasticism, that a few Christians at this late day may build it all over again. The Eastern Greek Church and the Western Latin Church have existed and still exist by the grace of God, as well as the modern Protestant Church or the latest Christian meeting that is called a church. Nor can we belittle their connection with the question as sentimental, academic, chimerical, or in any sense foreign to us. I do not refer merely to the few Greek congregations among us, on our eastern and western shores. Politically we are in the same boat with at least eight million Roman Catholic fellow-citizens; and sooner or later we may have to unite with them against the combined terrors of mutiny and shipwreck; in plainer words, against sectarianism and infidelity. As fast as that great spiritual organization under the plastic force of its new American environment sheds its Romanism and becomes simply American, national, and patriotic, will it prove an immense gain to our common Christianity as well as a safeguard to our common country. Already it is practically with us on the great moral questions of the day, bringing its rank and file as a compact fighting mass into the battle with social vice and sin. It is true, the *Filioque* in the Nicene Creed and the dogma of papal infallibility are present barriers to unity. But it is also true that reforming influences are at work, for which due allowance must be made. It remains to be seen whether existing obstacles may not be reduced to a dead letter or disappear in the unifying process. Moreover, it is a duty to make the terms of fraternity broad enough to embrace even those who erect barriers against it. Theoretically at least, if not as yet practically, the Greek and Latin communions must be included with the Anglican and American in any scheme of true church unity.

THE CLAIM OF THE REFORMED CHURCHES.

At the same time we must not wholly exclude from such a scheme the less historic churches which date from the Reformation, or even the denominations which have followed in their train. Protestantism, for all its faults, cannot be reckoned a sheer mistake and failure. No less than Catholicism, it has the reason of its existence in divine providence and its warrant in a divine success. For four centuries it has been making a history of its own. The Congregationalist, Baptist, and Methodist communions, though detached from the historic church, have largely restored the primitive Christianity. The Lutheran and Reformed churches claim to have renewed the historic church, not to have destroyed it, retaining its creeds and portions of its ritual. The Church of Scotland, as by law established, declared it had been "reformed from popery, not by prelates, but by presbyters as the only successors left by Christ and his apostles in the Church;" and to-day it has its own Catholic revival of ritual, as distinct from Oxford as from Rome, and by no means what is vulgarly termed among us "aping the Episcopalians." Now, even the straitest Protestant Episcopal churchman, who looks upon such bodies around him as pseudo-ecclesiastical or quasi-ecclesiastical sects having no right to the name of churches, must recognize among them certain ecclesiastical institutions, or ecclesiastical theories, or ecclesiastical aspirations, tending toward his own ecclesiastical system, together with acknowledged Christian methods and benefits which might well be legitimated and included within his own system. He would not deny their value merely as training-schools. Nor can he any longer, in this country at least, claim a monopoly of the culture and taste which once made the Anglican church a social caste in little sympathy with surrounding Christianity. Among liturgical denominations the prayer-book itself is ceasing to act as a social distinction. Other less cultured denominations may still hold doctrines of the church and sacraments which are hindrances to unity. But the most independent of Independents are not beyond the reach of churchly influences and unifying impulses. Many of the Baptists favor open communion; and some Unitarians would object less to the Nicene Creed than Greek Churchmen. In the long future, the extreme left wing of Protestantism as well as the extreme right wing of Catholicism may yet react toward the center. Neither should be cast outside the pale of Christian fraternity. In a word, if we would deal with all the facts, we must somehow prospectively, if not immediately, include both the historic churches, and the reformed churches, the oldest denominations and the latest sects, as alike within the scope of a true church unity.

THE NEED OF A PRACTICAL CONSENSUS.

The other practical principle is, that the true Church unity must be based upon the actual consensus of all existing churches in doctrine, ritual, and polity. With their ideal consensus we can have but little to do. In what doctrines or articles of faith they ought to be consentient; what dogmas should be rejected, or retained, or modified in order to make them rightly consentient, is largely a matter of pure speculation. Many of us could not agree as to the terms of such an ideal agreement. If some of us should frame such an agreement, satisfactory to ourselves, others would not assent to it. In the end we might only be adding one more sect to the medley, and so make confusion worse confounded. Church unity cannot thus be built up on the ruins of all existing churches.[1]

Nor have we any more to do with a future consensus of the churches, to be reached in the progress of learning and

---

[1] This may be the peril of the "Brotherhood of Christian Unity" and any like associations which ignore all existing churches for the sake of some meagre consensus of Christianity with other religions or some common Christian faith which contains only the minimum of Christian truth and is too vague and ideal to be made an organic bond of true Church unity.

liberty. In what doctrines they will be consentient ultimately in coming generations, or what dogmas will have been lost or gained in the Church of the millennium, is sheer beyond our ken. Some of us may doubt if such a perfect agreement will ever come; and any of us who hope for it could not now project it without the gift of prophecy, as well as the understanding of all mysteries. Church unity cannot be built after any prophetic model let down from heaven, ready made and complete, like the New Jerusalem in the Apocalypse.[1]

It is only with the actual, the existing, consensus of the churches that we can deal. Not the things which should be believed among us; nor yet the things which will be believed among us; but "the things which are most surely believed among us," as St. Luke expresses it—this is the practical question. To this practical question the catholic thought of the age is already addressing itself; and it has at length found voice and audience.

THE LAMBETH PROPOSALS.

It has become the rare honor and privilege of one of the smallest denominations—small in numbers but large in an intelligent survey of the situation—to lead all the rest in this great movement, and even to be followed by the mother Church of England. The Bishops of the Protestant Episcopal Church, from their high point of view, have undertaken to "set forth in order a declaration of the things which are most surely believed among us." In other words they have formulated an actual consensus of the churches as the basis of their unity; an existing creed, ritual, and polity in which they are already more or less consentient, and not some new or imaginary creed, ritual, and polity in which they cannot

---

[1] In this direction seem to tend those advocates of the Roman Catholic Church, or of the Protestant Episcopal Church, or of any other denominational church, who hope to realize church unity exclusively in their own organization at some remote millennium by destroying or supplanting or converting all the other churches and denominations of the country.

become consentient without utterly abandoning their respective standards or destroying their identity in some ruthless process of unification.

This practical quality of the Episcopal declaration is one of its chief merits. In its very nature it is a unifying manifesto. It exhibits to the world the great things in which Christian bodies can agree, and exalts them above the small things in which they differ. Each of the four articles, the Scriptures, the Creeds, the Sacraments, the Episcopate, will be found to serve this purpose as successively stated.[1] The Holy Scriptures are already accepted as the rule of faith by all Christian denominations between the extremes of Romanism and Protestantism, however varied may be their interpretation of those Scriptures. The Nicene Creed is the sufficient statement of the Christian faith, though it be supplemented with denominational symbols, such as the Augsburg Confession, the Heidelberg Catechism, the Anglican Articles of Religion, the Westminster Confession of Faith, or the latest American product of creed making. The two sacraments of Christ are administered with His appointed words and elements in all communions, the simplest as well as the most ritualistic, not less by the Baptist who insists upon immersion than by the Romanist who withholds the cup from the laity. The Historic Episcopate is everywhere adaptable to Congregationalists, Presbyterians, and Episcopalians of every type,

---

[1] The four articles, as proposed at Chicago, and amended by the Lambeth Conference, are as follows:

First. The Holy Scriptures of the Old and New Testament as containing all things necessary to salvation and as being the rule and ultimate standard of faith.

Second. The Apostles' Creed as the Baptismal symbol; and the Nicene Creed as the sufficient statement of the Christian Faith.

Third. The two Sacraments ordained by Christ Himself—Baptism and the Supper of the Lord—ministered with unfailing use of Christ's words of institution, and of the elements ordained by Him.

Fourth. The Historic Episcopate, locally adapted in the methods of its administration to the varying needs of the nations and peoples called of God into the unity of His Church.

as well to those without as to those within the pale of that Episcopate. In a word, if the Christian denominations of this land were in search of a canon, creed, ritual, and polity, which should express their consensus as against their dissensus, the essentials in which they agree as distinguished from the non-essentials in which they differ, they would find them in the four Principles of the Chicago Declaration.

CATHOLICITY OF THE FOUR ARTICLES.

Another great merit of that Declaration is its absolute catholicity. There is no denominationalism whatever in its terms. Although it emanates from one of the denominations, it proposes nothing peculiar to that denomination; not the Prayer Book, not the Articles of Religion, not even the Ordinal in its details. On the contrary the things which it proposes are also possessed or shared by other denominations. The Holy Scriptures are the common heritage of Christendom, Greek, and Latin as well as Anglican, American as well as European. The ecumenical creeds are professed by the Greek, Roman, Lutheran, Reformed, and Presbyterian communions, as well as by the Protestant Episcopal communion. The Sacraments of our Lord are scrupulously observed by many if not all other Christian bodies than those which follow the use of the English Liturgy. The historic Episcopate is a universal institution common to Eastern and Western Christendom, and not confined to the American House of Bishops. As this last point may not be as obvious as the other three points, and yet is pivotal to the whole discussion, it is important here to give it special attention.

CATHOLICITY OF THE HISTORIC EPISCOPATE.

The Historic Episcopate would remain in this country if the organization known as "The Protestant Episcopal Church" did not exist. It would still be represented to us by the Russian Greek and Roman Catholic Churches; encumbered, it is true, with various dogmas, but with dogmas no better, or no worse, than theories which encumber it in other communions and act as hindrances to unity. Indeed, it is quite conceivable that Roman bishops in some new reformation, more justly conservative than ours, may yet offer the episcopate to their Protestant brethren with some stronger motives than any that now appear in the tender of it from another quarter. In that event the whole ecclesiastical situation would be changed. The great Lutheran communion would be found more closely allied to the Roman than to the Anglican Episcopate. The Reformed bodies, Dutch, French, and German, might more naturally return to the historic primacy of Rome than to the local primacy of Canterbury. All Protestants, in fact, might then unite in recognizing a *de facto* headship of Western Christendom. And thus the Mother of Churches could grow as rapidly by conversion as she has been growing by emigration. Stranger things have happened. Be all this, however, as it may, treat it as a mere quixotic fancy, the fact remains, that the Protestant Episcopal Church has no exclusive property in the Episcopate, but only shares it, and shares it very largely, with other and greater historic churches in America as well as Europe.

It should also be remembered that at one time in the history of that church it was nearly on a par with other American denominations as to the episcopate now deemed so essential to its very being. For more than one hundred years, during the whole colonial period, the so-called "Episcopal churches" scattered along the Atlantic coast were practically without the Episcopate and even without episcopal visitations. Successive generations of communicants grew up unconfirmed, and the clergy had little more than the distant oversight of the Bishop of London. It is well known that the popular dread of an Episcopal establishment was one of the causes of the American Revolution. After the rupture with the mother country it became still more doubtful whether the Episcopate could be procured from the Church of England. In the emergency there was even some thought of applying for the foreign orders of Sweden. But the patriarchal Bishop White declared that in such circumstances "a scrupulous adherence to episcopacy would be sacrificing the substance to the ceremony,"[1] and lest the essentials of preaching and worship should utterly lapse he sketched a provisional polity with presbyterial ordination, and other features thoroughly Presbyterian. When at length the Episcopate was conferred by the English Bishops it simply supervened upon that provisional presbyterian organization as it might now supervene upon any other Presbyterian body; and it is still, in thought at least, as separable from the one as it is in fact separate from the other.

It should further be observed, that the college of Bishops has logically (I do not say formally) separated the episcopate from the communion over which they preside, by proposing it to other communions, at the same time nobly disclaiming any wish to absorb other communions, and declaring their readiness to forego the modes of worship and discipline peculiar to their own communion, and to co-operate with other communions on the basis of a common faith and order, in discountenancing schism and healing the wounds of the body of Christ. In distinct terms, "as Bishops in the Church of God,"[2] they have invited their fellow-Christians to meet them on the outside common ground of membership by baptism in the Holy Catholic Church, and there find further agreement in the four articles of unity. Suppose, for argument's sake, that the Presbyterian Church should adopt these articles, and at length select presbyters to be consecrated as bishops. Would the Episcopal college then bring forward

---

[1] "The Case of the Episcopal Churches in the United States Considered," p. 19. By the Rev. Dr. William White, afterward Bishop of Pennsylvania.

[2] The Declaration does not seem to have proceeded from "the House of Bishops" as a component part of the Protestant Episcopal Church, limited by its constitution and laws, but from the Bishops in Council at Chicago and in Conference at Lambeth.

the new requirement of an oath of "conformity and obedience to the doctrine, discipline, and worship of the Protestant Episcopal Church in the United States?" Would they amend their own terms by adding to the Holy Scriptures the church canons; to the Nicene Creed, the Articles of Religion; to the Sacraments of our Lord, the Book of Common Prayer; and to the Historic Episcopate, the entire ordinal of Bishops, Priests, and Deacons? Would they thus endeavor, in the face of their Declaration, to absorb other communions or impose upon them the laws, traditions, and usages of their own communion? In that case suppose the Moravian, or Swedish,[1] or Old Catholic Episcopate to have been elsewhere obtained, would they not gladly recognize and welcome it?

In order to make this point still clearer let us recur to the "case of the Episcopal churches" at the close of the Revolution. Their situation as to the question before us was analogous to that of presbyterial churches at the present time. They had assumed a thoroughly presbyterial polity, though as yet without Bishops. It is true, they had also the Prayer-book; and the English bishops would not confer the Episcopal character until assured that the Prayer-Book would be retained in its integrity. But that is not now made a condition of the conferment. The Prayer-Book is not even named in the terms proposed at Chicago or at Lambeth. There is nothing on the face of those terms to forbid the Presbyterian church, as it stands to-day, from acquiring the episcopate, if so minded. Nor would it thereby go over in a body to the Protestant Episcopal Church. On the contrary, the revered Bishop of Western New York, if correctly reported,[2] has distinctly said: "We have proposed a course which, if carried

---

[1] Lutheran clergymen have said that the proposed procurement of the Historic Episcopate from the Church of Sweden would have the effect of modifying the exclusive claims of the Protestant Episcopal Church among sister Protestant Churches.

[2] Sermon of Bishop Coxe at Buffalo, in New York *Tribune*, March 22, 1891.

out by any of the greater denominations of Christians, would compel us to join them."

ADAPTABILITY OF THE HISTORIC EPISCOPATE.

I may now add, that some learned canonists, if I understand them, are already advocating an extension of the American Episcopate to other denominations, as proposed by the late Dr. Muhlenberg of blessed memory, and as illustrated recently by the extension of the Roman episcopate over Uniate Greek congregations in this country, notwithstanding their married priests, trine immersion, presbyterial confirmation, and other tenets not held by Romanists, but held by Episcopalians, Baptists, and Presbyterians. The Lambeth Conference itself, if I read aright, has generously opened the way for a similar extension of the Anglican episcopate to other Christian communions abroad and at home, "without insisting upon the formularies which are the special heritage of the Church of England," and even with "large freedom of variation on secondary points of doctrine, worship, and discipline."[1] Both the Chicago and the Lambeth declarations also seem to distinguish the historic episcopate from its Greek, Roman, and Anglican varieties, by providing that it is to be "locally adapted in the methods of its administration to the varying needs of the nations and peoples called of God into the unity of His Church." This local adaptation has been begun in one of our denominations; but it will not be complete until it extends to all of them, or at least includes the Christian institutions, doctrines, and usages of the whole American people, and so becomes still more American and less Anglican, as well as less Roman. Then, and not till then, will there be a truly American variety of the historic episcopate.

The object of making these distinctions, I need scarcely say, is not to raise debatable questions, some of which are too

---

[1] Lambeth Conferences of 1888, p. 337.

difficult and delicate for me to handle, or perhaps even to suggest. I am simply aiming to emphasize the fact that the historic episcopate, like the other three articles, is only part of a common heritage, and more or less adaptable to all denominations with their respective standards and usages. In theory at least, it is as adaptable to the Presbyterian Church with its Confession of Faith, and Directory of Worship, as to the Protestant Episcopal Church with its Articles and Prayer-Book. In point of fact, however, such adaptation is not imminent and may not soon befall. Presbyterians as yet value the liturgy more than the episcopate, and could more easily accept the Articles and the Prayer-Book than the Ordinal. But should the day ever happily come when the high contracting parties would be ready for corporate reunion, we may assume that they would have wisdom and grace enough to adjust all canonical questions of ordination and jurisdiction in a spirit of Christian love and harmony.

Unifying Power of the Historic Episcopate.

The next point to be considered is the fitness of the four articles to serve as a basis of church unity. The fitness of the first three articles for such a purpose is scarcely in question. The chief reformed churches, at least, can estimate the scriptures, the creeds, and the sacraments as capital points of agreement and means of unification. But the unifying power of the historic episcopate is not yet so highly appreciated. Be it observed, the intrinsic value of that Christian institution is not now before us. As to what special grace or authority or advantage it conveys, opinions differ among those who view it from the inside, as well as among those who view it from the outside; and good churchmen may be found on both sides of the pale. Waiving the discussion of such opinions, not as unimportant by any means, but as not relevant to the present question, we are here only to estimate its external value as a unifying bond among the denominations. Never before has it been so presented. The simple fact that it has been so presented, marks an epoch, it may be a silent revolution, in the history of the church. Too often hitherto has it appeared in a polemic light as a bone of contention, an occasion of dissent and schism, and even a barrier to Christian intercourse between families, nations, and races. Now at length, as never before in three centuries, we are invited to behold it in an irenic light as an organic link of connection, a basis of reunion, and a magnetic centre of harmony. I can give but the heads of so pleasing an argument.

In the first place, it is the *de facto* government of three-fourths, if not of four-fifths, of Christendom. Reason about its *de jure* claims as we may, an immense majority of our fellow-Christians throughout the world, and nearly one-sixth of our fellow-citizens in this country, are tenaciously attached to it, and not at all likely to be detached from it; and these plain facts of the ecclesiastical situation must be dealt with in any scheme of comprehension which aims to be at once practical and complete. Otherwise, everything like church unity is simply out of the question. There can be no reunion of Christendom without the historic episcopate.

In the second place, it bases church unity upon church polity, not upon systematic theology. Until polity has been shaken loose from such theology we can never have organic unity. Exact theological agreement as a basis of church unity is already a failure. Denominations founded upon such agreement have been going to pieces all around us. Such agreement never has existed; not even in the Apostolic church, which allowed doctrinal differences without the unchristian results of schism and sectarianism. Such agreement never can exist, so long as human nature is diverse in its temperaments and many related truths are paradoxical in our logic. Such agreement never ought to exist, for the sake of Christian doctrine itself. Better far that two schools of theology should fairly contend in the same church than rush apart into two hostile sects. Never fear for our common orthodoxy, while special orthodoxies take care of themselves in the march of knowledge and under the laws of thought. Such agreement has not even been attempted by the strongest churches. No Calvinism has been so high and no Arminianism so low as the Calvinism and Arminianism nourished side by side within the ample church of England. The brief experiment to hold together that church on the theological basis of the Westminster Confession issued in disastrous failure. All history shows that church unity must rest upon an institution, not upon doctrines; and upon an institution ample enough and elastic enough to include all doctrines, even variant doctrines concerning itself. Such an institution is that episcopate, which not only embraces the national varieties of Catholicism, but shows a capacity for embracing the doctrinal diversities of Protestantism in the bonds of a reunited Christendom.

In the third place, it is comprehensive of all forms of polity as well as schools of doctrine. In its structure it involves in due organic relation the congregational, the presbyterial, and the episcopal elements of church government. The two former may exist apart from the latter; but not the latter apart from the two former. Episcopacy includes the other elements as the greater includes the less, and is upheld by them as the higher is upheld by the lower. Hence Congregationalism as a basis of church unity would on principle be inorganic, if not disorganizing. Presbyterianism, though organic and organizing, is separate and largely unhistoric, and so far as historic, has become too dogmatic and polemic. Episcopalianism also, when independent and unhistoric, becomes sectarian and schismatical, losing its unifying force. But historic episcopacy has ever included, while it surmounted, both the congregational and the presbyterial spheres of the church organism, and as locally adapted to the civil and religious institutions of this country, will neither sacrifice the liberties of the congregation, nor the rights of presbytery. Orthodoxy and liberty can dwell together in presbytery only under the mild sway of the historic episcopate.

In the fourth place, it is tolerant of all types of churchmanship as well as forms of polity and schools of doctrine. It neither enjoins, nor forbids, a doctrine of apostolical succession. Presented as a historic institution apart from any theory of its origin and claims, it allows all such theories without repressing any of them. Not the prelatic theory, not the presbyterian theory, not the rationalistic theory, not the ritualistic theory, alone can claim exclusive property in it without rendering it partisan and sectarian. Were any one of these theories made a basis of church unity, the church itself would be torn asunder, and its different schools of churchmanship fly apart as mere wrangling sects. The fact, however, that they are found loyally uniting in adherence to an institution which they estimate from so many diverse points of view—this fact proves its capacity to combine the Congregationalists and Presbyterians, still beyond its reach, with those like-minded churchmen already within its bounds. And unless different rules are applied to candidates and incumbents, it may be accepted in the interest of church unity, as it is maintained, on a presbyterian no less than a prelatic theory of its origin and merits. It will never be endangered by churchmen who have had presbyterian training; nor can it fully accomplish its mission in this country without the sort of ecclesiastical backbone which they furnish. The historic episcopate cannot do without the historic presbyterate.

In the fifth place, its exclusion of non-episcopal ministries, though otherwise deemed opprobrious, gives it in fact a unifying quality. By recognizing such ministries it could not help true church unity, but would really hinder and frustrate it. It would only make new schisms in trying to heal old ones. It would at once loosen and scatter the various schools of divinity, polity, and churchmanship which it now holds together in bonds as tenacious as they are elastic. I state the fact without explaining it: Differences which have elsewhere issued in sectarianism, are somehow restrained like balanced forces, or blended like discordant notes in a higher harmony. Episcopalians, Presbyterians, and Congregationalists in their relations as denominationalists are in a chronic state of antagonism and irritation; but the very same Christians, or others like them, in their relations as churchmen, holding to the unity of the visible church, simply lose all their sectarian rancor, without losing their distinctive beliefs. Denominational variety is thus visibly made consistent with church unity. It is not a matter of speculation. We have before us all the while the object-lesson of a unifying episcopate.

In the sixth place, it is the source and guarantee of the other three terms of church unity. Historically, the Sacraments, the Creeds, and the Sacred Canon emanated from the primitive episcopacy, howsoever that episcopate may have been connected with the apostles. Historically, they afterward continued in connection with episcopacy, though encrusted with error and superstition during the middle ages until the Reformation. Historically, ever since they have been more persistently maintained in Episcopal churches than in other Reformed churches. They may sometimes be found apart from episcopacy, but not episcopacy apart from them. To render them consistent and complete episcopacy is needed, and as connected with them it imparts strength and concord to them all. At once sustaining them and sustained by them, it is the very keystone of church unity.

In the last place, it is only through the historic episcopate that the primitive church unity can be restored. All parties seem agreed that the congregational, presbyterial, and episcopal elements of polity coexisted normally in the undivided church of the apostles. All must admit that they are now in an abnormal, dismembered state, where they are not more or less obliterated by an exclusive Congregationalism, or Presbyterianism, or Episcopalianism. In order to recover the lost organic unity of these elements, we must retrace the steps by which it was first found. According to the learned Bishop Lightfoot the primitive bishops gradually became centers of unity, and guardians of faith among the scattered congregations and presbyteries of the early church. In like manner the Congregationalist, Presbyterian, and Episcopalian denominations of our day can only recover true organic unity by returning by the same steps to that episcopate as it first arose in the apostles' time. Already one of those denominations has illustrated in its history this primitive evolution; having existed first in the embryonic stage of Congregationalism, as a cluster of detached parishes; thence, emerging into Presbyterianism, with its conventions of clerical and lay delegates; and at length acquiring the full ecclesiastical character in the Anglican episcopate. And other denominations, as yet congregational or presbyterial, are advancing, with various rates of progress and degrees of approximation, toward the same distant but inevitable goal of the whole organic development of American Christianity. If we are ever to have the one United Church of the United States, it would seem destined to find its flower and crown in the historic episcopate.

At this point comes into view the next important question: the mode of approaching church unity on the basis of the four articles of the Chicago-Lambeth declaration. Two methods, or schemes, have been proposed: confederation and consolidation. Without opposing either of them, I shall advocate organic reunion and growth as the more natural and hopeful process. Let us briefly compare them.

UNIFICATION BY CONFEDERATION.

According to the first of the three methods, as advocated by a Presbyterian divine,[1] the different denominations would meet by deputies in a general convention, and formally adopt the Lambeth proposals as articles of confederation, while

---

[1] Rev. Prof. Charles A. Briggs, D. D., of Union Theological Seminary, New York.

retaining in all other respects their respective standards of doctrine, polity, and worship, except so far as they might require modification and adaptation. Such federal councils of a single denomination have already been held by the Anglican body in the Pan-Anglican conference; by the Reformed body in the Pan-Presbyterian Conference; and by the Congregationalists and Methodists in their World's Conventions. Similar conferences may yet be held by the Lutheran churches, and perhaps by some of the Baptist denominations. "If these denominational conferences," says the learned Professor, "should accept the four propositions of the Lambeth Conference; or if accepting them, they should make some additional proposals; if the Presbyterian General Conference should propose to accept the historic episcopate, provided that a presbyterial organization of the church should also be adopted and the two systems be brought into harmony; and if the Congregational General Conference should propose to accept the historic episcopate, provided that the right of the Christian people, and the independence of the local church were guarded within certain definite areas; if we could have a general council of the Christian churches of America, on the basis of the four propositions of the House of Bishops, with any reasonable additions or modifications that might be proposed; church unity would, in my opinion, essentially be won."[1]

The advantages of this attractive scheme are apparent at the first glance. It proceeds upon the representative and federal principles with which we have become familiar in the history of our political unification; and it harmonizes with the genius of our religious institutions, especially in congregationalist and presbyterian communions. It would reduce the number of sects by compacting them closely in family groups or clusters, according to their hereditary and doctrinal affinities. It would satisfy the denominational spirit by according

---

[1] *The Churchman*, June 21, 1890.

to it an equal voice and vote in council, whatever may be the numbers or wealth or intelligence represented. It would offer at length the moving spectacle of great denominational leaders, meeting together not for conflict, nor for recrimination, as in former times, but to adjust the ancient disputes of Christendom in a spirit of love and harmony. And it is not unlikely that it may hereafter play some important part in the unifying process.

The difficulties of the scheme soon appear on closer view. It would substitute the artificial processes of federation and legislation for those of spontaneous growth and culture in the formation of public opinion and in social action. It presupposes radical changes in some denominations, and in others an immense increase of the ecclesiastical spirit. The Roman Catholics, of course, would not send deputies to such a council. The Baptists and Congregationalists could not, without abandoning their own principles; nor might their loose aggregation of churches be held by the decisions of such a council. The Methodists, with their sense of a denominational mission and lack of churchly feeling, are not yet ready for such a council. It would be practically restricted to the Reformed and Presbyterian churches, and the Protestant Episcopal Church, supposing the latter to appear in the conference. And then, should the first three Lambeth articles be adopted, the fourth would soon bristle with the delicate questions of episcopal ordination and jurisdiction, for which the whole Presbyterian body at least is not yet prepared. The result would not be ecclesiastical unity, but a mere league, made offensive and defensive by the reassertion of Presbytery against Prelacy on the one side, and against Papacy on the other.

UNIFICATION BY CONSOLIDATION.

According to the second method of unification, proposed by an Episcopal clergyman,[1] a single denomination would

---

[1] The Rev. W. R. Huntington, D.D., Rector of Grace Church, New York.

become the nucleus around which others would be crystallized, and at length consolidated in one ecclesiastical system, while yet retaining their admirable variety in doctrine, ritual, culture, and life. As the Protestant Episcopal Church alone possesses the four Lambeth conditions of agreement, it is natural to take it as such a rallying center, and hope to merge other Christian bodies into corporate union with it. The old-fashioned view seems to have been, that it is potentially the national church, destined, as it stands to-day, with its canons, liturgy, articles, and orders, to dissolve and recompose the other one hundred and forty-two denominations around it, and transform them into Protestant Episcopalian churchmen by the sheer force of propagandism. Such a view would demand the faith and zeal of a Hildebrand. The later and larger view seems to be that, by incorporating the four principles in the existing constitution of the church as the only ecclesiastical requirements, other denominations accepting those requirements might be included within its pale, substantially as they now are, with an allowed diversity in their methods of worship and work. "Every one of the denominations," says the eloquent advocate of this view, "has its own hallowed memories, its own roll of martyrs, its own cherished manner of worship, its own long-tried methods of missionary work. The theory of consolidation supposes not only their permitted but their constitutionally guarded continuance."[1]

No true lover of church unity could let mere traditional prejudice or sectarian jealousy mar this noble ideal of charity and harmony. If any one of the denominations is thus destined to become like Aaron's rod that swallowed up the rods of the magicians, this were better than that the serpent brood of sects and schisms should go on multiplying. Nor could any one of them better achieve such a consolidation than that one which stands among them, not only as the very flower of

---

[1] "The Peace of the Church," p. 42.

English civilization, but as the highest type of organized Christianity; which combines in its polity congregational, presbyterial, and episcopal elements that have elsewhere become separate and disjointed; which conserves in its liturgy the choicest formularies of the reformed as well as the historic churches; and of which, as an intermediary between Protestantism and Catholicism and in touch with both, it has been strikingly said,[1] it was like one of those precious chemicals capable of fusing substances otherwise unassociable. No wonder that even the Jesuit De Maistre was forced to admit its wonderful future, like Balaam blessing the distant tents of Israel which he had been fain to curse. No wonder that non-episcopal divines, as well as far-seeing bishops, are beginning to recognize "the majestic mission of the Anglican Church and of her daughter in America." Whatever other great and powerful denominations may yet wheel into the line of historic Christianity, the Protestant Episcopal Church must ever lead them in the march toward ultimate unity.

The difficulties of consolidation are more in the process than in the result, more in the way of approach than in the end attained. Though its aim be catholic, its point of departure would be denominational. Though in theory tolerant of other communions, it would in practice absorb them. However self-sacrificing in its spirit, it would look to them like zealous proselytism and ecclesiastical aggrandizement. While projecting before them an attractive goal of unity amid variety, it would seem to invite them thither only through the successive stages of concession, submission, absorption, extinction. In their view it would be somewhat like gaining the boon of immortality at the loss of personal identity. Here and there some detached Congregationalist society, ripe for the change, might melt away into the greater absorbing body. But compact national churches would not so easily

---

[1] De Maistre, as quoted by Bishop Coxe in a paper read at the Chicago Congress on Organic Unity.

surrender their corporate life. The Methodists would need to undo much of their history before they could return to the church whence they went out. The Lutheran and Reformed bodies, Dutch and German, never having gone out of the Anglican Church, could not very well be asked to return. The great Presbyterian communion, ever since it was driven out, has set up rival claims which it would not lower without at least a salute. And the greater Roman Catholic communion would simply reverse the invitation and bid us all come back to the mother church. Moreover, should the invitation be heeded, the little consolidating body, with all its conservative vigor, would soon be resisting the intrusion of so much foreign and uncongenial material, or find it not very easy of assimilation. At least one school of churchmen would view it suspiciously as a Trojan horse of masked sectarianism. Should the consolidating process become rapid and complete, the smaller absorbing body would soon be itself absorbed by the larger entering bodies; the transforming nucleus would be itself transformed by alien ideas and usages; at the rallying center would spring up repellent as well as attracting influences, and in the end Episcopacy would be obliged to reassert itself against denominationalism as well as against Romanism.

UNIFICATION BY ORGANIC GROWTH.

Between these extreme methods there is a third mode of unification, which I have ventured to call the process of organic reunion and growth. It would seek to combine the good in the other two methods without the evil. In distinction from the first, it would be an organic process of growth rather than an artificial act of legislation; and in distinction from the second, it would be an organic reunion of ecclesiastical elements in different Christian bodies, rather than a crude absorption by one Christian body of all the rest; a knitting together of the congregational, presbyterial, and episcopal politics wherever found, rather than a welding of the existing medley of churches. Its rallying center would be in the midst of the denominations, not aside in any one of them. Its crystallizing nucleus would simply be the four Lambeth articles of unity as detached from the Episcopal Church, no less than from the Roman Church, or from the Reformed churches, or from any other churches which may possess or acquire some or all of them. Especially would it find such a nucleus or germ in that catholic episcopate, which, if confined to the Protestant Episcopal Church, would itself become denominational and sectarian; but if extended over the other denominations, would recombine their congregational, presbyterial, and episcopal institutions not merely in one ideal polity, but as restored parts of the one undivided Apostolic Church. In a word, while confederation would arrange the denominations in a mere artificial mosaic, and consolidation would compact them as a crude conglomerate, organic reunion would develop them as an organism into the one body of Christ.

ORGANIC REUNION OF PRESBYTERY AND EPISCOPACY.

Take, for illustration, the Presbyterian and Episcopal Churches,[1] now engaged in hopeful negotiation on the basis of the Lambeth proposals. Were these two bodies at once either confederated or consolidated, it would be an incon-

---

[1] The Presbyterian Church is more closely allied to the Protesant Episcopal Church, both historically and doctrinally, than any other Christian body in the country. Its standards, as framed by the Westminster Assembly, were once legally established in the Church of England, as they are now maintained by the established Church of Scotland, with the Sovereign as a communicant in both churches. The two communions hold substantially the same doctrine of the ministry and sacraments, the one attaching the doctrine to presbytery and the other attaching it to episcopacy; and in other matters of polity and worship there has long been a growing assimilation and agreement.

The General Assembly of 1890 met the advances of the General Convention by passing without dissent the following resolution.

"The Assembly approves in general the spirit and position of the Committee on Church Unity in its correspondence with the representatives of the Protestant Episcopal Church, and desires a continuance of these negotiations with reference to a union on the basis of the four propositions of the House of Bishops, in order

ceivable catastrophe to both of them. It is not so inconceivable, however, that they should be brought together at points where they are in touch and admit of connection. Already they have such points of contact and agreement in three of the Lambeth articles; in the Scriptures, the Creeds, and the Sacraments. It only remains to attach them in the Episcopate. And that attachment might be begun by means of concurrent ordinations, on the principle advocated by a learned and accomplished bishop of St. Andrews (the late Dr. Charles Wordsworth[1]) for the reconciliation of Presby-

---

that all questions at issue may be discussed in a temper of Christian charity and brotherly affection, with a view to their full and final solution."

The last General Assembly at Washington continued its Special Committee on Church Unity, Rev. Dr. Joseph T. Smith and Rev. Prof. Francis Brown, and approved their report of progress, which contained this recommendation:

"The Assembly hereby recommends the holding of conventions, according to the terms proposed by the Episcopal Commission for the promotion of Christian unity. It also enjoins upon the members of the church represented in the Assembly, prayer, both in public and in private, for the realization of this unity."

[1] "The proposition of Bishop Wordsworth, made through a committee of the last Lambeth Conference, was substantially this: that the full ministerial standing of clergymen Presbyterially ordained be now recognized, provided that hereafter all their ordinations should be by bishops. . . . This proposition was not accepted by the Conference, and probably for two good reasons, if for no other: because it was not prepared to act so suddenly in so serious a matter, and also because, being only a Conference, it had no authority so to act. But it should also be said, that ten out of the twelve members of the committee voted for it, and that the Archbishop of Canterbury expressed his 'very full and hearty sympathy with it.' Altogether it is no doubt a very special expedient; but it is the only one so far proposed with any promise of likelihood in it. God grant that some way out of the dilemma may be found with honor to Him and to all!" *Address on Church Unity by the Right Rev. Boyd Vincent, S. T. D., Assistant Bishop of Southern Ohio.*

The suggestion above made differs from this proposition in two respects: In the Episcopalian view, the authorization would not be universal and indiscriminate, but gradual, as special cases arise; and in the Presbyterian view, the question of valid ordination would not be raised but left untouched in the sphere of private judgment, as at present. Many Episcopalians and Presbyterians already hold the principles involved in a concurrent ordination. Why not act upon those principles formally as well as practically, and in a frank and generous spirit?

terians and Episcopalians in the Church of Scotland. In such ordinations candidates would be presented to the bishop, with the concurrence of the presbytery, by priests who have had formerly Presbyterian ordination, or perhaps by Presbyterian ministers who have had formerly Episcopal ordination. The transaction might be kept within the rubric as well as the book, or at least within the Lambeth proposals, and would involve a practical sanction of all conceivable interests and claims, with no possibility of doubt or controversy. Both parties would have acted upon their respective theories of the Christian ministry, without conceding anything to each other, and without reflecting upon one another. The most extreme Episcopalian, from his point of view, would have fully legitimated a ministry which on other grounds he was prepared to appreciate and welcome ; and the most extreme Presbyterian, from his point of view, would have only gained enlarged authority for a ministry which he believed to be already valid and regular. As in a marriage of rival houses, former causes of warfare would disappear, and the contracting parties henceforth would have common aims and interests.

Nor would there be anything disingenuous or very novel in a concurrent ordination thus understood to represent Presbyterians and Episcopalians. Episcopalians see something like it whenever a postulant brings with him the commendation of twelve of his former co-presbyters. Presbyterians see something like it, whenever an Episcopal minister after due examination receives the authority of presbytery. Both Presbyterians and Episcopalians see something like it, whenever High and Low Church bishops and presbyters unite in conferring holy orders. What would be the essential difference, either in intention or in effect, between coördination in this last case and in the case before described?

The difficulty would not be in the rite of ordination so much as in the sphere of jurisdiction. And there it might not prove insuperable, if met cautiously and by degrees. The connection might first be made where there would be least embarrassment. On foreign mission fields, surely such ordinations ought not to bring any conflict of presbyterial and episcopal jurisdiction. On home mission fields there are as yet no vested rights and interests to prevent an arranged coincidence of jurisdiction. In the public service of the Army and Navy, and in purely academic positions, the coincidence would seem to be already practicable. There would be no more danger of free lances then than now in this free country. Moreover coördination would make re-ordination easy and reputable, when desirable. Gradually, as such examples became familiar and contagious, the parishes and presbyteries within a synod or diocese would come under bishops of their own choice through their own action. At length, by such a reunion of presbytery and episcopacy in all denominations, the very core of Protestantism would be unified on a church basis, and could bring its crude remainder under potent church influences. The chief ecclesiastical bodies in the land, all the historic Reformed churches, would stand compacted as a solid phalanx against sectarianism on the one side and infidelity on the other.

Ideal Fulfilment of Church Unity.

In order to complete this ideal sketch, let us now imagine the Lambeth articles of unity to have been thus adopted by the chief Christian bodies between the extremes of Protestantism and Catholicism. In that event, the historic episcopate would have been extended over all congregational, presbyterial, and episcopal denominations; but those very names would have lost their sectarian meaning, and serve only to indicate organic members and functions in the ecclesiastical body. The Apostolic and Nicene Creeds would have been accepted, the one as a symbol of church membership, and the other as a sufficient statement of the Christian faith; but while some communions, according to their origin, might still train under the polemic standards of Augsburg, Heidelberg, Geneva, and Westminster, other communions

Slow Growth of Church Unity.

might be content to display such standards as mere antique trophies in the castle of orthodoxy. The two sacraments of our Lord would be everywhere ministered with His appointed words and elements; but if in such ministration some parishes might still keep the Prayer-Book intact with its Protestant and Catholic formularies compacted as a finished product of liturgic lore and skill, yet other parishes might choose only its Protestant formularies, the Exhortations, Confessions, Prayers, Thanksgivings, Lessons, and Commandments derived from the Lord's Day Service of the Reformers, popular in style, and tending to spirituality in worship; while still other parishes might prefer the Catholic formularies, Matins and Evensong, Litany, Holy Communion, with their Versicles, Kyries, and Glorias, serving as an Englished Breviary and Missal, choral in structure, and admitting of the highest artistic embellishment when freed from their Protestant accretions.[1] In a word, the four articles would have become rallying centers for all our chief denominational varieties of doctrine and ritual, and served to reconcile a just Protestantism with a true Catholicism in one reunited Church of the United States. Meanwhile, too, let us hope, the great Roman Church, no longer antagonistic, already possessed of the essential principles of unity—the Scriptures, the Creeds, the two Sacraments, and the Episcopate—and being modified by American influences, would be ready to connect her old Catholicism with our new Catholicism, under the mild primacy of her Chief Pastor, in defense of a common faith, a common country, and a common civilization.

SLOW GROWTH OF CHURCH UNITY.

The approach to Church unity must be slow, and the way may be long and difficult. Not in one generation, perhaps not in several generations, can it be effected; not by spasmodic efforts, hostile to all religious life and growth; not by

---

[1] See Essay VIII, in this volume.

sporadic conversions, always personal in their significance, sometimes dubious, never unifying; not by coalitions with sectarian fragments, tending only to denominational aggrandisement and encumbering the ecclesiastical body with undigested material. No: Church unity can only be attained by a steady growth of Church principles in all denominations, by a generous recognition of Church institutions wherever found, Congregational and Presbyterial as well as Episcopal; and by a noble comprehension of such principles and institutions, together with their respective adherents, within one large and tolerant Church system. Confederation may play its part in some stages of the organic process; not decreeing unity by treaty or statute, but ratifying its spontaneous achievements; and consolidation may appear at the goal of the process; not as merging different denominations in the Episcopal Church, or in the Presbyterian Church, or in the Roman Church, but only as merging all churches and denominations in the one American Catholic Church.

The outlook for Church unity at the present time may not seem very hopeful. If we confine our attention to passing occurrences it will appear quite discouraging. Religious controversy has broken out afresh in some of the Churches, while yet they were devising means of agreement. Even the words of peace from Chicago and Lambeth, having since been surcharged with partisan meaning and distorted by sectarian misapprehension, have become like rallying standards hidden in the smoke of battle. But let us not judge by superficial and local signs. Great religious movements must be measured by the march of generations through centuries, not by current events of the day and the hour. If we will take into view the historic past together with the present, we shall see that the entire Protestant body, for more than a hundred years, has been steadily recoiling from the extreme sectarianism into which it was driven by the impulses of the Reformation, and that returning Church unity is made inevitable by the logic of tendencies, if not yet by the logic of events.

LOGICAL TENDENCIES TO CHURCH UNITY.

First among such logical tendencies is the decline of the polemic spirit. Despite some present appearances this is not a polemic age. Theological controversy is not now, as it once was, the most serious pursuit of life, when men crossed swords over a dogmatic distinction and consigned heretical writers with their books to the flames. Theological controversy is no longer the wordy combat that it was among the divines of the last generation, when rival schools flew apart as hostile churches. Nothing is now more censured and deprecated than such controversy. Bishops, Presbyteries, and Councils are slow in bringing erring brethren to book, although the questions are as vital as incarnation, probation, and inspiration. When the Church trial does come, the call to orthodoxy is blended with cries for liberty and peace. This is not the polemic, but the irenic period in the history of doctrine. The age of division is gone; that of reunion has come. Christian divines, meeting in conferences, alliances, congresses, are trying to see how much they agree rather than how much they differ. And the spirit of fraternity which is abroad among them will be satisfied with nothing short of true unity.

DECLINE OF THE DENOMINATIONAL SPIRIT.

Another of the logical tendencies toward church unity is the decline of the denominational spirit. This has largely ceased to be a mere sectarian spirit. The denominations do indeed continue among us, with their denominational titles and emblems conspicuously paraded, especially on anniversary occasions and in convivial moments. But some of them have lost their *raison d'être* by being translated to the New World, where their Dutch, German, French, and Scotch dialects are no longer spoken, and their political environment has become wholly American. Others have lost their sectarian bitterness with the dying out of the polemic feuds which made them Lutheran, Calvinistic, and Wesleyan, and through the social intercourse of their adherents. All of them have departed from their primitive standards and usages, and now linger as little more than mere anachronisms. There is not one of them that would be recognized by their respective founders and fathers, the Puritan, the Covenanter, the Methodist of a century ago. Now, the moment any system begins to be thus false to its own historic life and traditions, that moment it begins to die and its self-laudation is but a sign of its decadence. Already it is becoming unpopular, not to say unchristian, to assert bald denominationalism against church unity; and the disappearance of denominationalism is the disappearance of the last obstacle to church unity.

REVIVAL OF THE ECCLESIASTICAL SPIRIT.

With the decline of the polemic and denominational spirit has come a wonderful rise and growth of the ecclesiastical spirit. Throughout the Christian world there is a great revival of churchly ideas and catholic usages. Beginning fifty years ago in the school of Keble and Pusey, it has passed from the Church of England into the Church of Scotland. Even in that stronghold of Presbyterian worship, St. Giles' Church, at Edinburgh, the visitor to-day will find all the correct appliances of high ritual; an altar clothed in the color of the church season; lessons read from an eagle-lectern; creed and psalter musically rendered; a sermon on some Tractarian theme; and mayhap the very collect to which Jennie Geddes so forcibly responded. Our own churches are feeling a like reaction. The Puritan of our time loves to call his meeting-house a church; keeps Christmas and Good Friday as well as Thanksgiving and Fast Day; and sometimes forgets the local in the historic church. If he becomes a Unitarian, he has churchly tastes and affinities. The Hollander is restoring his antique liturgy. The Lutheran is looking after his lost episcopate. The Methodist is listening to a learned ministry with liturgical aids to devotion. The Presbyterian is reclaiming his version of the Prayer-book and pondering the advantages of episcopacy. The churchly Episcopalian is going to confession and early mass and looking forward to the archbishopric. Many Protestants would like to have brotherhoods and sisterhoods, and can heartily join our Roman Catholic friends in praising SS. Augustine, Aquinas, and Bernard, and even the Holy Father himself in his present American policy. There is not a Christian denomination in the land which is not becoming more or less consciously ecclesiastical in its aims and tendencies. And the growth of the ecclesiastical spirit simply means the growth of church unity.

POPULAR TENDENCIES TO CHURCH UNITY.

Besides logical tendencies to Church unity among Christian scholars and thinkers, we may discern certain more popular tendencies, none the less potent, because unconscious, and even illogical. Unlike their educated leaders the Christian masses are moving toward unity, not by the slow steps of reasoning, but with the swiftness of intuition and the force of passion. Sometimes they may seem to be unreasonable and blind in their impatience of all existing restraints and obstacles. Paradoxical as it may sound, they are even now ready for the Lambeth proposals without knowing it, and while repudiating each one of them. Do they not cling to the Holy Scriptures as the only rule of faith, while seizing those Scriptures as if handed down out of Heaven and utterly ignoring the historic Church through which alone they have acquired them? Do they not confess the Christian facts and truths set forth in the Apostolic and Nicene Creeds, while refusing either to say or sing those creeds, and treating them as mere ritualistic forms? Do they not receive the two Sacraments of Christ with His own instituting words and emblems, while rejecting the solemn and tender liturgy which has preserved those Sacraments amid the prayers and praises of saints and martyrs in all ages? Do they not call upon Congregationalists, Presbyterians, and Episcopalians to have done with their trivial disputes and come together like Christians in one church, while still sneering at an all-unifying episcopate as but the dream of a few sentimental ecclesiastics? In a word, although casting aside the words "one Catholic and Apostolic Church" as rags of popery, yet are they not in heart and hope ever yearning after what is meant by the words "one Catholic and Apostolic Church"? Some day these verbal disguises by which they are hidden from one another and kept apart will melt away like mists in the sunrise.

The Coming Campaign of Education.

It has been well said that we are entering "a campaign of education." In the most elementary sense, we all need information,—clergymen as well as laymen, Presbyterians as well as Congregationalists, Episcopalians as well as Presbyterians, Catholics as well as Protestants. All churches and denominations need to become better acquainted with one another. Therefore, it is with a wise forethought that the Lambeth Conference "recommends as of great importance, in tending to bring about reunion, the dissemination of information" not only "respecting the standards of doctrine and the formularies in use in the Anglican Church, but, on the other hand, respecting the authoritative standards of doctrine, worship, and government adopted by the other bodies of Christians into which the English-speaking races are divided." The former part of this Recommendation has already found its fulfillment in a "Church Unity Society," which cannot be too highly praised or too vigorously pressed forward in its high mission. The latter part of the Recommendation might find fulfillment in a less formal association or circle, freed from any suspicion of denominational propagandism by being composed of representatives of the three polities, Congregational and Presbyterial as well as Episcopal, and aiming to give to the public only the results of special research and studious conference.

But more even than information do we need that spirit of prayer out of which alone can be born a true unity. Such a spirit will dispose us to minimize our differences and magnify our agreements. Such a spirit will melt away our prejudices and jealousies. The need of such a spirit has been recognized by the highest Presbyterian authority, and the highest Episcopal authority has already voiced it for us in words which express the desire of all Christian hearts:—

"O God, the Father of our Lord Jesus Christ, our only Saviour, the Prince of Peace; give us grace seriously to lay to heart the great danger we are in by our unhappy divisions. Take away all hatred and prejudice, and whatsoever else may hinder us from godly union and concord, that as there is but one Body and one Spirit, and one hope of our calling, one Lord, one Faith, one Baptism, one God and Father of us all: so we may henceforth be all of one heart and of one soul, united in one holy bond of Truth and Peace, of Faith and Charity, and may with one mind and one mouth glorify Thee, through Jesus Christ our Lord. Amen."

IV.
DENOMINATIONAL VIEWS OF THE QUADRILATERAL.

IV.

DENOMINATIONAL VIEWS OF THE QUADRILATERAL.

The foregoing essay has been made the subject of a symposium of various clergymen, under the title of "Many Voices Concerning the Historic Episcopate." These voices, when heard apart, make pleasant melody and at times even their discords seem to blend in a higher harmony. The contributors to the symposium are agreed in lamenting our unhappy divisions, in recognizing unity as normal in the body of Christ, and in looking and longing for its fulfillment. It is only when the question of method is raised that the disagreement begins.

I must be content with a general acknowledgment once for all, of the many complimentary remarks upon the essay, and proceed at once, if I may without presumption, to estimate the valuable opinions brought together, in their bearing upon the problem of Church Unity. This will be no easy task, since the variety of these opinions is confusing and the aim of their authors is not always apparent. They will naturally group themselves for our purpose, according to the three church polities which they severally represent, as Congregational, Presbyterial, and Episcopal.

Congregational Opinions.

At the head of the Congregational group is the admirable introduction of Dr. Bradford.[1] The way to the question is

---

[1] The Rev. Amory H. Bradford, D.D., Montclair, N. J., Editor of "Christian Literature and the Review of the Churches":—

"The Chicago-Lambeth propositions are not understood by other denomina-

here opened by emphasizing the need for church unity as seen in the unchristian rivalries of the denominations, in the piteous appeals for missionary and humanitarian effort, and in the comparatively trivial differences which separate our churches. When looking for the remedy, Dr. Bradford has the sagacity, candor, and charity to see that the Lambeth proposals are not to be put aside as measures of mere church aggrandizement or denominational propagandism, but may be considered, especially the fourth article, as affording a practical if not acceptable basis of unification. His objection that they might produce a mere formal unity without the fullness of spiritual concord, though true in itself, is an objection which must ever inhere in all our schemes of church unity and is not peculiar to the scheme now under consideration. Such concord did not exist even in the golden age of the undivided Apostolic Church.

The new verbal distinction, which Dr. Bradford sanctions, between the Kingdom and the Church of Christ, if it means more than the old distinction between the invisible and visible church, does not seem to me quite scriptural and may prove misleading when pushed to its issues. Instead of forcing a breach between the teachings of our Saviour and those of His Apostles on this subject I would rather combine them as consistent, complemental, and inseparable. If the distinction be pressed it will be found that the divine ideal of the Church is depicted in more sacred terms than the Kingdom. The Church is the very " body of Christ " and " bride of the Lamb," while the Kingdom scarcely suggests such unity, life and love. In fact, the Kingdom of Christ would have been a mere abstraction without His Church, and His Church was

---

tions. We are not convinced that union is possible by means of them, but we gladly recognize that they are issued in the most catholic and fraternal spirit, and we can see clearly that the prominence which they give to the Historic Episcopate is not because it distinguishes the Episcopal Church, but because in the opinion of the Bishops it belongs to the universal Church of Christ. These propositions are worthy of a more careful consideration than they have yet received from the various denominations of Christians in Great Britain and America."

simply His organized Kingdom,—organized in part by Himself and then more fully by the Apostles under His teaching and guidance. That first organization, whether it be viewed as authoritative or simply as exemplary, has confessedly, like Holy Scripture itself, been more or less corrupted and perverted. For example, it involved Congregational, Presbyterial, and Episcopal elements which now exist as dismembered and conflicting denominations; and the practical question before us is whether they may not be organically re-combined by means of the Historic Episcopate.

Dr. Beach,[1] with his fervent enthusiasm and spiritual insight, discerns these three elemental polities as germs of unity, existing potentially in our Protestant Christianity; emphasizes the futility of mere sentimental schemes of unity, and voices prophetically the deep-seated yearning of the age amid all its discords, for catholicity as well as truth and freedom. It is encouraging to hear so stirring a call to unity out of the heart of New England culture.

While I might not fully agree with Mr. Cooley[2] in looking forward to a united church as in prophetic vision or in looking backward to it with a mere antiquarian interest, yet I can cordially concur in his thoughtful and practical view, that of the three factors of organized Christianity, Episcopacy rather

---

[1] The Rev. David N. Beach, D.D., Cambridge, Mass. :—

" I am confident that the intensity of the yearning after unity throughout large sections of Christendom, is very much minimized by many persons who write upon the subject. . . . The new education, the new science, the new philosophy, the new grasp of our age on essentials and on reality, carry this soul's cry with them as an inevitable intellectual corollary."

[2] The Rev. William Forbes Cooley, Stanley, N. J. :—

" Why, in the face of the historic examples of the Church of the Ante-Nicene period, the Mediæval Church and the more recent phenomenal advance of the Methodist Episcopal Church, should we shut our eyes to the fact that in periods of outward exigency, when great work is to be done and great secular foes are to be fought, rather than problems of faith to be solved or liberty to be won, the Episcopate, be its origin what it may, has by its victories and its services to the Church vindicated its claim to divine sanction?"

than Presbytery or Congregationalism is the chief need of the church of to-day. But the lesson of history, as I read it, is against the obliteration or inversion of any one of these ecclesiastical elements, and a true Puritanism may consist with all of them, when they are freed from mere false ecclesiasticism.

Dr. Stimson[1] puts himself genially in sympathy with the growing spirit of church unity. Perhaps he overlooks the fact that the three "prophets of the movement" may not be so much opposed as complemental to one another in the methods of unification which they respectively advocated— the "confederation" of Prof. Briggs and the "consolidation" of Dr. Huntington being simply different stages in the same social process of organic reunion and growth which I have advocated. His admission that the Lambeth articles are clarifying the views of some exclusive bodies of Christians is as just as it is frank; but it is to be hoped that he will not be content to remain as a mere sympathetic spectator of the discussions going on in such bodies, but find in Congregational bodies also the need and motive for church unity rather than for mere sentimental fellowship.

In the present movement the laity are in advance of the clergy, partly because they do not share the clerical sensitiveness as to the vexed question of orders and also because they are in more practical contact with the evils of sectarianism. For this reason the brief letter of Mr. Seward[2] is most signifi-

---

[1] The Rev. Henry A. Stimson, D.D., Tabernacle Church, New York:—
"The Lambeth Articles, whatever ultimate end they may serve in bringing about Christian unity, are accomplishing one good in enabling all Christians to clarify and adjust their own views of Christian truth and in helping some bodies of Christians who are to-day exceptionally exclusive, to get a new light upon their attitude toward their fellows."

[2] Theodore F. Seward Esq., President of the Brotherhood of Christian Unity:
"When the question of an actual union of Christian denominations is considered, and a system is sought which will, in the course of time, change a divided Christendom into a united Christendom, it appears to me that Dr. Shields' position is impregnable."

cant and hopeful as coming from an acknowledged leader of the Christian people who already foresees in church unity the fulfillment of his own zealous labors for the brotherhood of Christian unity.

Amid these cheering voices President Gates[1] raises the startling query, Is church unity a good thing in itself? A good thing! Is it a good thing that the body of Christ should appear dismembered? Is it a good thing that the household of faith should be divided against itself? Is it a good thing that the invisible community of saints should make itself visible only in sects and schisms, with rivalries and conflicts? Would the healing of such schisms and the removal of such conflicts be a mere "trivial step," an "unimportant matter," a "thing for ecclesiastics to play with"? Is there "no divine necessity" of manifesting to the world that oneness of believers in Christ which He likened to His oneness with the Father, and for which He prayed as affording demonstrative proof of His whole earthly mission? Church unity is set before us in the Scriptures not merely as a good end in itself, but as one of the highest ends of Christian hope and effort. Instead of being an incident or expedient, it is presented as an expressed attribute of the church itself, which is essential to its own normal perfection, and without which it must remain as a family broken by feuds or a body distracted with deliriums. If the church had no mission, such unity would be a good thing; and when its mission is fulfilled, it will be the most beautiful and glorious thing in the spiritual universe, even the realized ideal of Pentecost, the marriage supper of the Lamb and the nuptials of the new earth and heaven.

---

[1] President George A. Gates, D.D., Iowa College, Grinnell, Iowa :—
"If the Church is an end in itself, we can get on quite comfortably as we are. Whether we have one denomination or a thousand is of little consequence, so long as each one is contented in its own work, and satisfied to build itself up in its own way. But it ought to be impossible to consider church unity as an end. That is a matter interesting enough for us as ecclesiastics to work or play with, but no divine necessity seems to be about it."

When President Gates speaks of the main argument of the essay his words of praise are so cordial and generous that I regret the more any difference of view, and hope it may, after all, be more verbal than real. As to the practical value of church unity, he will find that it has been referred to, wherever the connection required it, as a remedy for the immense waste, loss, and conflict in our denominational charities and missions, for the evils of sectarianism and infidelity, and for the social anarchy of our times. In other writings, also, I have more fully shown that without organic unity the church can never accomplish its mission as the teacher, conservator, and regenerator of human society.[1]

It is quite probable that some sincere Christians are not merely inappreciative of church unity, but do not really want it upon any terms. They seem to be still under the influence of anti-church prejudices, inherited from ancestral conflicts with a false ecclesiasticism in the Old World. Anything like a union of denominations in one church system would, in their view, breed such ecclesiasticism in some of its lowest forms. Apparently, there is nothing they dread so much as ecclesiastical politics. It is pleasant to find that Dr. Ward, if taken seriously, does not share such scruples. He proposes to dismiss " ideals " and seize the question as an ecclesiastical politician. He tells us that " it is not a moral or religious question particularly," but " one of practical ecclesiastical politics ; " not even an " academical question," but a problem of " ecclesiastical statesmanship." And he has given an example. On behalf of some future Congregational Council he has formulated a new Quadrilateral, in lieu of the four articles known as the Scriptures, the Creeds, the Sacraments, and the Historic Episcopate. He has not, indeed, devised any new sacred canon, any new catholic creed, any new divine sacrament, any new historic ministry. He has only framed four new abstract propositions to take the place of canon, creed, ritual, and polity,

---

[1] See last Essay in this volume.

as bonds of church unity, and thus supersede the effete wisdom of the Christian ages, as well as the idealistic dreams of surrounding Christendom, by one stroke of the pen of ecclesiastical diplomacy.

I will not say of these propositions what their author has said of the overtures from Chicago and Lambeth, that "they are hardly worth discussing." I will only say that there is no need to discuss them or even to state them. They are the pleasantries of an ecclesiasticism which can view the question of church unity as neither a moral question nor a religious question, and only as an ecclesiastical question in a political sense.

It is still possible, however, to view it as a moral and religious question. There are those who can view it as a Christian question, even the highest Christian question of our time. And to such idealists it is beginning to appear as a very practical question,—I had almost said, as a question of practical politics in the literal sense. Distant as the reunion of Christendom may be in Greece and Rome, the Greeks and Romans themselves are at our own door, especially the Romans. Hopeless as it might seem to marshal the Salvation Army within the Quadrilateral, there are some Christian bodies almost inside without as yet perceiving it. The historic churches of the Reformation already possess the canon, the creeds, and the sacraments, and are in various stages of reaction toward the Historic Episcopate. Other less ecclesiastical denominations, we may hope, will better appreciate these existing bonds of church unity as they become familiar with them or grow more ecclesiastical in the best sense of the word. Indeed, a few Congregationalists, as well as Presbyterians and Episcopalians, are actually studying the Lambeth proposals and find them intrinsically worthy of consideration, as worthy of consideration as if they had emanated from the Congregational Council or from the Presbyterian Assembly.

Should other denominations act upon Dr. Ward's suggestion,[1] it is quite certain that the Baptist, Congregationalist, and Methodist Churches could not construct any platform of church unity, strictly so called, which would be more catholic, practical, and hopeful than the Quadrilateral, while the Lutheran, Reformed, and Presbyterian Churches could not adopt any other without largely ignoring their own standards and history, which already contain at least the first three of its articles.

Unless I do Dr. Strong[2] injustice he has fallen into an error common to many who have yet to examine this question carefully. True church unity does not require concession or compromise, but only mutual toleration and fellowship; and the peculiar value of the Historic Episcopate is, that it affords scope as well as basis for such unity. It includes both of the two views of churchmanship which Dr. Strong attributes to it; but it excludes neither of them, and could not exclude either of them without destroying itself. If evangelistic Christians will not tolerate and fellowship with ritualistic Christians in the same church system, as they did in the undivided Church of the Apostles, then there may be an end of church unity so far as they are concerned, but the blame of

---

[1] The Rev. William Hayes Ward, D.D., Editor of the *Independent*, New York:—

"The Episcopalians have offered their ultimatum, and the reception it has received proves that there is no hope in it as a basis of union. Now let Baptists offer theirs, Presbyterians theirs, Methodists theirs, Lutherans theirs, and let us see whether Episcopalians will be any more ready to accept these than other bodies have been to accept theirs."

[2] The Rev. Josiah Strong, D.D., Secretary of the Evangelical Alliance, New York:—

"Evidently the position of Congregationalists and Baptists is diametrically opposed to that of those who deem the Historic Episcopate essential to the validity of clerical orders and of church organization. There can be no possibility of compromise between them. The only alternative to conflict is unconditional surrender; and Baptists and Congregationalists could not surrender so vital a point without deeming themselves disloyal to the truth, which is true also of all non-Episcopal churches."

schism will not rest upon their ritualistic fellow-Christians. Baptists and Congregationalists are not asked necessarily to concede immersion and autonomy, nor should they ask their Episcopal brethren to concede the Episcopate as now defined, but be ready to practice tolerance and fraternity with them in the household of faith.

When we pass to the Baptist representatives in the Congregational group we expect to meet difficulties which are doctrinal and ritual in their nature as well as ecclesiastical. And yet the voices which greet us are in the tone of perfect unity. Dr. Boardman[1] is of so generous and catholic a spirit that one wishes to agree with every word that he writes. And, indeed, the disagreements arise mainly from a mere difference in the point of view. It is not material whether we speak of a "reunion" or of a "unification" of Christendom, if only we perceive that the various communions of the one Apostolic Church, notwithstanding their internal heresies and wrangles, did not excommunicate, unchurch, and disfellowship one another after the fashion of our times, but remained in compact unity until the great schism between the Eastern and Western churches and the greater schisms at the Reformation. Nor can we very well apply our Lord's far-reaching, prophetic prayer to the few trivial disputes among His Apostles and Disciples. If we will only keep ever before us the Pentecostal ideal of church unity we may gladly rejoice with Dr. Boardman in his vivid picture of a membership of denominations, as well as individuals, in the visible body of Christ.

The claims of true unity are also faithfully expressed by

---

[1] The Rev. George Dana Boardman, D.D., Philadelphia:—

"I have ventured to substitute the word "unification" for the word "reunion." For I am not aware that Christendom has ever been united in such a way as to make a reunion desirable. The sad fact seems to be that the Church of the primitive period, instead of having been, as we so often fondly imagine, a concord of brothers, was largely a discord of wranglers. * * * Like every other thing of life, it began in infantile imperfection, but subject to the blessed law of growth and perfection. Ideals, always excepting the one perfect Man, are ever before us, never behind us."

Dr. Tyler[1] in his scriptural and spiritual letter. I think, however, that the Christian unity of our churches, though far from being perfect, is already sufficient for the work of church unity; and it will decline rather than increase, if allowed to remain as a vague sentiment without some organic expression. If it be true that St. Paul bases Christian unity or spiritual oneness upon Christ alone, yet he also gives us a lively picture of church unity, in that structure which is built upon the Apostles and Prophets, Jesus Christ Himself being the chief corner stone. Some of us begin to think its unfinished walls and arches may yet find their keystone in the Historic Episcopate. The " Church of the Disciples," which Dr. Tyler represents, faithful to its liberal spirit, has proposed the Primitive Faith, the Primitive Sacraments, and the Primitive Life as essentials of Christian unity; and for their purpose they are excellent; but for the purpose of church unity strictly so called, they lack organic force, and ignore the ages of Christian experience and providential training through which the church has passed since it was instituted by Christ and His Apostles.

On the whole, the Congregationalist utterances are very favorable in their bearing upon Christian unity as requisite to church unity. Since no church unity can be real and lasting which is not thoroughly animated with Christian unity or spiritual oneness, all agencies and associations which practically promote such spiritual oneness ought only to be encouraged and fostered. But it is scarcely conceivable that historic churches should now find it their duty to wait for the Young Men's Christian Association, the King's Daughters, and the societies of Christian Endeavor to start them upon a long career through the successive stages of church coöpera-

---

[1] The Rev. B. B. Tyler, D.D. (Disciples of Christ), New York:—
" Instead of saying that the unity for which Christ prayed ' rests upon an institution, not upon doctrines ' (p. 90), why not say that it rests upon a person ? ' Other foundation can no man lay than that is laid, which is Christ Jesus.' And St. Paul was discussing this very subject when he made that statement."

tion, church federation, and church unity.[1] The end may be more directly sought by massing together those churches of the Reformation which represent the conservative forces of historic Christianity, in the hope of acting favorably upon a false ecclesiasticism on the one side as well as upon a crude evangelism on the other.

PRESBYTERIAN OPINIONS.

The Presbyterian voices in this symposium are too few to be fully representative. One of them, however, is clear and strong, and comes from a quarter of the field where the need and practicability of church unity are most apparent. Dr. Reid,[2] of the American Presbyterian Mission in China, faithfully represents the old Presbyterian doctrine of the "Catholic Visible Church," and vindicates the Episcopal proposals as not only generous in their spirit, but adapted to Presbyterian principles and having a unifying quality throughout Christendom.

On a first reading of the able and valuable argument of Dr. Waters,[3] of the Reformed Church, I thought his judgment

---

[1] The Rev. Lyman Abbott, D.D., Brooklyn, N. Y. :—
"I do not hope much from debates about Church union and conventions to promote it; but I hope very much from such movements as the Young Men's Christian Association, the King's Daughters, the Societies of Christian Endeavor, and from frequent meeting together in Christian and philanthropic gatherings. Out of these will grow gradually that unity of faith which is the indispensable pre-requisite to Church coöperation, and out of Church coöperation Church federation, and out of Church federation Church unity."

[2] The Rev. Gilbert Reid, American Presbyterian Mission, China:—
"Because the Historic Episcopate is made one of the points of the basis, this does not mean that the Episcopal Church of America or the Church of England, with all their canons, rites, ritual and personal preferences, is made the basis. It is a fair offer of Church union, not of swallowing up or being swallowed."

[3] The Rev. David Waters, D.D., Reformed Dutch Church, Newark, N. J. :—
"Summing up the whole matter and setting aside any objections which may be made to the adequacy of the doctrinal basis as something which might be overcome, it is to my mind perfectly clear that no general union of the churches can be formed on the basis of the proposals of the Lambeth Conference with the statement regarding the Historic Episcopate as one of the fundamental articles of the basis of union."

adverse to the feasibility of the Lambeth articles. But, after examining it more carefully, it seems susceptible of a different construction. While he deems the Apostolic and Nicene creeds insufficient as a statement of the Reformed doctrines, he still admits them to be sufficient as a statement of the common Christian faith of a united church in which different denominations might hold supplementary doctrines not inconsistent with those catholic creeds. The only serious objection which he raises has reference to a particular view of the Historic Episcopate, which is not required by that expression itself, which many Episcopalians as well as Presbyterians repudiate, and which need not, therefore, act as a barrier to the combination of Presbytery and Episcopacy in a united church.

In distinction from Congregationalism, the genius of Presbyterianism is more favorable to church unity than to church federation, which is at best but a half-way measure and often impracticable. The unification of the Presbyterian and Episcopal Churches would scarcely any more interfere with vested interests and existing institutions than federation, and would much more strengthen the cause of church unity than a league of smaller, younger denominations, which offer less resistance to the unifying process simply because they are weak in historic and ecclesiastical character. Moreover, we have been trying confederation for a hundred years in Bible, Mission, and Sunday-school unions, and have found it as inadequate as it proved to be in our political history. It is to be hoped that we are now entering a peaceful era of constitutional union and normal growth.

Episcopal Opinions.

The few Episcopal contributors represent nearly all the forms of Episcopacy which are concerned in the question.

It would have been a great advantage had Dr. Crooks[1] been

---

[1] Rev. George K. Crooks, D.D., Professor in Drew Theological Seminary:—
"The feeling which is uppermost in my mind when I think of the proposal, is

able to write more fully as an exponent of Methodist Episcopacy. In his brief note, I think, he falls into the common misapprehension of attributing to the Historic Episcopate a theory of the ministry and sacraments which it does not exclusively require, and he is, therefore, in danger of presenting the Methodist Episcopalian as really more obstructive to church unity than the Protestant Episcopalian.

I shall not be able to do justice to the thoughtful, generous, and catholic-hearted paper of Dr. Huntington.[1] Any remaining differences, as he states them, are quite trivial. He is unquestionably right in claiming that the Protestant Episcopal Church now holds the banner of unity in the midst of our divided American Christianity, and is entitled to the leadership by virtue of its English origin, ancestral connections, and full ecclesiastical type. But it would need to undergo great constitutional changes before it could incorporate with itself such vigorous historic bodies as the Lutheran, Reformed, and Presbyterian Churches, and it might by such changes depreciate its own churchly character. Nor are those churches likely to surrender their corporate life in an abrupt consolidation, without further organic growth of the latent ecclesiastical qualities which they traditionally possess and are steadily developing. It will be wise to treat them as professed churches, not as mere individual Christians. The

---

that the Historic Episcopate is Apostolic Succession disguised. The disguise imposes on the unsuspecting, and is used as a means of making what would be otherwise offensive, acceptable."

[1] The Rev. Wm. R. Huntington, D.D., Rector of Grace Church, New York:—

[I cannot resist quoting the following remark as tending to justify the title of this work.]

"If Dr. Shields had done nothing more than coin his felicitous phrase, 'The United Church of the United States,' he would have put the whole country in his debt. A telling cry is more than half the battle, and commonly the cry tells just in proportion to the distinctness with which it describes the object sought. To a far greater extent than is commonly supposed, the endurance of our national life hinges on our achievement of church unity. . . May he live to be a bishop in the United Church of the United States."

Lutheran Church will probably procure the Swedish Episcopate. The Reformed and Presbyterian Churches may be more ripe for the American Episcopate than is now imagined. There is nothing to repel them in consolidation, whether near or far off, as Dr. Huntington depicts it and would allure them toward it. He has said *Nolo episcopari* more than once, but in the ideal " United Church of the United States " he is already Primate by acclamation.

I need not say that the contribution of Dr. Satterlee[1] shares the same attractive qualities. His appreciative and discriminating analysis of the argument of the essay gives to it new force and clearness which its author had not perceived. In particular, I would emphasize, in his own language, his view of organic growth as a method of unification on the basis of the Lambeth articles: " It is divine and not human ; it is natural and not artificial; it is living and not mechanical ; it centralizes itself not in any one Christian body but in all of them. Though men may not create it, they can develop it by recognizing and yielding themselves up to this force of spiritual gravitation."

No voice could be more welcome in this Christian circle than one from the Church which is, in a sense, the mother of us all. Dr. Synnott,[2] in his excellent letter, has impres-

---

[1] The Rev. H. Y. Satterlee, D.D., Calvary Church, New York :—
" The four Chicago-Lambeth articles present an ideal toward which every Christian body can work. If it be a true ideal then it is the duty of each to propagate its influence ; if it be false in any respect then it is the duty of each to show exactly where it is false and how it ought to be modified, for to even the intelligent Christian observer the present divided state of Christendom is the crowning evil of the times."

[2] The Rev. Joseph J. Synnott, D.D. (Roman Catholic), Seton Hall College:—
"The present movement, defective as it is in its fundamental conception, may, we hope, be turned to good. It recognizes the need of union ; it admits the absolute necessity of organization in church matters; nay, it concedes the institution of the Church as a visible, social, organic body; it looks upon the Episcopate as the only means of achieving unity. It is on the right road: Let it go a step further, and it will see in the Church of Rome not only the Historic Episcopate, but also the Historic Primacy, the formal element and bond of union and strength."

sively set forth that aspect of solid unity presented by an episcopate claiming for its primate a succession from St. Peter as the vicar of Christ. The early Protestants could appreciate this appeal better than we do now. Melanchthon would have been content to remain under the Papacy had the liberty of evangelical preaching been allowed. Calvin, in the most pathetic terms, resented the charge of Cardinal Sadolet that the Reformers were breaking up the unity of the Church. And since that great rupture passed into history a more Christian spirit has been growing in spite of the bitter controversies which it engendered. When Pius the Ninth, in 1868, by an encyclical letter, affectionately invited all Protestants to return to the Roman communion, the Presbyterian General Assembly returned a courteous response, maintaining that they were not out of the communion of the Catholic Church, since they accepted the doctrinal decisions of the first six Œcumenical Councils, especially those of Nice, Ephesus, Chalcedon, and Constantinople, and only rejected certain later innovations. At the present moment also there is among intelligent Protestants an increasing respect for the consistent conservatism of the ancient church amid the abounding unbelief and license of the times.

As to the question before us, one main difficulty is that, while the Roman Catholic Church maintains a formal unity within its own pale, it does not exert a unifying potency throughout the rest of the Christian world. Until it has made peace with the oldest church in Christendom, the Orthodox Greek Church, its claim to catholic unity will be challenged; and while the newspapers are filled with reports of its own intestine conflicts even Protestant dissensions do not seem so scandalous. The clever picture which Dr. Synnott draws of denominational bishops, like so many trees, plants, and shrubs tied to stakes of the same size and kind, might be matched by another in which a divided episcopate and intelligent laity would appear attached to the Papacy by no less precarious ties. Thoughtful observers, without the least disrespect, believe that in this democratic country the Catholic Church is itself undergoing an internal reformation, of which it is not yet fully conscious, and by which it is to be brought into closer agreement with a like reformation which Protestants have already achieved. Should such hidden grounds of reunion ever appear it might not be difficult for communions of European origin to recognize a certain "Historic Primacy" of the Roman See in relation to a truly American Catholic Church.

The movement for Church Unity has been rapid and full of surprises. The ecclesiastical situation has changed, one might almost say, from month to month, and from week to week. In less than a decade, since the American Bishops lifted the standard of unity among the Christian denominations, there has been a growing interest in the question, which is not confined to our own country, but extends to all the English-speaking races. Nor can this interest be regarded as sensational and transient, much less as a dream of visionary reformers or a stock theme of the religious newspapers. It reveals a spontaneous movement of the whole Christian body. Thoughtful observers can see in it the impulse of great historic causes and reactionary tendencies which have been gathering force for at least a century, and which are making the unification of the American churches an inevitable and chief Christian problem of our age and country.

Let the evidences of progress first have our attention. Chief among such evidences should be placed the clearness with which church unity is becoming distinguished from Christian unity or from the spiritual oneness of all true Christians. This distinction is of primary importance. Valuable as the spiritual unity of Christian bodies must be deemed, it is still invisible, distorted, and largely sentimental and inoperative; while church unity would be visible, organic, potent, affording in its ideal fulfillment the only perfect expression of spiritual unity. Hitherto, this important distinc-

The Ecclesiastical Situation. 129

tion has been overlooked by those who did not appreciate church unity; and even those who theoretically appreciated it seemed to have practically adjourned it to the millennium, on the specious plea that Christians are not yet good enough to be united in one catholic church, thus making an excuse out of their own sin or trying to be too pious for the situation. It is certain that church unity will never befall us as a sort of blessed accident, or miraculous Pentecost, without any effort on our part. All true Christians are at least good enough to begin the work of church unification. A beginning must be made some time; and such a beginning the recent discussion has actually made, by calling attention to the duty and privilege, as well as need, of combining the legitimate denominations on a purely ecclesiastical basis, without suppressing their dogmatic differences and liturgical usages. Not merely individual ministers, but several Christian bodies, the Congregational and the Presbyterian, have already declared themselves in favor of some such corporate unity or church unity as the goal of Christian unity.

It is a further evidence of progress, consequent upon the advance just mentioned, that the Quadrilateral is beginning to be appreciated in its strictly ecclesiastical qualities, as affording the bases and bonds of the desired church unity. At first, neither churchmen nor denominationalists seemed clearly to understand why the canon, creeds, sacraments, and episcopate should be named as the only ecclesiastical requisites. By the one party it was thought that the omission of the Prayer Book, Articles, and Anglican Ordinal would imperil the integrity of the Church; and by the other party, that the acceptance of the Historic Episcopate would subvert the doctrine and polity of all the non-episcopal denominations. Both failed to see that the four articles simply secure to them what they both need without the least sacrifice of churchly feeling or denominational consistency, viz., a common rule of faith, a catholic creed, valid sacraments, and a legitimate ministry. If a Christian body has all these four essentials, it is in good church standing; if it lacks any of them, its church claims are more or less defective. And the recent discussion has put to test these criteria. By leading to a comparison of the various denominational standards with the Quadrilateral, it has revealed their respective degrees of churchliness, and has shown that their church unification must be approached along the lines which it has projected. As yet, indeed, only a few advanced thinkers have discussed it in this light; but at least one large body, the Presbyterian Church, has formally approved the first three of the articles of church unity, and has been engaged in friendly conference with the Episcopal commissioners as to the fourth article.[1]

Still another step in advance is the discovery of the catholic spirit and unifying value of the Quadrilateral. For a long time, non-episcopal divines viewed it askance, as a mere stroke of denominational propagandism, and some episcopal divines treated it as a dubious measure of church aggrandizement. Neither side seemed to perceive that the first three articles were already possessed by other reformed churches besides the Protestant Episcopal Church, and that the fourth article was not the exclusive property of that church, since the Moravian or Swedish or old Catholic Episcopate is theoretically as available as the Anglo-American Episcopate for the purpose of church unity, as well as for any other spiritual benefit to be conveyed. Both parties, in fact, were infusing into the four tenets their own denominational significance with more or less interested motives. But the recent discussion has changed the point of view. It has lifted the Quadrilateral out of these narrow misapprehensions, and planted it where it belongs, in the midst of the denominations, as the rallying standard of a united church. And although but few recruits have openly espoused it, yet it has at least been favorably

---

[1] Report of Assembly's Special Committee on Church Unity, 1893.

discussed in a symposium of ministers representing all the leading denominations, both Catholic and Protestant.[1]

The advantage of this new departure and approach to church unity may not appear at once to all minds. It may even cost some Protestant Episcopal churchmen an effort to admit that the Quadrilateral is not bounded by the four sides of their own denomination; that no single denomination can now claim to be the national church, not even the Roman, which is the largest catholic Church in the country; and that other Protestant denominations may yet acquire full and unimpeachable church standing. The great Lutheran Church, for example, has the historic episcopate of Northern Europe within reach, and is even now considering the advantage of acquiring it.[2] Equipped with that advantage, it might offer to some other churchmen a prestige older than the Reformed Church of England, a confession less Calvinistic than the Thirty-nine Articles, and a Liturgy more Tractarian than the Prayer Book. I have no fear of being here misunderstood. Personally, as I have elsewhere stated, I might gladly hope that the chief church of our English civilization should dissolve, recast, and absorb all the other one hundred and forty denominations of continental as well as British origin. Already it is nobly leading them toward unity, and in the church of the future may give more than it will receive. But there is a right and a wrong way of putting things. There is an imperial churchmanship which would embrace all communions within one united church of the United States; and there is another sort which would pursue catholicity only by the methods of a denominational policy. Christian bodies, in their intercourse, are keenly sensitive to anything that looks like propagandism and proselytism. They will

---

[1] The Question of Unity. Many Voices Concerning Dr. Shields' Book, "The Historic Episcopate," and His Response to the Many Voices. Chris. Lit. Pub. Society.

[2] The Episcopate for the Lutheran Church in America. Second edition. By the Rev. J. Kohler, D. D.

not be attracted to the exclusive ground of the Protestant Episcopal Church, as a basis of unity; but they might be attracted to the broader, common ground of an American catholic Church. Such a common ground is afforded them in the Quadrilateral, and by opening it to the public view as an undenominational platform, the late discussion has brought a distinct gain to the logic and the policy of the movement for church unity.

This survey would not be complete without including two other features of the situation which are not so favorable. They should be frankly stated and carefully considered. One of them is the recent symposium of bishops and ministers, in a New York journal.[1] It must be granted that this discussion has wounded some friends of church unity and touched a clerical sensitiveness more to be respected than resented. But it must also be granted that these untoward effects are due not so much to the bishops as to their critics; that they have been greatly aggravated by the denominational papers; and that they may soon pass away. At best, the question of pulpit exchange is a side issue of trivial interest; one which ought not to be raised until the more important points of the Quadrilateral have been settled, and one which could not be raised at all if they are wisely settled. Least of all should it have been raised while they were under consideration. Its interjection into the pending negotiation between the Episcopal and Presbyterian communions has had all the effect of an apple of discord thrown by an unfriendly hand. Moreover, the question itself, as proposed in the symposium, is simply preposterous. Does anybody favor indiscriminate pulpit exchanges? Could the bishops have given any other direct answer? Half the critics would themselves have given the same answer as that by which they were offended. Presbyteries, at least, are no more ready

---

[1] "A Barrier to Church Unity: Can it be Removed?" *N. Y. Independent*, March 8, 1894.

than bishops to admit heretical teachers and unauthorized evangelists to preach and administer the sacraments, whatever individual pastors and rectors may sometimes do. The line of authority, regularity and decorum must be drawn somewhere. As a matter of fact, Congregationalists draw it at one point; Presbyterians at another; and the bishops have shown where Episcopalians draw it. Instead of erecting "a barrier to church unity," they have simply indicated a boundary of church unity; and, as marked out by the Quadrilateral, it will be found to be a boundary ample enough to include Congregationalists and Presbyterians, as well as Episcopalians, within the fold of a united church.

The other unfavorable sign in the ecclesiastical horizon is the appearance of rival schemes of mere vague Christian unity, which if not designed to take the place of church unity, are suited to raise a mist of confusion and perplexity around it. Of these the most remarkable is the so-called Quadrilateral of the Congregational Association of New Jersey. If this declaration had proceeded from any other denominational source, Baptist, Methodist, Presbyterian, or Episcopalian, I would still say of it that it seems to me utterly wanting in historic Christianity, ecclesiastical quality and organic force. Instead of the four church tenets of canon, creed, sacrament, and ministry, it offers four misty propositions which may mean almost anything or nothing, and which could not hold together any two churches or denominations for a single hour. Its noble professions of charity and fraternity toward other denominations are in themselves praiseworthy, and may increase the spirit of Christian unity; but on their present unstable basis they cannot promote church unity, except in an indirect and remote way. Indeed, it does not pretend to be a scheme of church unity. The only scheme deserving to be so called is that which has emanated from Chicago and Lambeth. No other is in the field. No other has even been suggested. And notwithstanding all the misapprehension and perversion to which it has been exposed, it remains unshaken and unimpaired, and in the future seems likely to become a standard by which to measure and guide the various Christian denominations in their educational advancement toward a truly American Catholic Church.

The present situation suggests two practical reflections. The first is, that the denominational controversies of the hour are not irreconcilable with catholic unity. The very same differences in respect to the Scriptures, the creeds, the sacraments and the episcopate exist among churchmen, which have been developed among denominationalists. There is not an opinion on these points advanced by the various non-episcopal divines who are discussing them in denominational journals, which has not been also avowed by as many clergymen now in Holy Orders and of unquestioned standing. This does not mean that Church Unity is "an iridescent dream." It means simply that all American churchmen, in an ideal Catholic Church, might still differ among themselves as other Christians do now.

The other reflection is, that the differences between denominationalists and churchmen are largely confined to clergymen or ministers, especially those already committed as leaders. Learned rectors and eloquent pastors, in one symposium after another, have so infused their own various partisan meanings into the four terms of unity, that now the terms themselves are obscured and lost from view. But the great Christian heart of the people still beats true to them. The Holy Scriptures are still the basis of all Christian denominations: the Apostles' and Nicene Creeds still express their essential faith; the two sacraments are still ministered among them with unfailing use of Christ's words of institution; and the Historic Episcopate is still adaptable to the Episcopalians, Presbyterians and Congregationalists beyond, as well as within, its pale. In a word, the Christian masses despite their wrangling leaders, are still in heart and hope one American Catholic Church.

V.

THE QUADRILATERAL STANDARD AMONG THE DENOMINATIONS.

V.

THE QUADRILATERAL STANDARD AMONG THE DENOMINATIONS.

Our review of the ecclesiastical situation has led us to the general conclusion that the Quadrilateral is likely to become a standard by which to measure and guide the various Christian denominations in their educational progress toward an American Catholic Church. It affords the only favorable outlook for Church Unity. If we take our position in any existing church, hoping to see it absorb into itself all the other hundred and fifty denominations, everything like Church Unity will seem as far off and nebulous as the millennium. But if we take our position in the midst of the denominations, hoping to rally them around the Quadrilateral as an undenominational standard, they will appear in various stages of unification as they severally approximate the requirements of that standard. Let us try this latter point of view.

It will help the survey to arrange the chief Christian denominations in fancy on either side of the standard, according as they possess all the four Lambeth articles or only one or two of them. By such an arrangement the right wing will include the great historic Churches, the Greek, the Latin, the Anglican, the Scandinavian, which need more or less church reformation before they can be thoroughly reunited; while the left wing will embrace those reformed churches and denominations which largely require a work of church restoration in order to be unified on a Church basis. Dismissing the former for the present, we confine our view to the Protestant bodies in our country which have yet to be brought back into full connection and harmony with historic Christianity.

These bodies will naturally fall into three groups, according to their ecclesiastial structure: the congregational, the presbyterial, and the episcopal. As to each of them, a general remark may here be in place. The congregational polity, so long as it asserts the absolute independence of the local church, could not, of course, come within the scope of the Lambeth articles, since it would accept neither canon, nor creed, nor ritual, nor ministry as imposed by any external church authority. It could only enter a loose confederation of churches, somewhat like our former union of states, with reserved rights of secession and self-control. But a congregationalism which liberally adds the principle of church fellowship to that of autonomy might adopt the Quadrilateral as embracing only the common duties and interests of all Christian churches, without interfering with their interior self-government. In like manner the presbyterial polity, if held to be inconsistent with every form of episcopacy, could only adopt the first three Lambeth articles, and maintain the historic presbyterate in place of the fourth article. But a presbyterianism which consistently applies its doctrine of presbyterial oversight, as well as of Church Unity, might find its own complement in the fourth article and at the same time recover all the elements of catholicity. The episcopal polity, also, cannot come up to the full measure of the standard, if wanting in any of the first three articles or holding the fourth in a partisan or sectarian sense. Only that episcopalianism which will tolerate ritualists as well as evangelists and evangelists as well as ritualists, can deal with the problem of Church Unity.

It will be seen that the three polities vary somewhat in their capacity or readiness for unification, each having its own special difficulty or facility. Congregationalism, though wanting in all four articles, would leave each congregation free to act for itself in reference to them. Presbyterianism, though binding each congregation in a compact organization, would only need to have that organization completed in the fourth article. And Episcopalianism, though in some of its forms needing legitimation or completion, in one of its forms already offers the model and germ of a complete Church Unity. At the same time, it will be found that these inherent difficulties or facilities are greatly complicated with others more adventitious and extraneous, such as the prejudices, dogmatic, national and social, which have been acquired in this country. Congregationalism is Unitarian and Baptist as well as Orthodox in doctrine. Presbyterianism is German, Dutch, French and English as well as Scotch in origin. And Episcopalianism is evangelistical as well as liturgical in worship. All this will more strikingly appear as we proceed to compare the leading denominations in the order of their approach toward the Quadrilateral, and toward that denomination which most fully illustrates it, the Protestant Episcopal Church.

CONGREGATIONAL DENOMINATIONS.

At the extreme left of the standard are the Unitarian Congregationalists who would probably now repudiate it, if made binding in any such sense as would preclude their own views of canon, creed, sacrament and ministry. The only hope is that, like other denominations, they have reached an extreme from which there may yet be some conservative recoil toward a more normal type of Christianity. This hope is favored by their English blood, their Puritan training, their liturgical culture and their churchly affinities. It is even rendered plausible by the large agreement between them and the so-called broad Churchmen of Old and New England. We have had object-lessons, not in King's chapel only, but in the Church Congress, if not in the episcopate. In the event of such a reaction our Unitarian brethren would be in a position to draw after them certain religious bodies still less ecclesiastical or Christian than themselves, such as the Friends, the Jews and other Theists, who as yet are quite beyond the scope of the Quadrilateral. Indeed, from this point of view, the Parliament of Religions and the Brotherhood of Christian Unity, in which Unitarians have taken an active part, might be reckoned as unconscious first steps toward the distant goal of Church Unity.

In the next position are the Orthodox Congregationalists, who, while much nearer to the standard, have been held back from it through long centuries of separation, insulation and consequent narrowness. What was, at first, a calamity in the old world and then a necessity in this new world has been perpetuated as a normal condition, even a permanent form of polity; and although enjoying to the full all and more than all the religious freedom for which their forefathers contended, they seem to have inherited a morbid terror of ecclesiasticism, which is now their chief obstacle to unity. Over against this obstacle, however, must be placed not only their Puritan breeding, their broad scholarship and their growing historic sense and catholic spirit, but also their practical adherence to the canon, their substantial agreement with the creeds, their formal observance of the sacraments and their ready susceptibility to the episcopate without loss of denominational pride. These germs of Church life among them only await development. In fact, they have already been largely developed on their own soil. It has been said that a New England diocese is congregationalism tinctured with episcopacy. The ease with which any Congregationalist society, if so minded, could pass into such a diocese, would be impossible for a Presbyterian parish; and it is quite conceivable that some absorption or consolidation, on the terms of the Quadrilateral, like that which Dr. Huntington advocates, might become spontaneous and general without agitating the Congregational body at large. But it would be unwise to place among the signs of such a movement the so-called Quadrilateral of the New Jersey Congregationalists, since it is covertly based upon vague anti-Church principles.[1] That manifesto can only be viewed as a preparatory expression of Christian fellowship or as a crude sugges-

---

[1] " A Declaration by the Congregational Association of New Jersey." It proposes, " the Bible for creed ; Discipleship of Christ for rule of life ; the Church for instrument of service ; and liberty of conscience in the interpretation of the Bible and administration of the Church."—*The New York Independent*, June 28, 1894.

tion which, by its failure, may make clearer the need of true Church Unity.

In the same group are the Baptist Congregationalists, differing by a stricter independency, but sharing some of the same churchward tendencies. Their chief difficulty lies in a view of the third article, which isolates them from the rest of Christendom, and seems to build around them a barrier to anything like unity. They might accept the canon, the creed, and even the episcopate, but they could not commune with any but immersed believers. On the other hand, it cannot be said that this strict adherence to a divine rite is in itself without ecclesiastical value as a potential germ of church life. Nor might it be quite impossible for them to develop it in a larger church system on their own principle of local autonomy. The Prayer Book not only allows immersion as well as sprinkling, but offers a form of "Baptism to such as are of riper years and able to answer for themselves;" and the sight of Baptist and Pædo-Baptist congregations under the same episcopate would be scarcely any more incongruous than that of certain other ritualistic and anti-ritualistic parishes. What is asked of our Baptist brethren is not concession, but tolerance and fellowship. And such a spirit is growing among them. The expressions of Christian fraternity which come from them are very encouraging in view of the acknowledged difficulties of their position; and a few efforts to unite among themselves such as those of the "Christian" and "Free Baptists"[1] and Disciples of Christ[2] on a Bible basis, though without historic creed or ministry, may be viewed as first steps toward some more organic unity.

The whole Congregational group of denominations, it will be seen, is as yet in the preparatory stage of church restoration, being largely wanting in ecclesiastical elements and

---

[1] Quadrennial Convention, Haverhill, Mass., Oct. 15.
[2] General Convention of Disciples of Christ, at Richmond, Va., Oct. 25.

hindered by anti-ecclesiastical prejudices. But its most intelligent and influential bodies are already turning churchward. The International Council of 1891 "unanimously expressed a hope for the federation of Christian bodies,"[1] and the last National Council "recommended the affiliation of other Congregational churches upon the basis of the common evangelical faith and a substantial Congregational polity."[1] Such a denominational unity, with the growth of the church spirit, may hereafter become ready for church unity.

PRESBYTERIAL DENOMINATIONS.

As we pass to the presbyterial group, we shall find that the preparatory work is not so much one of church restoration as of church completion, the development and fulfillment of already existing ecclesiastical elements. First in this group, in close alliance with the Congregationalists, but much nearer to the standard of the Quadrilateral, are the Calvinistic Presbyterians, adhering to the Westminster Confession. The practical impediments among them to unity are their inflexible Scotch and Scotch-Irish temperament, their polemic spirit, their inherited dread of liturgical worship, and their embittered recollections of a persecuting prelacy in the old world. Many of them are still echoing the war-cries of the Covenant, while themselves extemporizing new episcopates, making Prayer Books and building cathedral-like houses of worship. But, offsetting such impediments, there is a strong infusion of English and Huguenot blood in their Covenanter stock, a growing tolerance in their virile orthodoxy, and a reviving catholicity in their intense ecclesiasticism. Moreover, their own standards already maintain at least three of the Lambeth articles. Their Confession formally defines the canonical books of Scripture. Their Directory prescribes the Apostles' Creed and the valid conditions of the two sacraments. And their Form of Government recognizes the offices

---

[1] The *Congregationalist*, Oct. 25.

of bishop, presbyter and deacon as Scriptural and divine. These standards, too, have hidden historic affinities with those of the English Church and its American scion. The Articles of Religion were but the original skeleton of the Westminster Confession. The Ordinal does not claim a higher doctrine of the apostolic ministry than was lodged in the Scottish presbyterate. The Daily and Communion Offices are largely Calvinistic in purport and structure, as well as in traceable origin. In a word, the entire Prayer-book, as amended by the Presbyterian divines of 1661, is so much like the present book of the Protestant Episcopal Church that, if now living, they would be more at home in that church than in any other American communion. It is true that these historic bonds are obscured or ignored and forgotten, but they are none the less enduring and vital. The plain fact is, that the Presbyterian General Assembly is the only Christian body that has met the Episcopal commissioners in a churchly spirit; and the untoward pause to which they have come may simply mean that each has something to give as well as to receive in any negotiation or alliance.

In the same Calvinistic group, but a little nearer to the standard, are the Reformed Presbyterians, Dutch and German, adhering to the Confession of Dort and the Heidelberg catechism. They seem to be hindered from unity largely by their conservative habit, their denominational pride, and their long vested property rights and interests. Hitherto they have declined proposed alliances with Presbyterian churches which have adopted their own Heidelberg symbol; and the Dutch and German wings of the denomination have not yet been able even to federate, although their standards are identical. At the same time—some counteracting influences have arisen from their commingling with other races, creeds, and cultures. Their Calvinism, though of the highest type, is mild and pacific. They possess the first three Lambeth articles more perfectly than other Presbyterians, with the same structural aptitude for the fourth article. Their liturgy also connects them æsthetically as well as historically with the Prayer-book. And it is not unlikely that strong ancestral and social ties are drawing them toward the Episcopal Church in New York rather than toward bodies which are really more congruous with them in doctrine and polity. It will be remembered that the House of Nassau gave freedom to the Kirk of Scotland, but cast its lot in the Church of England.

Nearest in the Presbyterial group to the standard, are the Lutherans, adhering to the Augsburg Confession. As this great cluster of churches becomes more Americanized, it may take a leading part in the problem of Church Unity. Its genial type of piety, its ritualistic tendencies, its growing culture and direct connection with German erudition will be reckoned by many as promising features. In some respects it is the most conservative Church of the Reformation. Its standards set forth most fully the first three Lambeth articles, and it already has the historic episcopate in abeyance or within reach. The Swedish[1] succession is less questioned than the Anglican; and if it has not always claimed apostolicity dogmatically, yet it has not taken polemic ground against it, like the Reformed Episcopalians in this country. Its validity is at least a puzzle to the canonists. The Lutheran ritual also has liturgical affinities with the English and American Prayer-book. The offices of Baptism, Matrimony, and Burial are largely indebted to the formularies of Melanchthon and Bucer, while the Evangelical Mass is not only higher in doctrine but purer in structure than the Communion Office, which has certain Calvinistic accretions more popular than artistic in their aim. The church of the saintly Muhlenberg is beginning to feel the general impulse, and has met the Chicago Declaration in a thoroughly appreciative spirit. Indeed, the

---

[1] "If anything outside the domain of pure mathematics may be said to be capable of demonstration, Dr. Nicholson [of Leamington, England,] has demonstrated the reality of the Swedish Succession." Presiding Bishop Williams, of Connecticut, as quoted by Rev. J. B. Remensnyder, D. D.

movement of its leading divines for recovering its lost episcopate is a distinct ecclesiastical advance toward unity.

While the various presbyterial denominations are thus found to be in different stages of nearness to full church standing, they are also moving together in a mass toward the same result. The great Pan-Presbyterian councils in Europe and America are born of the Presbyterian instinct for "one Catholic, visible church;" and the last General Assembly has formally proposed for adoption a plan of federation, to include at least seven presbyterial denominations or reformed churches under one "Federal Council" or "Ecclesiastical Assembly, for the glory of God and the greater unity and advancement of the church."[1] Such a Presbyterian church unity, involving ecclesiastical elements and animated with an ecclesiastical spirit, would only need to acquire the historic episcopate as the next and last step to Catholic unity.

EPISCOPAL DENOMINATIONS.

When we come to the episcopal group, the outlook is more confused and perplexing, for the reason that the work to be done is that of legitimating ecclesiastical elements which lack mere form rather than substance. The Methodist Episcopalians, for example, have substantially the first three Lambeth articles, with a new episcopacy developed out of the Anglican presbyterate. Their inherited dislike of formalism, their evangelistic fervor, their want of churchly taste, and their immense denominational spirit hold them back from the Quadrilateral standard with a recoil which is not yet spent. Nevertheless, historic causes, though hidden, are potent. Methodism at first was an Oxford movement, no less than Tractarianism; and it may yet react from its extremes. Many of the causes which once justified its rise in England scarcely remain in this country, and the need of it as a pioneer denomination decreases with the spread of civilization

---

[1] Minutes of General Assembly, 1894.

and the growth of Christian culture. Some ecclesiastical influences are already permeating it in the large cities. The time may come when such dormant germs as the Wesleyan Prayer Book and Articles shall be evoked into life, and Methodist Episcopacy return into connection with historic Christianity.

The Reformed Episcopalians are a somewhat similar offshoot from the Anglo-American episcopate. They have attempted to erect that episcopate upon partisan, if not sectarian ground, in the interest of one-sided views of the ministry and sacraments. Their dogmatic opposition to apostolical succession and baptismal regeneration may promote a pure type of evangelical piety among themselves and bring them into sympathy with other Protestant denominations; but it necessarily puts them in a polemic attitude toward Catholic unity. The next bad thing that could happen would be another seceding episcopate in pronounced sympathy with Roman error and with a hostile front toward all the reformed churches. And after that the very worst thing that could happen would be some authoritative definition in the interest of either of these Church parties. That would rend the historic episcopate itself asunder, and end the dream of Church Unity for our time. No General Convention or Lambeth Conference is likely to undo its work in this manner.

The Protestant Episcopalians alone in this group fulfill the standard. Their Prayer-Book and Articles prescribe the canon, creeds, and sacraments, while their Ordinal enjoins the historic episcopate. In the movement toward unity, they are still somewhat impeded by their early British antecedents, their elaborate liturgy, their fashionable associations, and some occasional infelicity in their Church claims. Although, during the first two hundred years of their nominal existence on this continent, nearly twice as long as the whole apostolic period, they were practically without the episcopate, without the three orders in their ministry, even without confirmation in their membership, yet they now must make these things the conditions of any church standing or privilege and treat other great national churches around them as if they were mere sectaries and dissenters who had assisted at the execution of Charles the Martyr. Gladly we hasten to add that such impediments are fast disappearing. With the decline of international hatred this Church is coming to the front in our Anglo-American civilization. Its liturgy has been made flexible by revision and thrown open to evangelistic influences. It is becoming distinguished by missionary and popular efforts as well as fashionable attractions. And after having been long deemed a mere narrow Christian caste, it has suddenly sent forth a call to unity the most catholic and fraternal that has been heard since the Reformation, if not since the day of Pentecost. It is not the Roman Church, nor yet the Anglican, nor even any reformed church, but the Protestant Episcopal Church, which is now leading the grand movement for the reunion of Christendom.

The entire group of episcopal denominations, though so near the standard, is not yet rallied around it. At their origin, however, there was intercourse between them and some effort for unity. The elder Muhlenberg knelt with White in Lambeth Palace to receive ordination for Lutheran parishes in Colonial Virginia. After the Revolution, Bishop White himself favored union with the Methodists as well as the Lutherans. The Moravians are already in touch with the Lutherans through the Augsburg Confession, and with the Methodists through the pietism imparted by Zinzendorf to Wesley, and have been formally recognized by the highest authorities as possessing the historic episcopate.[1] Such filaments as yet may seem to be slight, but the beginnings of all organic life are faint and feeble.

If we would compare the groups of denominations as to

---

[1] "Presiding Bishop Smith, of Kentucky, proposed an organic union between the Methodist Episcopal and Protestant Episcopal Churches, through the medium of the Moravian Episcopate, which both Churches acknowledge." The Right Rev. Paul de Schweinitz, D. D. (Moravian).—*Century Magazine*, 1887.

their numerical strength, we shall find that the number of their ministers, congregations, and communicants might be roughly estimated by the following figures:—[1]

	Ministers.	Congregations.	Communicants.
Congregational,	39,000	62,000	5,000,000
Episcopal,	46,000	70,000	11,000,000
Presbyterial,	24,000	32,000	3,000,000

It will be seen that the ecclesiastical denominations, Episcopal and Presbyterial, outnumber the Congregational nearly two to one; and when we remember that in the Congregational group are included many evanescent sects, without historic or ecclesiastical life, while in the Episcopal group is included that most historic ecclesiastical body in the world, the Roman Catholic Church,—the outlook for Church Unity from a purely ecclesiastical point of view will not seem so discouraging as at first sight might be inferred from the divided state of our American Christianity.

The results of our survey are now before us. It has become apparent that the work of Church Unity must consist in restoring ecclesiastical elements to congregational denominations, in completing ecclesiastical elements in presbyterial denominations, and in recovering or legitimating such elements in episcopal denominations. If these views be correct, it would seem to follow that the educational process may most hopefully begin in the most churchly denominations and thence react with cumulative power upon the least churchly, until all have regained the four conditions of unity. Such a massing or fusing of the chief ecclesiastical bodies, or historic churches, would also exert a tremendous conservative influence, as much needed in our whole civilization as in our Christianity. Could the Lutheran, Reformed, and Presbyterian Churches, by gaining the historic episcopate, become annexed or consolidated with the Protestant Episcopal Church within the limits of the Quadrilateral they would stand

---

[1] Taken in round numbers from Dr. Caroll's "Religous Forces of the United States."

together, like the impregnable square at Waterloo, against all the assaults of surrounding infidelity, irreligion, and vice.

It has been well said that anomalies are incident to a state of transition. They appear in social movements as well as in organic processes. The independent colonies before they became the United States were a sort of political hydra or many-headed body politic. We may have to endure such anomalies during the transition to a united church. In fact we already have them, in clusters of legitimate bishops claiming the same jurisdiction, such as a Roman Catholic and a Protestant Episcopal bishop of New York. Imagine also in that city a Moravian, a Lutheran, and a Presbyterian Bishop, all having the true historic episcopate, and Church Unity would look like a monstrous spectre. Yet the very appearance of such anomalies would hasten their decline. As fast as the grounds and bonds of true unity came into distinct consciousness, the rival episcopates would become consolidated in one official personage or in some true hierarchical, system. Besides, these inconsistencies are not yet upon us as matters of practical concern, and may even be prevented by rapid unifying processes, some of which are already conceivable. Adjacent congregations, by their own fellowship, might pass at once under the same bishop; presbyterial bodies might unite with episcopal in electing the same bishop; and episcopal colleges might readjust diocesan and provincial boundaries. Some passing events may show that the visionary future of church unity is not all a region of chimeras.

The most practical question now emerging relates to the method of promoting an understanding and adoption of the Quadrilateral standard of church unity by the Christian denominations. Two methods may be pursued; the one denominational, the other undenominational. The former would identify the Four Articles with the denomination which possesses them most fully and make the work of extending that denomination throughout our American Christianity equivalent to the work of Church Unity.

CHURCH UNITY SOCIETIES.

This is the method adopted by the Church Unity Societies of the Protestant Episcopal Church. It has some obvious advantages. At first sight, indeed, it would seem to be the most natural, if not the only method to be pursued. The denomination which alone professes the Quadrilateral standard might claim to be primarily and especially fitted to rally around it other denominations or individual Christians who do not as yet profess it. Moreover, as a mere manifesto or abstract declaration it would lack that social force and propagandist zeal which it would gain as attached to a compact denominational organization, moving like a Roman legion or with the effect of a strategic wedge, among the less disciplined sects around it. It may be added, that the Protestant Episcopal Church, besides already having the prestige of the Lambeth articles, has also some accessional attractions arising from its place in English history and its increasing adaptability to our own American civilization, as well as its organic affinities with both Catholicism and Protestantism. If that church can be so expanded and popularized as to gather within its pale all other denominations with their various standards of doctrine, polity, and worship so far as not inconsistent with the Lambeth Articles,—I for one would bid it God speed. I would throw no obstacle before the chariot-wheel of such a church triumphant. The obstacles in the way are not wholly external. They inhere in that denomination itself rather than in the Quadrilateral standard which it now bears to the front. Let me state them frankly and in the most friendly spirit.

At the outset, Church Unity Societies encounter a popular suspicion of denominational proselytism seemingly inconsistent with their own avowed aim. This suspicion may be and often is wholly unreasonable, but it exists and must be dealt

Church Unity Societies. 151

with by all who approach the question. It even finds some color in a few forward churchmen who are always antagonizing the other churches and denominations around them, and giving the impression that church unity means confessing the sin of dissent and conforming to the Protestant Episcopal Church. Whether their contention be true or not, it is not wise to say it under the olive branch. It savors more of a battle than of truce and peace. It is true, many other churchmen have the true conciliatory spirit and catholic feeling; yet they honestly believe that the way to the goal lies through the national predominance of their own church; and it is not easy for the unthinking observer to distinguish even such church unity from mere church aggrandizement. These difficulties, it must be granted, are largely sentimental, and may wear away in the progress of opinion and the lapse of time. They are already disappearing from generous minds. "Of course," says the Presbyterian Dr. DeWitt, "the Episcopal Church hopes to 'capture' American Christianity. Nor do I think it an unworthy ambition for them to cherish. They are convinced that they possess an element of primitive Christianity in the grace of orders conferred through the historic Episcopate, which we should find highly valuable; and their desire to communicate it we ought not to confound with arrogance. No doubt some of them are arrogant, but some of us can match them."

A more inherent difficulty lies in the exclusive claim which must be put forth by Church Unity Societies. They belong to a denomination which denies the church standing of other denominations, and even largely ignores any church-like elements which they possess. The legitimacy of such a claim is not here in dispute. The fact only of its existence at present concerns us, and it is a stumbling block in our path. There can be no misunderstanding a churchman who intelligently believes that other Christian bodies are badly organized, pseudo-ecclesiastical types, which he would rather see exterminated than preserved and perfected toward a purer, fuller type of church life. He may be right, on the principle of the survival of the fittest, could that principle be applied. But right or wrong, it is a great infelicity in his position as an advocate of church unity among such Christian bodies. It looks to them as if he only wished to build up church unity on the ruins of other churches by undermining them, dissolving them, and absorbing them as individual Christians, or as congregations, into his own organization. Even if this must be the final issue, to openly avow it and proceed toward it is a repellant and mistaken policy. Enlightened churchmen may, indeed, and often do, nobly disclaim such aims and methods, but the difficulty still inheres in the very bearing of their church toward other Christian denominations professing and calling themselves churches. It has been brought into public view by the recent Bishops' Symposium, and has caused a temporary arrest to the whole movement.

Another difficulty arises from the ecclesiastical parties of which Church Unity Societies must be composed. They hold esoterically such variant views of the Quadrilateral itself as make it more or less repugnant to the other denominations to which they proffer it. There is no need to discuss these views, but only to state them in order to see their embarrassing effect. Easily enough, a high churchman attaches the dogma of apostolic succession to the historic episcopate, makes the sacraments depend upon a sacerdotal theory of the ministry, accepts the creeds as all but inspired symbols and subordinates the Scriptures to a form of ecclesiastical infallibilism. Such opinions are favored by some expressions in the Prayer-book and by the tenor of modern Anglican teaching. Perhaps they are considered as sound by a majority of the American clergy. But sound or unsound, if infused into the Quadrilateral, they simply destroy it as a basis of unity with other Protestant denominations. They do not even allow as much standing room as is already allowed the low and broad church parties, and if pressed to their due issue would make church unity as impossible inside as outside the pale.

Generously as liberal churchmen may repudiate such partizanship and insist upon the breadth and freedom of the new platform, yet behind them may still be discerned a more dominant school who would narrow its limits or abolish it altogether. The result is that the Quadrilateral has become surcharged with the most extreme interpretations, attracting or repelling the surrounding denominations as one church party or the other expounds its terms of unity. While such misrepresentation of it continues among its own adherents, it can only appear to others as a scandal, or as a paradox.

It should be added that Church Unity Societies are encumbered in their efforts by certain purely denominational tenets, which are less acceptable than the Four Articles. They hold to the Quadrilateral as already imbedded in their Prayer-book and Ordinal, in connection with doctrines, rites and canons peculiar to the Protestant Episcopal Church in distinction from other denominations. It is true, that it is separable in thought from these church standards; but it is not yet so separated in fact, or in the popular mind. It is true, also, that it has been proposed to separate it in form, as a new constitutional provision for including other Christian bodies within the pale of the Church, and guaranteeing to them their own special doctrines and usages, so far as not inconsistent with the Four Terms of Unity. But this portentous policy has not yet been fully discussed and adopted; and were it adopted it is not certain that some other Christian bodies, especially those of continental origin, would care at once to merge their power and prestige in the Anglo-American episcopate. Moreover, have not the bishops themselves expressly disclaimed any wish to absorb other communions? For the present, at least, whatever the future may have in store for us, Protestant Episcopalians are somewhat embarrassed by their own church standards in the movement for Catholic Unity, on the basis of the Lambeth articles.[1]

---

[1] " It is true as well of the Protestant Episcopal Church, as of all the churches, that nothing in her which is really catholic is inconsistent with organic Christian

Having thus frankly stated these difficulties, I may now the more freely add that I do not think them insuperable, or even so grave as to prevent a great and good work from being done by those who can subordinate denominational advancement to catholic unity, or even by some who are fain to make the one identical with the other; nor would I disparage the great good which has already been done in spite of these difficulties by large-minded churchmen in the cause of unity. Dr. McConnell becomes conscious of them only to rise superior to them, when he says: " In this process of rebuilding [the Church of the future], what shall become of *us?* Dare we venture to throw our jewels into the crucible and trust them to the fires? If they are pure metal we may, otherwise we may not. I for one am so thoroughly assured of the intrinsic excellence of the things we value, our Orders, our Liturgy, our religious traditions, that I am willing to trust them to the regenerating fires!" [1]

My object in this discussion has been simply to open the way for considering another wholly undenominational agency which is free from the difficulties mentioned, whatever other difficulties may attend it, and which at the same time would not antagonize the Church Unity Society, but only supplement and complement its effort by moving from a different point of departure, over a different quarter of the field, toward the same general result.

CATHOLIC UNITY LEAGUES.

A Catholic Unity League or Circle (the name is not essential) would embrace representatives of the leading Christian denominations or church polities, congregational and presbyterial, as well as episcopal, voluntarily associated on the basis of the Quadrilateral with the view of promoting its better

---

Unity; but that everything which is inconsistent with that unity is essentially sectarian."—" The Stumbling Block," Rev. Wm. Chauncy Langdon, D. D., *Christian Literature*, January, 1894.

[1] Address to Church Unity Society of Pennsylvania, by Rev. S. D. McConnell, D.D.

understanding and general adoption. These objects it might seek by studious conference and friendly discussion, by attracting other like-minded inquirers and leading them to form affiliated leagues or circles, by embodying consentient results in carefully written papers, and at length by taking public measures, through the periodical press or by a special organ of publication, to develop, express, and organize the growing church unity feeling which pervades in various degrees all the Christian denominations. Some grave objections to such an agency at once start into view. It will be said that it would appear somewhat vague in its aims; it would combine the most heterogeneous opinions, traditions and tastes; it would hold its members together by the mere threads of brotherly feeling, intellectual enjoyment and spiritual recreation; it might even seem to compromise their existing relations to denominational pulpits, chairs and editorships, from which they must officially speak on other occasions; and should it find solid ground of agreement in the Four Articles, it might then lack, as a mere voluntary association, the organic force and propagandist zeal needed to give it full practical effect. So far as these objections are inherent in the scheme and peculiar to it, let us at once admit them and proceed to consider some advantages which may outweigh them.

From the start an advantage is gained by the undenominational point of departure taken by such a Catholic League. There can be no suspicion or fear of sinister or secondary aims in a circle which welcomes all denominations to equal rights and powers within the ample limits of the Quadrilateral. In fact it presents the only alternative to some purely denominational effort like that of the Church Unity Society. The members of other churches could not consistently and freely combine with that Society in promoting the Lambeth standard until it is planted somewhere outside of the Protestant Episcopal Church. Even if other churches should adopt that standard, or anything like it, there would still be room and reason enough for some more catholic circle in which their representatives might meet unembarrassed and free to converge their common aims toward the one desired result. After all that can be done in awakening Christian brotherhood, in securing denominational federation, in expanding a historic church, there will still remain a more extensive sphere of thought and action where these same parties might complete their several efforts and bring them to harmonious issue and full effect. In other words, Brotherhoods of Christian Unity, Schemes of Congregational or Presbyterial or Episcopal Federation, Church Extension Societies, need not be inconsistent with, but only preparatory and auxiliary to, a League for the promotion of the Catholic Unity of Christendom.

Another advantage of such a league is the varied composition of its membership. It would include all the parties interested in the problem of church unity and bring them together under circumstances favorable to the frankest and fullest comparison of views. It is a common remark, that the churches need to become better acquainted before they can even intelligently consider the question of unity. They are separated, not merely by known doctrinal differences, but by barriers of inherited prejudice, popular ignorance and denominational jealousy, which melt away in social intercourse and free discussion. Even their doctrinal differences under such influences will appear in a true light, not necessarily as diminished or even modified, but as real convictions and formidable difficulties, which must be honestly and carefully considered in seeking a just agreement. The Pedobaptist, who may have thought the question of immersion trivial, will learn to respect it in a Baptist who presents it with learning, logic, candor, and courtesy. The Congregationalist, who may have eschewed all creeds as mere ecclesiastical figments, will more truly estimate them in a churchman who exposes their essential truths as common to our Christianity no less than to that of Nicæa. The Episcopalian, who may have regarded

Catholic Unity Leagues. 157

Presbyterian sacraments as wholly invalid and ineffective, as well as irregular, may be surprised to find them animated by the doctrine of his own ritual. And all these parties, who might otherwise have been indifferent or estranged, will see themselves drawing more closely together, should they find that they could accept at least the first three Lambeth articles without any sacrifice of principle, of consistency, or of dignity.

There would be a special advantage in bringing together in such circles representatives of the three polities, congregational and presbyterial as well as episcopal. The crucial point in the whole inquiry is the Fourth Article, and since the historic episcopate, when divested of all dogmas and theories concerning it, presents itself simply as a question of church polity, it is of prime importance that such dogmas and theories should sink out of view while we are considering its claims and merits as a Christian institution. Let this be done, and the problem of unity becomes at once simplified and disengaged from everything adventitious. The advocates of the three polities will appear as the only parties properly concerned in the question; and their conferences in these new and direct relations may soon reveal existing bonds of organic unity, where otherwise would have been heard only the wrangle of ritualist and evangelist, dogmatist, and rationalist, each claiming the episcopate as his own property. The purest Congregationalist would see that the self government of the local church might be guarded even while admitting presbytery and episcopacy into the outer sphere of associated and consociated churches. The staunchest Presbyterian would find that the parity of the ministry need not be sacrificed by choosing a permanent moderator, like the primitive bishop, to exercise the episcopal functions of presbytery. The highest Episcopalian would discover, not only that he already has much practical presbyterianism and congregationalism in his own system, but also that new forms of episcopacy are emerging in the congregational and presbyterial bodies around him. In a word, the representatives of all three polities, becoming thus conscious of organic bonds rather than of mere sentimental professions or doctrinal compromises, would be ready to accept the Fourth Article as the most unifying point in the Quadrilateral, and realize in their own circle a miniature, if not an embryo of true church unity.

Besides these advantages such a circle would afford the only educational agency adapted to the present state of opinion. As we have seen, the denominations and churches are not yet ready for the Quadrilateral, but only in various stages of approach toward it under reactionary influences and educational processes; and no existing agency or organization can fully express those influences and rightly guide those processes. A Church Unity Society largely expresses denominational views and only affords the teaching of a propaganda. A conference of ecclesiastical commissioners, like that between the Presbyterian and Episcopal Churches, could not exceed the binding instructions which had been received, and would in its very nature and tendency be more conservative, if not obstructive, than progressive. But a voluntary group of inquirers, freed from everything sectarian or official, would also be free not only to study the Four Articles in relation to their respective denominations, but to give the results of their studies to the Christian public in the manner most likely to be effective and practical. All denominations would have before their eyes a visible embodiment of the Lambeth ideal of unity in a band or league of loyal Congregationalists, Presbyterians and Episcopalians, loving denominationalism not less, but only Church Unity more. There might even be thus formed a model or nucleus around which other bands or leagues or like agencies could gather, developing, expressing and organizing the growing ecclesiastical tendencies of our American Christianity. At length, by such means, it is conceivable, the Church Unity Society might see its own aim accomplished differently, and the inter-ecclesiastical commission would only meet to ratify a unity which had already been spontaneously achieved. As Dr. Langdon profoundly remarks, " Great discoveries in thought and great revolutions in religious truth, as little as in the realms of geography and physics, are made not by official and responsible committees duly appointed by authority and formally charged with that duty; but by or through irresponsible enthusiasts who represent no one, it may be, but the Divine Spirit by whom alone they hold themselves impelled."

Let it be added that the Lambeth Conference itself has recognized the propriety as well as the advantage of such an educational agency. It has virtually planted the Quadrilateral standard outside of the Church of England and the Protestant Episcopal Church, among the Christian denominations, by recommending them to study it in connection with " the authoritative standards of doctrine, worship, and government adopted by the different bodies of Christians into which the English speaking races are divided." We may therefore repeat with emphasis the statement that a Catholic League would be not only concurrent with all general efforts for Christian Unity but complemental to the special effort for Church Unity. On the one hand it would include Congregationalists and Presbyterians who elsewhere may be laboring for congregational and presbyterial federation ; and on the other hand, Episcopalians who elsewhere may be laboring for the expansion of the Episcopal Church. It might even include Lutherans who are seeking to recover the Swedish episcopate, and Old Catholics who would aim to reform the Roman episcopate, should such advocates of Church Unity arise. In a word, it would rally typical representatives of all the Christian denominations around the Lambeth standard in a supreme effort to combine them, at least ideally and at length actually, in one United Church of the United States.

STUDIES IN THE QUADRILATERAL.

The studies of such a circle will be many and sometimes perplexing. Frequent conferences may be needed in order to settle even preliminary questions referring to the Quadrilateral, before it can be intelligently and cordially accepted as a tentative basis of agreement.

At the threshold will arise some general questions as to the church unity in view; its nature, value and feasibility. Distinctions will be drawn between the kingdom of God as proclaimed by our Lord in the Gospels, and the church of Christ as instituted and described by his Apostles in their Acts and Epistles; between this church of the Apostles as established in their own time and the church of history as succeeding it through the Christian centuries; between the visible church of to-day as a human organization and the invisible church of all time as a divine organism. Against the opposite views resulting from these distinctions, it may be urged that the distinctions themselves are unwarrantable, fallacious and misleading; that the gospels and epistles are inseparable, either being useless without the other; that the apostolic church was simply the organized kingdom of Christ; that the historic church is distinctively a providential, not a merely Satanic development of the apostolic church; and that the church visible is necessarily but the embodiment and expression of the church invisible, being divine as well as human. Between the extreme views, a safe intermediate ground may be found in the Quadrilateral as affording the conditions of one Catholic and Apostolic Church.

More special difficulties will be raised as to each Article. From the Holy Scriptures, as the first rallying point, the ways will be seen parting, on the one side through the successive stages of biblical infallibilism, ecclesiastical infallibilism, papal infallibilism, and on the other side through the consecutive stages of critical rationalism, exegetical rationalism, dogmatic rationalism.[1] Amid all this divergence the limiting way-mark will be the acceptance of the Bible as a "common rule of faith containing all things necessary to salvation."

As to the Second Article it will be objected that the Nicene

---

[1] See the author's "Philosophia Ultima," vol. ii, pp. 372-391.

Creed is antiquated in its origin, metaphysical in its terms, and incomplete in its statement of doctrines. It will be replied that it is antiquated as eternal truth is antiquated, and guards against errors as active in our age as in the first age of the church; that it is metaphysical as all divinity is metaphysical, and no more recondite than the first chapter of St. John; that if it does not include some special dogmas of the Reformation, yet neither does it exclude them, but contains them germinally and allows them so far as they are supplemental and consistent. The essential point is that it is the only "statement of the Christian faith" that the whole church has ever put forth and maintained, and therefore is "sufficient" for the purpose of unity as serving to connect the whole church of the past with the whole church of the present.

As to the Third Article more serious difficulties will emerge into view. On doctrinal grounds the Baptist will object to the church membership of infants; on lexical grounds to any mode of baptism but immersion; and on ecclesiastical grounds to communion with any Christians but those who have been immersed. The Pedobaptist can only reply that the membership of infants is made complete by their own confession of faith when they have reached years of discretion; that immersion is legitimate as well as sprinkling; and that even a local Baptist communion might be maintained provisionally in a large church system. In like manner, the circle will seem divided by ritualistic and evangelistic views of the Holy Supper, as celebrated at an altar or a table, and by the new questions of the temperance chalice, individual cups and other details of the ministration. But in spite of accumulating difficulties in regard to both sacraments all will be able to unite in the requirement of an "unfailing use of the very words and elements appointed by Christ himself."

The Fourth Article will remain as the crucial point around which all other difficulties become intensified. Evangelical and rationalistic theories of the ministry will stand contrasted with sacerdotal and hierarchical theories. Congregationalism,

Presbyterianism, and Episcopalianism will assert their respective claims. How these questions will adjust themselves has been shown in a former essay and also may appear in the next essay. The emphatic point is, that the historic episcopate is to be accepted not as a theory of the ministry but as including all such theories; not as the Roman papacy or as the Anglican prelacy, but as the one catholic ministry, "locally adapted" to the Congregationalist, Presbyterian, and Episcopalian denominations of our own American Christianity.

The connection of the four articles may also be found important. The first as joined to the second article makes the catholic creeds accordant with the Holy Scriptures. The second as joined to the third makes the Apostles' Creed the baptismal symbol or confession of faith, and the Nicene Creed the eucharistic confession of the communion of saints. The third as joined to the fourth secures the validity of the sacraments by a legitimate ministry. And the fourth article as connected with the other three articles secures the maintenance of sound doctrine and holy living in the church.

Even the order of the four articles might be made significant and advantageous. They are stated, not in a doctrinal but in a practical order, not according to historical but logical sequence. If it be true, doctrinally or historically, that in the age of the apostles the ministry gave forth the gospel sacraments, the sacraments led to the formation of the catholic creeds, and the creeds were at length followed by the completed canon of Scripture; yet practically and logically, in the present state of opinion, the Scriptures must first be accepted as the rule of faith, and then the creeds as the sufficient statement of Scriptural doctrine, and then the sacraments as conveying the benefits expressed in the creeds, and at length the episcopate as the complement of the congregational and presbyterial elements of polity. The denominations now must retrace the steps of the early church and recover in an inverse order its bonds of unity. Already it is apparent that they can accept the first three articles long before the last. While then the four points may be considered with advantage separately and in any order, yet the best order in which to approach, study, and accept them is the order in which they have been presented.

If now we seek for a full yet concise expression of the principles of such a league as has been described there would result some formula of concord like the following :—

THE LEAGUE OF CATHOLIC UNITY.

We, whose names are subscribed, devoutly seeking the Divine guidance and blessing, hereby associate ourselves as a League for the promotion of the Catholic Unity of Christendom.

Without detaching ourselves from the Christian denominations to which we severally belong, or intending to compromise our relations thereto, or seeking to interfere with other efforts for Christian unity, we accept, as worthy of the most thoughtful consideration, the four principles of Church Unity proposed by the bishops of the Protestant Episcopal Church at Chicago, in 1886, and amended by the Lambeth Conference of 1888, as follows :—

"I. The Holy Scriptures of the Old and New Testaments, as containing all things necessary to salvation, and as being the rule and ultimate standard of faith.

"II. The Apostles' Creed, as the baptismal symbol, and the Nicene Creed, as the sufficient statement of the Christian faith.

"III. The two sacraments ordained by Christ himself, Baptism and the Supper of the Lord, ministered with unfailing use of Christ's words of institution, and of the elements ordained by Him.

"IV. The historic episcopate, locally adapted in the methods of its administration to the varying needs of the nations and peoples called of God into the unity of His church."

We believe that upon the basis of these four principles as

articles of agreement, the unification of the Christian denominations of this country may proceed cautiously and steadily, without any radical alteration of their existing standards of doctrine, polity, and worship, and with only such concessions as they might reasonably make in a spirit of brotherly love and harmony, for the sake of unity and for the furtherance of all the great ends of the Church of Christ on earth. This will appear the more closely each of these articles is examined.

The *Holy Scriptures* are already our accepted rule of faith, however we may differ among ourselves concerning the mode of their inspiration and interpretation.

The *Apostles'* and *Nicene Creeds*, being in accordance with the Holy Scriptures, do already express the catholic belief and doctrine, without precluding the more particular confessions, to which we are severally attached, such as the Augsburg Confession, the Heidelberg Catechism, the Thirty-nine Articles, the Westminster Confession, and other symbols or formularies not inconsistent with these two catholic creeds.

The *Sacraments of Baptism* and the *Lord's Supper*, as instituted by Christ himself and administered with his own appointed words and elements, are already recognized among us as the badges and media of church membership and communion, although we do not yet agree as to particular modes of their administration or special qualifications for their reception, or even theories of their efficacy.

The *Historic Episcopate* in various forms already prevails extensively throughout the Christian world; and as connected with the Scriptures, the Creeds, and the Sacraments, it would secure a legitimate catholic ministry to all Christian denominations, and might become a bond of organic unity among them, by completing their congregational, or presbyterial, or episcopal systems, and at length recombining them normally in one Catholic Apostolic Church.

In order to promote a better understanding of these articles, we recommend, as proposed by the Lambeth Conference,

The League of Catholic Unity. 165

that they be carefully studied in connection with " the authoritative standards of doctrine, worship, and government adopted by the different bodies of Christians, into which the English-speaking races are divided;" and we reverently and lovingly invoke the countenance and aid of the Bishops of the Protestant Episcopal Church, and of all other catholic bishops and Christian ministers of every name, who may join this League or any like associations for studious, prayerful and brotherly conference with a view to the unification of Christendom.

May our united prayers be so blended with the prevalent intercession of our ascended Lord, that we shall all become one in Him, for the glory of His eternal Father, for the good of His Church, and for the redemption of the world.

VI.
THE HISTORIC EPISCOPATE AND THE THREE CHURCH POLITIES.

VI.

THE HISTORIC EPISCOPATE AND THE THREE CHURCH POLITIES.

The chief Christian denominations may be grouped in three classes according to their structural principles : the congregational, as including the Baptist, Congregational and Unitarian Churches; the presbyterial, as including the Presbyterian, the Reformed (Dutch and German) and the Lutheran Churches; the episcopal, as including the Moravian, Methodist, Protestant Episcopal, Reformed Episcopal, and Roman Catholic Churches. As nearly all these bodies both in law and in courtesy are entitled churches, the question of their consolidation as united Churches, or their comprehension in one united Church, may be termed in general, the question of Church Unity. And the problem is to find a bond or system under which they may all be embraced in their integrity, or with as little sacrifice as possible of their several views of doctrine, polity and worship.

PRELIMINARY PRINCIPLES.

In approaching this great question we need to remind ourselves of one or two premises from which to reason. The first is our common Christianity. We already agree in those essential tenets which distinguish the Christian religion from other religions and warrant us to call ourselves Christians. Between our Roman Catholic brethren at the extreme right and our Unitarian friends at the extreme left, the other denominations stand together around the great central facts and truths of Christianity. This Christian unity, as a matter of fact, now pervades all Christian bodies in so far as they are truly Christian, and becomes expressed in more or less Christian union whenever they associate for great Christian ends. But Church union or Church unity, in addition to our common Christianity; the association of Christian bodies by means of the same ecclesiastical principles in one ecclesiastical system —this is yet to be attained. Does the historic episcopate afford the bond or link of such Church unity?

A second premise is the legitimacy of the Christian denominations. They have won their right to be. They have a clear providential warrant for their existence. Congregationalism, Presbyterianism, Episcopalianism may stand severally for great ecclesiastical principles or institutions, which are taught if not delineated in Holy Scripture, which appeared together in the apostolic Church, which were reaffirmed separately at the Reformation, which since then have been maintained through fierce struggles in the Old World, and in the New World have at length found free scope and full development. Such principles are not to be risked lightly in any scheme of Church unity. They cannot be ignored or over-ridden. They should at least be weighed carefully and estimated. At the same time, these same principles, it must be granted, are often pushed to sinful extremes and have become an occasion of immense evils. They have been made to exalt the sect above the Church and to dismember the body of Christ. They have torn its organization limb from limb. They certainly do not cohere now, as once in the church of the Apostles. And the question is, whether through the historic episcopate they might not be restored to their pristine normal relationship, become legitimated and recombined and ever kept in harmonious action?

A third premise is the subordination of denominationalism to Church unity. Not the extinction of denominations, or, at least, not the extinction of any ecclesiastical principles which they may contain, but their incorporation in the Church as legitimate parts of its organism. Let there be the greatest freedom and variety as to modes of worship and lesser doctrines, but all within the same ecclesiastical system. Let existing denominations still continue, but only with the hope of becoming more congruous and coöperative as living members of one body. If we cannot come to the question in this spirit, we shall only waste time in discussing it. If we begin by preferring mere denominationalism to Church unity we shall simply end by inviting one another into some congregational, or presbyterial, or episcopal millennium, or else fall back upon some sentimental invisible unity which only glorified saints and angels might realize. The invisible Church or Church of the Future is not within our reach. We have to do with the visible Church of the present. Taking its various denominations as we find them, let us study their actual consensus of doctrines, their organic affinities, their points of vital contact, their complemental relations, their growing similarities. Let us ask if Baptist and Pedobaptist congregations, Lutheran and Reformed presbyteries, Methodist and Protestant Episcopal bishops might not combine, not indeed at once in one Church organization, but at least in the same general Church system, the congregation concurring with the presbytery and the presbytery with the bishop as to all matters outside their several spheres. In a word, let us see if through and within the historic episcopate the chief Christian denominations might not find comprehension without compromise, concord without concession, unity without uniformity, oneness amid variety.

But what is the historic episcopate? It may mean very much or very little, according to its definition; and its definition will be full or meager, according to our point of view. At present we can only view it in its external relations, as a Christian institution appearing among other Christian institutions and organizations. I do not here pretend to define it per se as an ecclesiastical dogma; much less to give an inside view of its powers and effects upon those who devoutly receive it. I will aim at little more than a verbal definition of the phrase itself.

Christianity is historic. It has had organic life and growth from the beginning. It was more than mere sentiment or doctrine. It was a church as well as a gospel. It has ever been visibly organized, with fixed institutions persisting from age to age until the present time. Among those institutions is the historic episcopate. Thus viewed it may be defined negatively and then more positively.

The Scriptural Episcopate.

In the first place, the historic episcopate is distinguishable from the scriptural episcopate. It may or may not have been enjoined in the Scriptures. On this point all are not agreed, but all must admit the historical fact that sooner or later the Episcopal institution did exist in the church and ever since has been accepted by an overwhelming majority of Christians in all ages and countries. As to the mode of its origin we have the high authority of the late learned Bishop of Durham, Dr. Lightfoot. In his commentary on the Epistle to the Philippians he maintains that the episcopate was formed out of the presbyterate as the need for central unity became felt among the scattered congregations and presbyteries which the apostles had planted. And this is the very need which is now felt by the very same parties, by the congregational, presbyterial, and episcopal denominations of this country.

The Apostolic Episcopate.

In the second place, the historic episcopate is distinguishable from the apostolic episcopate. Whether the apostles as such had any official successors is in dispute; but no one can deny that they were actually followed in course of time by bishops presiding over presbyteries and congregations. The learned prelate before cited traced the growth of this episcopate historically as a rational process, the bishops at first becoming centers of unity, and at length claiming succession from the apostles as guardians of faith and order. In the same way ministers now refer to church founders for their authority and doctrine; and however we may theorize about it, the fact of some apostolic succession is as certain as the fact of transmitted power in any regular ministry, presbyterial as well as episcopal. Indeed, some of the fathers, Irenæus, Clement of Alexandria and St. Jerome, found this succession in both presbyters and bishops, and it was only by degrees that the apostolate was claimed for the bishops alone.

THE MODERN NEW-MADE EPISCOPATE.

In the third place, the historic episcopate is distinguishable from the modern new-made forms of episcopacy. Whatever else these may be, they are not historical. The Reformed Episcopalians can claim to have a non-apostolic episcopate; the Methodist Episcopalians may claim to have an evangelical episcopate; the Irvingite Episcopalians, or Apostolic Catholics, lay claim to a miracle working episcopate; but none of these parties could claim to have the historic episcopate. In fact, they have already disclaimed or renounced it. For this reason, were there no other, the Reformed Episcopal Church cannot become the conciliator in our unhappy divisions. It has taken dogmatic ground openly against historic episcopacy, if not against all Catholic Christianity. It may have some other good and high mission, but its mission is not to promote church unity. In such unity the claims of episcopal as well as other churches must be duly satisfied, and ritualistic as well as evangelistic views of the ministry must be at least tolerated.

By urging these distinctions I do not mean to prejudge the scriptural, or the apostolic, or even the Reformed episcopate. The things distinguished, though separable in thought, are not always separate in belief. On the contrary, the great majority adhering to the historic episcopate believe it to be both scriptural and apostolic, having the didactic force of inspiration and the special grace of a divine institution. Other adherents, however, think that it arose providentially out of the wants of the early Church, in accordance with apostolic example and Scripture doctrine, but with no exclusive legitimacy. Still others, waiving the authority both of the Scriptures and of the Apostles, find their warrant for it in its mere expediency or fitness to the existing circumstances of the Christian religion. All these views are found consistent with loyal attachment to the institution itself, and their concurrence in upholding it may show at once its breadth and its stability.

COMPREHENSIVENESS OF THE HISTORIC EPISCOPATE.

As we pass to a positive definition or description we shall see still more clearly how comprehensive is this great Christian institution. Not only did its original structure involve congregational and presbyterial elements, synagogues and elders as well as bishops, but its historic growth has pervaded the whole Christian world. As instituted at first by our Lord himself in the work of the apostles, they exemplified it in their acts and epistles, while planting and training the first parishes and presbyteries. Thenceforward, it extended over the entire Church through the centuries before the Council of Nice. After the great schism it was continued in both the eastern and western sections of Christendom until the Reformation. At the present day on its Catholic side, as maintained in the Old World, it embraces the ecclesiastical principles of the Greek, Roman, and the Anglican Churches, while on its Protestant side as developed in the New World, it has also embraced the ecclesiastical principles of the Lutheran, the Reformed, the Presbyterian, the Methodist, the Congregational, the Baptist Churches. It has embraced them actually, even if not consciously or avowedly. Without sacrificing the episcopal principle, it has incorporated the presbyterial principle in diocesan conventions and standing committees and the congregational principle in free parishes and vestries. As good Congregationalism and as sound Presbyterianism can be found inside the American Episcopate as outside of it. And could our various congregational and presbyterial denominations now come together under the same stringent yet elastic bond, through bishops of their own choice, with their creeds and usages untouched, they would do no violence to their respective missions in this new age and country. They would simply retrace the steps by which unity was reached in the New Testament Church, when the first congregations and presbyteries became united under bishops after the apostles had ceased from their labors.

No other church system is at once so large and cohesive. Not the congregational, because of its localizing tendency and inorganic state; not the presbyterial, because of its brittle structure and lack of centralizing force; not the episcopal alone, without the congregational and presbyterial institutions, with which it must ever be in living connection. The three elements as fitly joined in one organism make an ideal unity; and it is a unity which might become actual. At the center of our divided and distracted Christianity we have before our eyes the spectacle of Episcopalians, Presbyterians, and Congregationalists, in all but the name, loyally held together by this Historic Episcopate in the catholic faith of Christendom.

ITS ALLEGED HIERARCHISM.

But here we are met by two grave objections. It is alleged that this historic episcopate has ever tended to hierarchy, as seen conspicuously in that Roman papacy and Anglican prelacy from which we have escaped only through grievous wars and persecutions. Undoubtedly such scruples would have had force in Europe some generations ago. Whatever good ends the abnormal sway of the Latin episcopate may have served providentially in the mediæval civilization, its greater evils could only be cured by the Reformation. Such evils however, do not menace us now in this free land. Nor can we imagine a prelatic peerage among its free churches. A congestion of church power in bishops is about the last danger that we have to fear. The whole drift of our times is the other way, and with terrific momentum toward the wildest license in Church and State. We have to face the anarchy of the nineteenth century, not the hierarchy of the Middle

Ages. Good Christian people, I sometimes fancy, can be frightened by the mere word hierarchy, and seem often to cherish an inherited dread of it, which religious demagogues may but too easily inflame in thoughtless moments. And this, too, while the Pope himself is but a prisoner in the Vatican and the church of Archbishop Laud seems to be on the verge of disestablishment.

Its Alleged Sacerdotalism.

It is further charged that this historic episcopate has bred sacerdotalism in the ministry.[1] The candid Bishop Lightfoot has replied that the priesthood of believers only becomes expressed through the priesthood of ministers, who faithfully represent the people to God as well as God to the people, in divine service. Without pursuing the question, however, it is enough here to say that it is misplaced in a discussion which bears upon the terms of Church Unity rather than upon the truth or falsity of special doctrines. You need not agree with ritualists while making common cause with them against sectarianism, infidelity and vice; nor approve, because you tolerate them as differing brethren in the household of faith. If I read aright, some ritualists as well as revivalists, were allowed in the one Church of the Apostles, neither of them without good advice. That episcopacy has no invariable connection with sacerdotalism is shown in its evangelical pulpits and plain services as well as by Moravian spirituality and Methodist fervor. That it is not exclusively committed to any partisan view of the ministry and sacraments is but a proof of its unifying capacity and organizing power. Moreover, at a time when great foes of our common faith are mustering before us, we need a leadership which can marshal into battle both the extreme right and left wings of the Church militant.

---

[1] This popular hindrance to Church unity has been judiciously treated by the Rev. G. Woolsey Hodge, of Philadelphia, in a tract entitled "Sacerdotalism and Sacramentarianism."

In justice let it be added, that neither hierarchical nor sacerdotal claims have been put before us as terms of Church unity. Not the Roman papacy nor the Anglican prelacy, but simply the historic episcopate as adapted to American Christianity; not the priestly view of the sacraments, but simply the sacramental words and acts themselves, whatever theories may be held as to their meaning and efficacy. The truth is, the Fourth Article of the Quadrilateral is being subjected to a double misrepresentation. On the one hand many are surcharging it with doctrines which it does not require, and on the other hand many are discharging it of doctrines which it does not exclude. But as the mists clear away we may hope to see the Historic Episcopate standing out in full view simply as a primitive and catholic institution, in which Congregationalists and Presbyterians as well as Episcopalians can find a broad, yet firm basis of ecclesiastical unity. That it is possible thus to treat it may appear in the following programme of studies, which has been used by some representatives of the three polities in their conferences on the subject.

STUDIES IN THE HISTORIC EPISCOPATE.

I.

Christianity began historically as a church no less than as a gospel; with institutions as well as with doctrines; having an organization to secure the ministry of the Word and Sacraments. And in some organized form it has ever since continued for nearly twenty centuries.

The lover of church unity must recognize the fact of this historic continuity, whatever he may think of its origin and value.

II.

The historic continuity of the church may be considered in three forms:—

First, as Congregational; the continuance of a Christian people from the Apostles' time.

Second, as Presbyterial; the continuance of a Christian ministry of the Word and Sacraments.

Third, as Episcopal; the continuance of Bishops as well as Presbyters in the Christian ministry.

The lover of church unity may personally hold any one of these three views of historic continuity, but not any one of them to the exclusion of the others.

The historic episcopate alone includes all three views, without excluding any one of them; and therefore affords the only practicable basis of church unity.

III.

This historic episcopate may be estimated variously:—

First; That it simply secures the advantages of order, regularity, and good government in Christian society.

Second; That it secures a divine authority in the ministry of the Word and the Sacraments, without which other ministries are merely human and unauthorized.

Third; That it conveys a supernatural grace, without which the Word and Sacraments fail of their due and full effect.

The lover of church unity, instead of discussing these estimates, accepts the historic episcopate simply as a fact, having his own doctrine or theory of its value. Its practical fitness as a basis of unity appears in the variety of such theories and doctrines among its loyal adherents.

IV.

In view of these principles the general problem of Church unity may be distributed into several special inquiries:—

(1) The Relation of Congregationalism (Orthodox, Unitarian, Baptist) to the Historic Episcopate.

(2) The Relation of Presbyterianism (Lutheran, Reformed, Presbyterian) to the Historic Episcopate.

(3) The Relation of Episcopalianism (Methodist, Reformed, Protestant) to the Historic Episcopate.

(4) The Relation of Special Episcopates (Greek, Roman, Anglican) to the Historic Episcopate.

VII.
THE HISTORIC PRESBYTERATE AND THE HISTORIC EPISCOPATE.

VII.

THE HISTORIC PRESBYTERATE AND THE HISTORIC EPISCOPATE.

It has become plain that the historic episcopate is the pivotal question in the debate upon church unity. The three other points proposed by the House of Bishops have raised but little discussion. Indeed, they scarcely need to be discussed; at least, not in the Protestant Episcopal Church, nor in the Presbyterian Church. These two bodies, without changing their standards or forfeiting their autonomy, could to-day, if so minded, unite in confessing the Holy Scriptures, the Nicene Creed and the two Sacraments as an actual consensus, setting forth the great things in which they agree in distinction from the small things in which they differ. But under such a league the historic episcopate would still be viewed as a remaining barrier between them rather than a ground or link of organic affinity. As to that matter no consensus has yet been defined, and it may even be thought that none exists.

It cannot be denied that some effects of the Chicago declaration appear discouraging. Amid many expressions of Christian feeling it has brought the old denominational lines more sharply into view and provoked, in some quarters, a fresh outburst of the sectarian spirit. The responding churches have simply re-asserted their respective positions and for the moment seem farther apart than ever. But such strange manifestations of division on the face of a deep-seated popular movement toward church unity can only be regarded as deceptive and transient. Look beneath them at the facts. For a whole generation the Young Men's Christian Association has been undermining denominationalism throughout the land. Great revivals have been breaking down the barriers between the churches and fusing them into practical oneness. Liturgical forms of prayer and praise have been fostering their common faith and worship. The Evangelical Alliance, the American Congress of Churches, the Washington Conference, have successively brought together their leaders on national platforms for consultation and coöperation. Nearly every historic church has been seeking closer relations with its neighbors. At length one of them proposes four terms of unity, only to be assailed at once on all sides. Why such a volley at a flag of truce? Why such a recoil in mid progress? Surely it is worth while to look deeper into the subject.

APPEAL TO BOTH EPISCOPALIANS AND PRESBYTERIANS.

In offering some thoughts upon church unity, addressed at once to Episcopalians and to Presbyterians,[1] I beg to disclaim any sense of special vocation or mission. Nothing could be more absurd or more thankless than a self-appointed mediation. Whoever breaks from the ranks on either side can only risk a cross-fire from both sides. He may also be charged with ignorance as well as rashness. Nevertheless, it is a Christian duty to study this great problem in a catholic spirit; and if any one reaches conclusions which he thinks important and timely he can respectfully tender them, and let them pass for what they are worth. He will at least have bestowed his mite in a cause which all should have at heart. In such a spirit I would submit a view of the fourth term of unity which I have not seen anywhere clearly stated or fully discussed. It is briefly this:—

The historic episcopate, as neither enjoining nor forbidding any doctrine of apostolic succession.

It will be seen that I use that happily chosen phrase, " the historic episcopate," in its literal meaning. It gives no hint

---

[1] The first part of this paper appeared simultaneously in *The New York Evangelist* and *The Churchman.*

of any doctrine of apostolical succession. Yet many such doctrines are known to exist. Old-fashioned Presbyterians hold to an apostolic succession in the presbyterate, though attaching to it but little value. Episcopalians of all schools, except such as deny it outright, find it in the episcopate, but rate it variously in a scale somewhere between zero and infinity. According to some, the doctrine is not set forth in the Scriptures, nor even in the Prayer-book, but is simply an inferential tenet or incidental fruit of church growth in history. According to others, the apostolate which has been transmitted was not a divine institution, but a mere ecclesiastical office, securing the advantages of good government. According to others, only the apostolic functions of oversight and discipline have been transmitted. According to others, with these functions have been continuously illustrated simply the true apostolic doctrine, character, and spirit. According to others, over and above such gifts, a divine authority has been committed by our Lord himself through his apostles to their successors, rendering all other ministries illegitimate, irregular, and dubious. According to others, a special supernatural grace inheres in the apostolic episcopate, without which the word and sacraments cannot become means of salvation. And so on, until we reach the climax in the learned Dodwell, who wrote a treatise to prove that immortality itself, not being natural to man, is a supernatural gift in baptism, which only the bishops as successors of the apostles can confer.

Now all these various doctrines do indeed touch upon vital interests. It cannot be a matter of indifference which of them is true. It may be important, it is important, for every one to decide which is true for him and which he will maintain to the end. But this is not the question here before us; nor is it the burning question of the hour. The present problem is to find a basis of church unity broad enough and firm enough for existing church organizations. And you will certainly narrow and weaken that basis by either selecting for it or rejecting from it any of the doctrines mentioned. As an

Episcopalian, you will commit your own church to a mere party and vainly ask other churches to unite with it on a ground where it is not itself united, and perhaps never can be. As a Presbyterian you will forego all claims of your own church to true catholicity and leave no ground on which to unite with other Catholic Churches. In either case you will not help forward the cause of church unity. Glance for a moment at some of the injurious effects of such partisanship on both sides.

Apostolical Succession not Enjoined.

On the one hand it would only be hurtful to enjoin a doctrine of apostolical succession. Dear to you as such a doctrine may be, and fundamental as it may seem, you could not make it a term of unity in the existing state of opinion. By taking such ground you would at once assail the liberal and evangelical portion of the Protestant Episcopal Church, and repel all the other Protestant Churches around you, together with all the ecclesiastical elements which they contain. You would repel the Evangelical Lutheran Church, that bulwark of the Reformation, with its six thousand ministers, its high ritual, its rich erudition, its conservative traditions and catholic affinities. You would repel the Presbyterian Church, that backbone of American orthodoxy, with its twelve thousand ministers, its historic presbyterate, its solid learning, its earnest spirituality, organizing skill and potent ecclesiasticism. You would repel the Methodist Episcopal Church, that pioneer of American Christianity, with its forty thousand ministers, its dormant prayer book and Articles, its scriptural simplicity, apostolic zeal and pentecostal fervor. In a word, you would repel nine-tenths of our ecclesiastical Protestantism and be left with a mere formal catholicity.

Apostolical Succession not Forbidden.

On the other hand however, it would be as hurtful, if not more hurtful, to forbid a doctrine of apostolical succession.

Weak and untenable as such doctrine may be deemed by you, it runs through all historic Christianity, and should you exclude it from your basis of unity you would thereby exclude the great Catholic churches of Christendom. You would exclude them not merely as European but as American organizations to which we are bound by common aims and interests. You would exclude the Roman Catholic Church, the mother of churches, the church of scholars and saints such as Augustine and Aquinas and Bernard and Fenelon; the church of all races, ranks and classes, which already gives signs of becoming American as well as Roman, and the only church fitted by its hold upon the working masses to grapple with that labor problem before which our Protestant Christianity stands baffled to-day. You would exclude also the Protestant Episcopal Church, the beautiful daughter of a beautiful mother, claiming a lineage of apostles, saints and martyrs, the church which still hails from the home of our Anglo-Saxon Christianity, from altars at which Knox and Bucer ministered, from cloisters in which our Westminster standards were born, and from colleges out of which came our Whitefield and Wesley with tongues of flame; the church which daily offers Lutheran, Reformed and Presbyterian prayers in its liturgy, and the one church which now seeks to win back the wrangling sisterhood of churches home again. In a word you would exclude five-sixths of Christendom, and be left with a mere sectarian Protestantism.

Moreover, through such partisanship your rallying-point of unity would actually become a starting point of fresh divisions. You would drive whole groups of Christians and churches around new sectarian centers. Those, on the one side, who begin to value the Episcopate as a custodian of the Prayer-book, a complement of presbytery, and a guarantee of regularity, would seek such advantages in Reformed Episcopacy or in Methodist Episcopacy, or in a liturgical Presbyterianism. Those, on the other side, who have learned to prize the historic Christianity which gathered the canonical Scriptures, set forth the ecumenical creeds and framed the orthodox system of doctrine, would find it within that Roman Catholic episcopate which still spurns at all our parvenu churchmanship, with claims everywhere unchallenged. At the same time those larger Christ-like souls, who can take both sides of Christendom into view, would lose all hope of any true Catholicity and matured Christianity. It is because the Protestant Episcopal Church stands between these extremes, at once protesting against Roman error and maintaining Catholic truth, that to many she seems called of God to this very crisis, and they would not see her yield an inch of hard won ground on either side by presenting a mere partisan Episcopate in place of one truly historic because both Catholic and Protestant.

PRACTICAL UNION BY IGNORING THE QUESTION.

We have thus seen that it would only hurt the cause of church unity to press the question of apostolic succession. Add now, that it would greatly help that cause and harm no other interest, to leave the whole question open. At least, to leave it open between Presbyterians and Episcopalians. As to that question, they could agree to differ for the sake of closer oneness in essentials. In the historic episcopate, as freed from that question, they could retain severally their own view of the ministry and sacraments, and at the same time find a large consensus for organic reunion throughout Christendom. The Catholic Episcopalian could still find in it what he finds in it now, a ministration of that apostolate which he believes to have been perpetuated in the Greek, Latin, and Anglican Churches alone, and the catholic Presbyterian could again find in it what he found in it once, a complement of that presbyterate which he believes to have been continued in the Lutheran, Reformed, and Presbyterian Churches, as well as in the whole Church before the Reformation. In all this there would be nothing strange or incongruous. Such a union of the Episcopal and Presbyterial orders has prevailed throughout the universal Church from the apostles' time. Such a union of Presbyterians with Episcopalians formerly obtained in the Church of England. Such a union of Episcopalians with Presbyterians has lately been proposed for the Church of Scotland. And something like such a union may be found to-day in the Protestant Episcopal Church in the United States.

ONLY GRADUAL UNION PRACTICABLE.

Here let it be emphasized that there is no thought of one communion absorbing another. Surely nobody is foolish enough to dream of any immediate fusion of Christian denominations into some newly-organized body bursting forth, like the flower of a night, as the " American Catholic Church." Nor would the mere melody of that grand title ever soothe them into oneness. The glorious ideal if reached at all, must be approached step by step, with prayers and tears, through many trials, it may be, and after much mistake and failure. Doubtless existing church organizations will long continue with their standards intact and their autonomy undisturbed. Organic unity could only supervene upon them, or slowly supersede them, as discussions give rise to conferences, and conferences issue in leagues, and leagues ripen into more vital relations. In this process the two Churches before us might lead the way through the four stages proposed. The Holy Scriptures could be recognized at once as their common foundation. The Nicene Creed could be accepted as equally consistent with the Articles of Religion and the Confession of Faith. The sacraments of Baptism and the Lord's Supper would be found doctrinally the same in the Prayer-book and the Directory. And the Ordinal and the Form of Government might have some practical agreement, enough at least for a good beginning.

Meanwhile it is of the utmost importance that the question of Church unity should be kept distinct from other and lesser questions. It does not turn upon denominational tenets or party claims. Neither Presbyterians nor Episcopalians, neither evangelical nor ritualistic Churchmen may dictate its terms. If Christian sects and factions cannot sink their differences and find some common ground of mutual tolerance in the same Church or within the same Church system, there is an end to everything like organic oneness as distinguished from mere sentimental fellowship.

Accordingly, the proposed terms of Church unity are so stated as to exclude most thoroughly all denominational tenets and partisan opinions. Even the denominational tenets of the Protestant Episcopal Church are largely ignored, as well as the ecclesiastical parties within its pale. The Holy Bible is insisted on, but not the Prayer Book; the Nicene Creed, but not the Thirty-nine Articles; the two sacraments, but neither the evangelical nor the ritualistic view of their efficacy; the historic episcopate, but neither the high nor the low theory of its prerogative. In like manner, the Presbyterian Church in acceding to such terms could not insist upon its own Directory for Worship and Confession of Faith, nor dictate any special views of ritual and polity. The two bodies, while adhering to the same Scriptures, creeds, sacraments and ministry, would still have a wide margin for their denominational forms of doctrine and worship.

These distinctions apply with special force to the last of the four conditions. The historic episcopate if defined in any particular sense by Church authority, would cease at once to afford a ground or bond of unity. Its own supporters would rush apart into schism. According to the definition made, the ministry and sacraments would either be declared void of all that they meant to the High Church party, or charged with a meaning wholly repudiated by the Broad Church party. And among the denominations of the Church at large, such a doctrinal definition would be still more divisive, repelling them toward the extremes of Protestanism and Romanism. It is but a truism to say that the right and left wings of Christendom could never be conjoined in an episcopate which should take sides dogmatically with either against the other.

Pulpit Exchanges.

If this be a correct view, it is not easy to see how true church unity would be promoted by interchanges of pulpit services between episcopal and non-episcopal ministers. Sooner or later such interchanges could not but involve a divisive definition of the Christian ministry itself. For a time, indeed, they might serve some good ends. Superficial observers might rejoice in them as signs of Christian fellowship and clerical amity. In some worshiping assemblies they might lead to effusive manifestations of fraternal feeling, and on charity platforms to more or less practical co-operation. But at length a breach would be opened which had been concealed, and harsh recoil would follow the hasty union. When the black-gowned preacher in the pulpit stood contrasted with the white-robed priest at the altar, a difference would become visible to their respective adherents in the pews—a difference as absurd as irritating, should it be known that the priest meant to recognize the validity of the preacher's ministration, while the preacher claimed to have the presbyterial functions from which he was debarred. Each party would be put in a false position. The visiting minister would publicly take the place of a layman, and his low church brother would be forced to appear against him in the Absolution or the Communion, though both held substantially the same views of the clerical office and the Holy Supper. Is it not to be feared that a few such object lessons might put an end to every hope of church unity in the pulpit as well as at the altar?

Let it be observed that we are now looking at this question from the standpoint of church unity alone. I am not here maintaining the truth or falsity of any doctrine of the Christian ministry, nor asking others to take high or low church ground as to its powers. Indeed, it is not upon such ground merely that intelligent Episcopalians may be supposed to withhold recognition from learned divines of unimpeached orthodoxy and piety. It is because they know that the recognition would draw after it a train of other questions involving at length the unity of their whole church. And they value such unity more than any chance fraternization or mere visionary fellowship. In other words, the historic episcopate holds them together in the essential faith, notwithstanding their diverse views of the ministry and sacraments, and in spite of their leanings toward either extreme. Now, in like manner, it might draw together other denominations with which it has more or less affinity. On a larger scale in the Christian world it might embrace the same schools and parties which are now found within its pale. Its expansive, unifying power is no mere theory, but an exemplary fact. All this power, however, it would lose were it dragged aside to any partisan ground, high or low, evangelical or sacerdotal. By recognizing faithful ministers or preachers not episcopally ordained, no doubt it would meet many noble Christian impulses and please some sections of Protestantism, but it would alienate the rest of Christendom, as well as rend its own body asunder. Whatever else it might retain, it would forfeit its potential capacity for collecting and combining the scattered ecclesiastical elements of our divided American Christianity. For such reasons it is quite conceivable that a true lover of church unity might deprecate the proposed interchanges, not as undesirable in themselves, but as likely to do more harm than good to the cause which he had at heart. He might think a lasting peace better than any hollow truce, and be disposed to shun mere sentimental compacts for the sake of more intelligent agreements.[1]

---

[1] Another view of this question has been clearly and forcibly presented by Prof. John DeWitt, of Princeton Theological Seminary, in a letter to the Rev. Dr. S. D. McConnell, published by the Church Unity Society of Philadelphia.

Unity is a plant of slow growth. It cannot be forced. It will require time and thought and study, as well as prayer and effort. The present race of clergymen may have to pass away. Another generation may need to be educated to a higher point of view. In future ordinations which cast no seeming reflection upon a former ministry, or which may involve some more practical legitimation of Presbyterian ministrations, a degree of essential unity may be reached before which the freest interchange of pulpit services would sink into insignificance.

PRESBYTERIAN ORDERS.

What is true of pulpit exchanges is true of the whole question of Presbyterian orders? Important as that question may be, it is as yet irrelevant and premature. As a matter of personal duty, it might have much significance, for a Presbyterian minister seeking admission to Holy Orders in the Episcopal Church; but as a question of ecclesiastical policy between the Presbyterian and Episcopal Churches, it is the very last one to be raised in any formal conference or negotiation. Were the two churches already agreed on the Lambeth basis in accepting the historic episcopate as a bond of re-union or unification, the question would then be both timely and hopeful, and might almost settle itself with but little discussion. Only in view of such an event is it worth while to consider it, and only in that view do I now propose briefly to present it.

It should be observed, at the outset, that the question has become a very simple one as transferred from the old to the new world, amid the changed circumstances of the two churches in this country. It is no longer complicated with the political institutions which made both Episcopacy and Presbytery monarchical and aristocratic in their associations. It is no longer complicated with the needs of a State religion, which made the church of England Episcopalian, and the church of Scotland Presbyterian, before the union of the two kingdoms. It is no longer complicated with the racial influences which through successive generations made Presbytery distinctively Scottish and Episcopacy as distinctively Anglican. It is not even complicated with the difficulties which beset it during the colonial period of our own history, when Presbyterians, in common with Puritans, opposed the intrusion, not of the episcopate itself, but of its civil establishment over the colonies with all the evils of British taxation and patronage. "We hope in God," wrote the Legislature of Massachusetts to their London agent, "such an establishment will never take place in America, and we desire you would strenuously oppose it." "We would by no means have it understood," gravely declared the Synods of New York and Philadelphia, "that we would endeavor to prevent an American bishop, or archbishop, or patriarch, or whatever else they might see fit to send, provided other denominations could be safe from their severity and encroachments."[1] The Episcopal churches themselves joined in opposing the project. The Virginia clergy, with only eight exceptions out of a hundred, resisted it; and the House of Burgesses unanimously thanked the protesters "for the wise and well-timed opposition they had made to the pernicious project of a few clergymen for introducing an American bishop."[2] After the Revolution, when all danger of any State religion was gone, the episcopate, pure and simple, was procured, and the Protestant Episcopal Church took its place among sister churches without opposition or even criticism. "As far as the Presbyterian Church is concerned," says Dr. Hodge, "we should be sorry that it should lie under the imputation of having resisted the reasonable wishes of another denomination to the enjoyment of their own ecclesiastical system." The whole question of Presbyterian orders has thus become divested of foreign issues: and it is a mistake to be ever injecting into it

---

[1] Dr. Hodge's Constitutional History of the Presbyterian Church, p. 372.
[2] Dr. Hawks' Ecclesiastical History of the United States, Vol. i, p. 127.

the old feuds of Cavalier and Covenanter, Churchman and Dissenter, Whig and Tory, after a century of friendly intercourse.

It should also be borne in mind that both churches hold substantially the same theory of holy orders, the one attaching it to presbytery and the other to episcopacy. Practically at least, Presbyterians, no less than Episcopalians, maintain the Christian ministry as a divine institution, conveying divine authority and apostolical doctrine and piety, all in fact that is transmissible from the apostles, by means of regular ordinations in a succession presbyterial rather than merely prelatical. "So far as apostolical succession can be verified," says Dr. Alexander, "the Presbyterian Church in the United States possesses it, as really and fully as the Church of England. In making this assertion we assume as proved already, that a superior order in the ministry to that of presbyters is not essential to the being of the church, but that from the beginning presbyters have exercised the highest powers now belonging to the ministry. If so, it is through them that the apostolic succession must be traced, and we accordingly maintain that our orders may be just as surely traced in this way up to apostolic times as those of any other church through bishops. The denial of this fact has, for the most part, been connected with the false assumption that the ministry of our church has been derived from that of Geneva, and depends for its validity upon the authority of Calvin; whereas we trace our orders, through the original Presbytery of Philadelphia, to the mother-church of Scotland, which is well-known to have been reformed with the concurrence and assistance of men regularly ordained in the Church of Rome. The principal admixture of this Scottish element, in our earliest presbyteries, was with New England Puritans, among whom only two examples of lay-ordination are believed to have occurred, and whose ecclesiastical system was originally founded by regularly ordained priests of the Anglican establishment."[1] The point to be emphasized in this reasoning is, that it clearly puts the question before us as not so much a difference in doctrine as in polity, and almost reduces it to a matter of ecclesiastical policy.

Even as to this mere ecclesiastical question, it is well to remember that both sides have long since made admissions and advances by which they have met midway and all but exchanged positions. On the one hand, the highest Episcopal authorities have repeatedly recognized the validity of Presbyterian orders. During the first century after the Reformation, as it is well known, foreign divines such as Bucer, Laski, and Peter Martyr, who had only presbyterial ordination, were admitted to benefices in the Church of England, and on the invitation of Cranmer assisted in framing the articles and liturgy. Knox also officiated in English parishes and himself wrote the "Black Rubric" against transubstantiation in the Communion office. It is useless to argue that the orders of such men were not recognized. They were legalized by Act of Parliament (Eliz., 1571), and the Primate, Archbishop Grindal, applied the act, not to Roman priests only, but to Presbyterian clergymen, as for example, in the typical case of Morrison, described in his licensure as "called to the ministry by the imposition of hands according to the laudable form and rite of the Reformed Church of Scotland. And since the congregation of the county of Lothian is conformable to the orthodox faith and sincere religion now received in the realm of England, we, therefore, approving and ratifying the form of your ordination and preferment, grant you a license and faculty in such orders by you taken. You may and have power to celebrate the divine offices, to minister the sacraments, etc."[2] Travers pleaded the same statute successfully in maintenance of Dutch

---

[1] "Primitive Church Offices," p. 177. By Prof. J. Addison Alexander, Princeton Theological Seminary.

[2] "History of Presbyterians in England," p. 132. Rev. J. H. Drysdale, London.

as well as Scotch Presbyterian ordination. The greatest names in the English Church might be cited to the same effect. "There may be sometimes," said the judicious Hooker, "very good and sufficient reason to allow ordination made without a bishop."[1] It was admitted by Bishop Hall, of the divine right school, that many such ministers were in holy orders without exceptions against the lawfulness of their calling. "The peerless prelate," Andrews, declared that a man must be blind who does not see churches standing without episcopacy. "I love not herein," said the devout Bishop Cosin "to be more wise or harder than our own church is, which has never publicly condemned and pronounced the ordination of the other Reformed Churches to be void."[2] Such authorities and precedents were openly plead by the Presbyterian clergy at the Restoration, in their protest against re-ordination: "When," said they, "a canon amongst those called the Apostles', deposeth those that re-ordain and that are re-ordained; when it is a thing that both Papists and Protestants condemn; and when not only the former bishops of England that were more moderate, were against it, but even the most fervent adversaries of the Presbyterian way, such as Bishop Bancroft himself, how strange must it needs seem to the reformed churches, to the whole Christian world, and to future generations, that so many able, faithful ministers should be laid by as broken vessels, because they dare not be re-ordained."[3] It was only by the triumph of the high prelatic party in the Act of Uniformity that Presbyterian orders were for the first time made unlawful and Presbyterianism itself thenceforth extinguished in the Church of England. But though extinguished there, it re-appeared on this side of the Atlantic with undiminished vigor, after our Revolution, when the patriot-bishop White, dismissing the resort to a Swedish

---

[1] Ecclesiastical Polity, B. vii, chap. xlv.
[2] Anglo-Catholic Library, Vol. iv, p. 403.
[3] Documents relating to Act of Uniformity, p. 186.

episcopate as ludicrous, and contenting himself with a general approbation of the English episcopate, if it could be had, proceeded to give the Protestant Episcopal Church that presbyterial constitution which it now has in common with the Presbyterian Church and in distinction from the mother Church of England.

Candid churchmen of the strictest school, admit all these facts, and while favoring no abatement of existing canons, generously allow good standing to other churchmen, who view the episcopate as a development or complement of the presbyterate. "That it is not competent for one in Holy Orders to hold and affirm such views," says the Bishop of New York, "can only be alleged by one who is grossly ignorant, whether of the history of the Church of England or of our own, or deliberately determined to misrepresent both."[1] With the same comprehensive view the Bishop of Western New York, in a public letter with which he has honored the writer, almost identifies English Presbyterianism with American Episcopacy on the basis of the Lambeth proposals: "With entire consistency therefore the Presbyterian position might be thus stated in answer to our proposals, viz.: 'We affirm (1) that no bishop has a right to ordain a presbyter without the consent of presbytery and the conjoint imposition of their hands; and (2) that the concurrence of presbyters and laymen in synodical sessions and consistories is requisite to the rightful exercise of episcopal government,'—which is our doctrine confirmed by the teaching of St. Cyprian, and as we suppose the teaching of Holy Scripture itself."[2] There has thus been a catena of Episcopal authorities from the beginning favoring in some form or degree the claims of presbytery.

On the other hand, it is well also to remember that the

---

[1] Third Triennial Charge to the Convention by the Right Rev. Henry Codman Potter, D. D., LL.D.

[2] "Second Letter to the Rev. Dr. Shields," from the Right Rev. A. C. Coxe, LL. D.

highest Presbyterian authorities have often recognized the legitimacy and even desirableness of a pure Episcopacy. The reformers, with scarcely an exception, not only held such an episcopacy to be scriptural, but lamented the political circumstances which prevented them from reforming and continuing the existing historic episcopate. Calvin, in delineating the primitive Church, says that "in each city the presbyters selected one of their number to whom they gave the special title of bishop, lest, as usually happens, from equality dissension should arise.[1]" And so far from thinking it necessary in reforming the Church to destroy even the Roman episcopate, he grows indignant at the thought, if it could only be freed from papal corruptions and restored to primitive purity: "Let them show us such a hierarchy that therein bishops should so preside as not refusing subjection to Christ, but from Him as their only Head should be derived and to Him should be related; in which their brotherly fellowship with one another should be so disposed that by no other bond than that of His truth they should be allied; then verily I must allow that there is no anathema of which they would not be worthy, if any such should be, who would not reverently and with consummate obedience yield them recognition."[2] In the Reformed Kirk, from the time of Knox, for the first hundred years, there was a species of episcopacy or superintendency, and the Confession, in distinct terms, long required the induction of Church of England clergymen, if sound in doctrine, without re-ordination. The English Presbyterians, from Cartwright to Baxter, did not so much oppose episcopacy as the hierarchical corruptions with which it had become overlaid, especially the suppression of the powers of presbytery. Their views were fairly set forth in Archbishop Ussher's famous Reduction of Episcopacy unto the form of Synodical government in the Ancient Church.[3]

---

[1] Institutes, Book IV, Chap. 4.
[2] De Necessitate Reformandæ Ecclesiæ, Edinburgh Trans., Vol. 1, p. 217.
[3] Ussher's Model of Church Government, Documents, p. 22.

At the Restoration in 1661 the English Presbyterian clergy, many of whom had sat in the Westminster Assembly, themselves proposed this pure episcopacy, in the following terms: "Although upon just reason we do dissent from that ecclesiastical hierarchy or prelacy, disclaimed in the Covenant, as it was stated and exercised in these kingdoms, yet we do not nor ever did renounce the true ancient primitive episcopacy or presidency as it was balanced and managed by a due commixtion of presbyters therewith, as a fit means to avoid corruptions, partiality, tyranny and other evils which may be incident to the administration of one single person.[1]" It is interesting to notice, among the reasons which they give for such episcopacy are those which now animate the American Bishops in their proposals; "First. We have reason to believe that no other terms will be so generally agreed on, and it is no way injurious to episcopal power. Second. It being agreeable to Scripture and the primitive government, is likeliest to be the way of a more universal concord, if ever the Churches on earth arrive at such a blessing."[2] This is more than a coincidence. There is even something prophetic, as well as pathetic, in the voice which thus comes to us across the centuries at this juncture:—

"And here we leave it to the notice and observation of posterity, how little the English bishops had to say against the form of primitive episcopacy contained in Archbishop Ussher's Reduction, in the day when they rather choose the increase of our divisions, the silencing of many hundred faithful ministers, the scattering of the flocks, the afflicting of so many thousand godly Christians, than the accepting of this primitive episcopacy; which was the expedient which those called Presbyterians offered, never once speaking for the cause of presbytery."[3]

Why recall this sad argument? Surely not to fight the

---

[1] Documents relating to Act of Uniformity, p. 15.

[2] Documents, p. 50.   [3] Documents, p. 82.

battle over again. Not to renew the plea of presbytery or the claim of prelacy; but simply to show how much common ground Episcopalians and Presbyterians have gained since they parted company two hundred years ago, and how little ground of difference would remain were the Lambeth basis adopted. In fact, even that remaining ground disappears between them. By their own mutual concessions and approaches they are already virtually committed to the Quadrilateral. The mere logical battle for church unity is won. It may be long before it is followed by the logic of events. Doubtless, the wretched wrangle will go on among us for some time to come, like the guerrilla warfare of men who know not that a treaty of peace has been signed; but it cannot go on forever. The issue is only a question of time.

In a word, were the Presbyterian and Episcopal Churches now formally, as they are historically and doctrinally, agreed upon the Lambeth basis, the vexed question of orders would at once sink between them into a mere provisional matter, to be treated as an anomaly or exception incident to the practical process of unification. In view of such an event several modes of settling the question present themselves. We need not stop to consider it as it figures in the popular caricature of twelve thousand Presbyterian ministers going straightway to the Bishops for re-ordination. Instead of looking for so catastrophic a millennium, let us approach the problem more quietly, with caution and circumspection. It may be found that within the Quadrilateral, as affording mutually accepted bounds of church unity, ecclesiastical correspondence between the two communions might begin and proceed through three stages: Mutual recognition; hypothetical ordination; and concurrent ordination and jurisdiction.

MUTUAL RECOGNITION.

The Episcopal recognition or authorization of Presbyterian ministers, as it may become desirable and practicable within the prescribed church limits, would be no novel measure. To say nothing of ancient precedents and analogies, it was long practiced, as we have seen, in the early churches of England and Scotland. In 1661 it was definitely proposed by Archbishop Leighton of Glascow, for the comprehension of Presbyterians with Episcopalians in the Scottish church when prelacy was enforced by Charles II; but the rancor of the times showed it no favor, and the saintly prelate retired from his see, it is said, to die broken-hearted at the failure of his scheme. Quite recently the proposition has been renewed for the comprehension of Episcopalians with Presbyterians in the existing church establishment, by the late Bishop Wordsworth of St. Andrews, who advocated it at the last Lambeth Conference. His suggestion was to recognize the full standing of Presbyterian ministers on condition that bishops and presbyters be united in all future ordinations. Assuming Episcopal ordination to be a rule within the Anglican communion alone, which casts no reflection upon other ministries, the Bishop says: "A rule if applied without exception, may defeat its own end. Accordingly it has been felt by the greatest divines whom God has ever raised up within His church, such as St. Augustine and Hooker, that the rule of ordination, if it were enforced without suspension or relaxation in all circumstances, so far from tending to maintain unity, must serve to render unity impossible." The proposition is understood to have been carefully considered by the Committee of the Conference and even attracted the commendation of the Primate himself. It has also been favorably noticed by several bishops and learned clergymen on this side of the water.

The question, as it may emerge between the two corresponding churches in our own country, is happily free from the embarrassment of a state religion and from some social influences which are of a divisive tendency. Its settlement is favored by their new political condition and their more homogeneous structure and culture. But unfortunately, at the present time, it is held in suspense by the arrest put upon the deliberations of the Episcopal and Presbyterian Commissions on church unity by the last General Assembly. Friendly discussion would seem to have been shut off at the point where alone it might begin. To stipulate, in any ecclesiastical sense, for "the doctrine of mutual recognition and reciprocity" as a condition precedent to even entertaining the Episcopal proposals is simply meeting large concessions with a demand for larger, and begging the very question in dispute. It remains to be proved whether on the basis of the historic episcopate, as properly understood, the fullest mutual recognition and reciprocity might not be found as feasible as it is desirable. The commissioners were feeling their way toward such results, however distant as yet, and had made good progress when their brotherly conferences were interrupted. The leaders on both sides take this view of their commission. Dr. Joseph T. Smith tells us that the two "Committees were required in express terms to proceed on 'the basis of a common faith and order.' They were to inquire, first of all, as to their agreements, and ascertain how far and in what particulars they were at one. Their differences were to be held in abeyance until the preliminary question was settled, whether there was any such 'common faith and order' as would furnish a basis for closer relations."[1] Bishop Coxe also says emphatically: "I should never have consented to be one of the commission for brotherly conference with a like committee of the General Assembly, had I not supposed that mutual acquaintance and the eradication of long estrangements and feuds which have been the bane of our intercourse for centuries would naturally promote important results. . . . To reach the *terminus ad quem* by making it the starting point, instead of the goal, appears to me a *hysteron proteron*, illogical and involving impossibilities."[2] What makes the momentary breach the more unfortunate is

---

[1] The *New York Evangelist*, May 10, 1894.
[2] Letter to Rev. Dr. Shields, in the *Churchman*, September 29, 1894.

the fact that it was not caused by any real change of opinion in the two churches, much less in the two committees, but by outside parties forcing into the negotiation a wild issue with which it had nothing whatever to do, that of an indiscriminate exchange of pulpits with all denominations, good, bad, and indifferent. It is not probable that two great ecclesiastical bodies, so intelligent and self-respecting, will allow a misunderstanding brought about by such influences, to continue after the mists which have obscured the situation have passed away.

Without speculating as to the future course of opinion in this matter, I can only state in a word or two the general argument for mutual recognition as attainable on the Lambeth basis. As Presbyterians have always recognized the validity of Episcopal orders, it is natural that they should desire it to be mutual for the sake of both parties. It would seem that among non-episcopal denominations a discrimination might be made in favor of a church which historically and doctrinally is already in so full accord with the Episcopal Church, especially in regard to the ministry and sacraments and other ecclesiastical questions. It should be remembered that Presbyterian ordination was made unlawful only by the civil authority of a state-religion; that it has never been pronounced invalid by any purely ecclesiastical authority, though always deemed irregular; and that its validity in mitigating circumstances has often been recognized by the most illustrious prelates and divines of every school of churchmanship. Add to this, that the acceptance of the Lambeth articles even provisionally, would remove traditional prejudices and former causes of difference. Finally, it would be an act of magnanimous reparation for a great public wrong, which some historians have likened to a second St. Bartholemew, and all have lamented as a calamity, to restore relations of ecclesiastical comity in this land and age of greater light and freedom and at this distance from the scene of the original conflict.

A generous admirer of the Episcopal Church, who was

not less a thoroughgoing Presbyterian, the late Dr. Vandyke, has said : " If the Episcopal Church could come back to the spirit and practice of her earlier and in this respect her better days, and acknowledge non-episcopal ordination as valid, though in her judgment irregular, this would put us upon an equal footing. Zealous Episcopalians will probably resent the bare suggestion of such a concession on their part. Some, like Dr. Blunt, will look upon it as a renewed attempt of foreign Protestantism to bring them down to the same abject level. But vehement protests, though they express the sincere conviction and desire of individuals, are not always the prophecies of what great bodies of people will do. Extreme opinions are never the most stable. Stranger changes than the one suggested have swept over even the Episcopal Church."[1] While it has proved true that this suggestion has been resented by some Episcopalians, yet many others are now showing themselves ready not, indeed, to formally recognize the validity of Presbyterian ordination, but to secure all the substantial advantages of such a recognition so far as it can be done consistently with rubrics, canons, precedents and usages. And in seeking this result there need be no sweeping changes of a revolutionary nature, but only the successive steps of an orderly progress. This at least is the conservative view of the Bishop of Long Island, who is known to have been the author of the Chicago Declaration and may decisively speak of the motives and hopes which animated it. After noticing favorably the Episcopal and Presbyterian Conference at Baltimore, he says,[2] " On the other hand, I cannot but think it was wise in the House of Clerical and Lay Deputies not to consent, under existing circumstances, to the incorporation into our organic law of the principles which we have set forth as the basis of

---

[1] " The Church, Her Ministry and Sacraments," p. 159. By Rev. Henry J. Vandyke, D. D.

[2] Annual Address to the Clergy. By the Right Rev. A. N. Littlejohn, LL.D.

any possible unification of the sundered Communions of Christendom. Had such incorporation been authorized, the whole body of our canons would have required immediate adjustment to it. For one, I believe this would be too radical a step to take in view of the very slight favor that has, as yet, been shown by other bodies toward the very liberal overtures we have already made. What we have done has answered the very important purpose of exciting widespread and earnest discussion of the whole subject. This is all that can be safely or wisely done at this time. In one way or another the discussion will go on, now that it has been begun, until it shall produce some practical fruit."

The first practical step in an orderly progress has already been taken by the appointment of an Ecclesiastical Commission, representing the learning, wisdom, and piety of the two churches. Should its conferences be continued, it could lay the foundations on both sides of a connecting arch destined to find its keystone in the episcopate. It might even span the gulf with an airy outline or temporary framework of provisional agreements and arrangements in the building process of unity. One of these might be a sanctioned interchange of sermons between Episcopal and Presbyterian preachers of the two communions, understood to be agreed in accepting the four Lambeth conditions of good church standing. This would put the vexed matter of pulpit exchange, otherwise quite insignificant, on a basis of ecclesiastical principles, and would protect it from the evils of an indiscriminate and unauthorized practice.[1] By such a step neither party would or could have conceded anything whatever. The ministry of the

---

[1] The guarded proposal of the Presbyterian Committee was in the following terms:—"We recognize the right and duty of each Church to protect its pulpits from the intrusion of all unauthorized or self-appointed preachers of the Word, and to take such measures as shall best secure the teaching of sound doctrine. Also this custom, if established between us, should not be in unregulated liberty, but under such rules and limitations as the episcopal authority of both bodies may agree upon."—Dr. Joseph T. Smith, in *The Evangelist*, May 10, 1894.

Word is separable from that of the sacraments, as may be seen in the Presbyterian licentiate and the Episcopalian deacon, neither of whom has the latter function. Were it proposed to take a step farther in the mutual recognition, the path would become thorny with perplexities. At the start would appear the obvious inconvenience that Presbyterian ministers are no more fitted to officiate in liturgical offices without the training of the diaconate than an Episcopal clergyman to conduct extempore services without long familiarity with spontaneous worship. Against this difficulty it might justly be urged, that the third Lambeth article does not require the use of the Prayer-book, at least not as a condition of church comity, and Episcopal and Presbyterian ministers might unite in other Reformed liturgies or directories which ensure the unfailing use of the validating words and elements appointed by our Lord. Even then, however, it would still be objected, that the fourth Lambeth article, as connected with the third article, would seem to make the efficacy or validity of such ministrations depend upon Episcopal as distinguished from Presbyterial ordination, and the conflicting claims of the two kinds of ordination would need to be somehow reconciled. It has been proposed to meet this last crucial point by the device known as hypothetical ordination.

HYPOTHETICAL ORDINATION.

This device seems to have been first proposed at the Revolution under William of Nassau, when the latitudinarian Bishops Tillotson, Stillingfleet and Tennison united with Doctors Baxter, Calamy and Bates in an effort for the comprehension of the ejected Presbyterian clergy in the re-established Church of England. The office for ordaining " Priests, *i. e.*, Presbyters"[1] was to be amended by the addition of the words,—"*If they shall not have been already ordained.* By

---

[1] These titles were to be made equivalent, as in Laud's Scottish Prayer-book " Presbyter" was everywhere substituted for " Priest."

which the church, as she retains her opinion and practice, which make a Bishop necessary to the giving of orders when he can be had; so she does likewise leave all such persons as have been ordained by Presbyters only, the freedom of their own thoughts concerning their former ordinations."[1] It was expressly provided that this measure must not become a precedent and that its operation would cease after a given date. The Ordinal was still further to be amended by converting the imperative form, "Receive ye the Holy Ghost," into the precatory form of an invocation of the Holy Spirit, according to primitive as distinguished from papal usage. The Letters of Orders granted to such persons would also disclaim any intention of condemning their former ordinations or of determining either their validity or their invalidity. It was the opinion of Calamy that upon these terms at least two-thirds of the Presbyterian ministers would have returned into the establishment. There had been some reaction in their favor against the rigors of the Act of Uniformity. The Calvinistic King William naturally viewed the inclusion of such Protestants to be as consequent upon his coming to the throne as the exclusion of the Romanists. But he had permitted the downfall of Episcopacy in Scotland, where the Presbyterians were having their turn at ejecting the prelatists. Moreover, the scheme was weighed down with other more radical amendments. The result was that the attempted compromise was a failure, and the Act of Uniformity gave place to the Act of Toleration as the only substantial advantage then attainable.

Different as the circumstances of the parties are in this country and in this age, yet the idea of a conditional ordination, analogous to conditional baptism, has been broached in recent discussions by some earnest inquirers into the grounds and conditions of church unity.[2] It has even been gener-

---

[1] Procter's History of Prayer-book, p. 158.
[2] Address of the Bishop of Western Texas, Right Rev. James S. Johnston, D.D.

Hypothetical Ordination. 207

ously proposed to insert it in a conspicuous rubric as a standing welcome to other ministries, to show that the Quadrilateral has been issued in good faith and in the earnest hope of its adoption. Perhaps, however, as to the Presbyterian Church at least, it is too soon to discuss the wisdom of an expedient which presupposes a degree of intelligent agreement that has not yet been reached. If the measure would meet the scruples of some Episcopalians who take a strict view of episcopal ordination, yet it might not so readily meet the scruples of some Presbyterians who take a like view of presbyterial ordination and would not care to have a slur or shadow openly cast upon their former ministry. Presbyterians who doubt of their former ministry, or take a low view of it, would not scruple at unconditional re-ordination, but even prefer it as affording proof of their church loyalty, their good fellowship with high churchmen, and their desire to receive the full benefit of holy orders. Moreover, anything that is good in the proposed rubric for hypothetical ordination seems to have been already provided in the American Ordinal by the alternative form "Take thou authority," as contrasted with the earlier form, "Receive ye the Holy Ghost." If the new form merely expresses the outward call of the church, while the earlier expresses also the inward call of the Spirit, a Presbyterian minister so re-ordained might think he was simply gaining new ecclesiastical authority and larger province for a ministry to which he had already been called of God in his former ordination. Unless he held high sacramentarian views of the rite itself, the mere repetition of the ceremony might not violate his convictions nor be inconsistent with some usages and precedents.

All this, however, is somewhat aside from the real question before us. It applies merely to the case of a Presbyterian clergyman seeking holy orders in the Episcopal Church, and would have importance only for those who expect that communion somehow to absorb other communions, in spite of the disclaimer of the bishops. It does not apply to the relations of the two communions. As yet there is no such open and candid understanding between them as would justify on both sides the episcopal ordination or even authorization of Presbyterian ministers. The difficulty remains, to find some more mutual recognition not only in ordination, but also in jurisdiction. To meet that difficulty a method has been proposed on page 99 which may now be more fully considered.

CONCURRENT ORDINATION.

The principles involved in concurrent ordination are not new in the history of the two communions. The Church of England from the beginning has associated presbyters with bishops in giving presbyterial orders, and the American Church has admitted them to a participation to some extent in the Episcopal jurisdiction. In like manner the Presbyterian Church, during its early days in Scotland and through the Westminster divines in the Savoy Conference, may be said to have committed itself to a pure episcopacy, as both scriptural and apostolical, and might now find in it a wise stable administration of the episcopal functions of presbytery. These mutual principles historically underlie and logically connect the two churches. The only novelty proposed is that they should now be formally professed and openly acted upon; in other words, that both authorities should visibly concur in future ordinations, when a coincident jurisdiction is found feasible without destroying or impairing the normal relations of Episcopacy and Presbytery, as already existing or illustrated in both communions. How this might be attempted has been explained with some detail in the previous essay.

If this suggestion have no other merit, it may at least serve to confront the parties with the real difficulties of the situation. These are serious enough, but not so amusing as represented by some critics who have imagined a Presbyterian minister armed with a sort of "double ordination" and turned loose as a knight-errant of church unity. That might not be possible under existing relations, since he would have to renounce his former allegiance, if he could not retain it, or else sink into mere individual insignificance. But it should be borne in mind that here, as throughout the whole argument, we are still proceeding on the assumption that the Lambeth conditions of church standing and comity have been accepted and are to be adopted and acted upon as far and as fast as possible. In that view the suggested concurrence of authorities is to be regarded as a mere transitional expedient in the unifying process. It would provide for a gradual coincidence of jurisdiction wherever possible, as on mission fields and in the army and navy,[1]—leaving meanwhile existing Presbyterian clergymen, in cases requiring it, to be episcopally licensed, as in the early Church of England, or to receive a purely ecclesiastical ordination like that proposed in 1689 and apparently adopted in the American Ordinal.[2] Against such a scheme it is easy enough to magnify and multiply difficulties, constitutional and canonical, on both sides,—in a word to show how not to do the thing proposed. The present writer is trying to show how to do it; and if any one will show a more excellent way he will be the first to welcome it.

What are the alternative methods? One of them would be to use the Quadrilateral as a solvent for breaking up and absorbing the Presbyterian Church, but that would be contrary

---

[1] A highly esteemed Army Chaplain writes me, that whenever he invites the visiting Bishop to the Chapel at his post, he is only recognized by being publicly thanked for his courtesy. "Concurrent ordination" he says, "would relieve the situation."

[2] If this dormant provision was inserted by Bishop White with a purpose, it may yet be found available; and new meaning might appear in Archbishop Bramhall's form of licensure to a Scotch Presbyter,—"not destroying his former orders, nor determining their validity or invalidity, but only supplying what the canons of the English Church require and providing that occasion of schism be removed, and the faithful assured that they may not doubt of his ordination, or be averse to his presbyterial acts as invalid."—Anglo-Catholic Library, Vol. I, p. xxxvii.

to its own professions. Another would be to let it stand as a bond of theoretical and sentimental fellowship between the two communions; but such a bond could not last long unless some more organic filaments were woven into it. Still another method would be to wait until the Presbyterian Church by its own development shall have secured the historic episcopate in some other quarter. That course will doubtless be taken very naturally by the Lutheran Church, and its acquisition of the Swedish episcopate, besides perfecting its own church order, will be an immense logical gain to the Lambeth standard by freeing it from Anglican and Protestant Episcopal implications in the popular mind and thus demonstrating that the proposed terms of church unity are catholic and undenominational, as well as practicable. Yet even then two such rival episcopates could only secure church likeness, or church union, not church unity. The problem of jurisdiction would still remain unsolved and only more complicated. Surely, when Presbyterians begin to appreciate the historic episcopate for its unifying qualities, they would want nothing foreign or sectarian in it, but rather gladly welcome what Dr. Huntington fittingly terms "the episcopate of the race which gave us our language and at least a good fraction of our law."

It may still be objected that the Chicago Declaration presents the historic episcopate as one of the "inherent parts of a sacred deposit of Christian faith and order committed by Christ and his Apostles to the Church," which would be compromised or surrendered in any concordat with the Presbyterian ministry.[1] Some Episcopalians have detached this qualifying preamble from the terms themselves, and do not find it in the Prayer-book. Nor does it necessarily inhere in the Fourth Article as it has been held historically and doctrinally throughout the universal church. In fact, it has not

---

[1] "The Historical Position of the Episcopal Church." By Rev. Prof. Francis G. Hall, Western Theological Seminary, Chicago.

even been adopted by the great Pan-Anglican Council of Bishops, whose amended version of the Quadrilateral must now be accepted by all parties. They attach no qualification to it, but simply offer it as the basis of a "United Church to include the chief Christian Communions," and recommend brotherly conference with their representatives, "in order to consider what steps can be taken either toward corporate re-union or toward such relations as may prepare the way for fuller organic unity hereafter;"[1]—which seems to be the very policy here advocated. Even if it be held that the Chicago preamble was implied or involved in the action of the Anglican Bishops, it would still remain true that their claim of trusteeship is unhappily repudiated by an immense majority of historic episcopates throughout the Christian world, to say nothing of churchmen like Dr. Harwood, who hold that episcopacy is not a divine, but an ecclesiastical institution.[2] This would be an Episcopalian answer to the objection before us.

There is, however, a more positive and satisfactory answer from the Presbyterian side. We may unhesitatingly and gladly yield the chief place to our American Bishops as custodians of the primitive faith and order, and still maintain that the proposed re-union would involve no compromise or surrender of their trust. In the first place, the Presbyterian Church also claims to be part of that "Catholic Visible Church unto which Christ hath given the ministry, oracles and ordinances of God,"[3] and has preserved its sacred trust by means of a presbyterial succession from the Apostles, which is as certain and unquestionable as any merely prelatic succession in Christendom, for the simple reason that it underlies and shares all such succession until the Reform-

---

[1] Lambeth Conferences, 1888, "Resolutions Formally Adopted," p. 280.

[2] "The Historic Episcopate and Apostolic Succession." By Rev. Edwin Harwood, D. D., New Haven.

[3] Confession of Faith, Chap. xxv.

ation, and since then has been maintained with scrupulous regularity in both the Scottish and American presbyteries. But let that pass for what it is worth in this argument.[1] In the second place, the trusteeship of our honored Bishops, even in the highest possible estimate of it, could not be imperiled but would only be confirmed and secured by the loyal return of a free presbytery into normal relations with a pure episcopacy on their own proffered terms of unity. The result would simply be a gradual enlargement of episcopal jurisdiction without any sacrifice of presbyterial integrity, and a practical mergence of interests rendering any assertion of rival claims and rights both useless and distasteful. The time would have come to let bygones be bygones and generously end the old family quarrel in a true apostolic love-feast. Episcopalians and Presbyterians, forgetting their "endless genealogies and contentions," would have met together on the Lambeth basis, like good Christians and good churchmen, determined to get the full benefit of both episcopal and presbyterial ordination, as no longer to be practiced separately, but henceforth to be re-combined in a United Church.

The circumstances of the two communions in this new world are highly favorable for their organic reunion. After dominating one another by turns in the old world, they are now upon an equal footing before the law and in the view of surrounding denominations. They have become assimilated in their constitution. They are theoretically one in ecclesiastical doctrine. Already they have a proposed basis of ecclesiastical intercommunion. They are drawn together by early

---

[1] It will be remembered that when the Archbishop of Canterbury in 1850 declared that there were not two bishops on the bench or one clergyman in fifty who would deny the validity of the Presbyterian orders, solely on account of wanting the imposition of episcopal hands, the learned Dr. Goode in his "Vindication," produced a long chain of authorities, including the most eminent prelates and divines, all maintaining that bishops and presbyters were of the same divine order, and must therefore be included in the same apostolic succession, however much they may differ in ecclesiastical office and dignity.

affinities and by the Christian spirit of the age. Their union would be a mutual benefit, would strengthen historic Christianity amid our unhistoric civilization, would combine the two most ecclesiastical denominations against sectarianism, and would lead the American churches toward catholic unity. They seem charged with the fate of Protestant Christendom.

Let us now suppose, for the sake of illustration, a concurrence of Presbyterian and Episcopalian authorities to have been effected in the future ordination of candidates for mission fields, either with or without a joint imposition of hands, any priests present with the bishop, having had formerly Presbyterian ordination or being themselves Presbyterian ministers who have had formerly Episcopal ordination. Under some such agreement the utmost claims of both churches would be practically recognized and satisfied and all requirements merged in one common sanction. A missionary thus ordained would go forth with double authority, into a wider field, for a fuller service, and everywhere represent a united Church at least to heathenism abroad if not to infidelity at home. Even re-ordination under such a system could not be offensive to those who deny any sacramental grace in the mere rite itself, but might rather be approved by a sound Christian feeling for the sake of the great ends in view. Meanwhile the two communions, though still distinct, would be touching at other vital points. On the one side, as such concurrent ordinations became frequent, bishops and rectors, without losing consistency or regularity, could yield to Presbyterian ministrations a practical recognition, far more genuine and complete than any for which some are now pleading. On the other side, as such relations grew closer, by means of an elective episcopate presbyteries might be made coincident with deaneries, synods with dioceses, and assemblies with conventions in one national system. And so at length both communions might find it a good and comely thing to join forces and fall into line with the great Catholic Church of the past and of the future.

THE HOPE OF REUNION.

The Bible is full of ideals no more feasible than this. In estimating them, we dare not belittle those divine powers and promises which are stronger than any human reasoning and before which all human passions and prejudices melt away like morning mists. That fraternal impulse which is now abroad in the churches, vague though it seems, if kindled by the Holy Spirit, may yet sweep all our polemics aside. Perhaps ministers as a body do not want church unity, but the Christian masses do want it, and would have it on any just terms that can be devised. Should the terms proposed be found feasible they might not share the sensitiveness of the clerical mind on points of coördination or re-ordination as raised against unity. Nor need we fear that sacred trusts, endowed interests and revered traditions are to be roughly overridden in the unifying process. Providence in bringing about great social changes often gently smooths the way, until foes are glad to meet as friends and welcome as a blessing what they had dreaded as a calamity. The Old and New School Presbyterians of the past generation once seemed farther apart than the Presbyterian and Episcopalian Churchmen of to-day.

The Church of Christ, like the kingdom of nature, is yet to be strong in its unity as well as rich in its variety. Its full glory can never come until different denominations shall appear in the same ecclesiastical system, showing forth their essential harmony amid trivial diversity. That denominationalism, or ecclesiasticism, which fancies that it has no need of any larger and fuller organization, is but a vain hallucination of the members dreaming among themselves that they can do without one another in the Body of Christ. Not until their sleeping catholicity awakes; not until their mere sentimental oneness becomes organic; not until their invisible unity makes itself everywhere visible, will the living Church stand forth, "fair as the moon, clear as the sun, and terrible as an army with banners."

VIII.
THE HISTORIC LITURGY AND THE HISTORIC CHURCHES.

VIII.

THE HISTORIC LITURGY AND THE HISTORIC CHURCHES.

In a previous part of this volume attention has been drawn to the unifying influence of the English liturgy among the Christian denominations, as seen in their growing observance of the Christian year, their increasing taste for liturgical worship, and their occasional use of such forms as the Lord's Prayer, the Creeds, the Commandments, the Psalter, and the ancient Canticles. It is proposed now to show this more fully and clearly by analyzing the Prayer-book into its constituent elements and exhibiting them as historically connected with our oldest Churches and as still adapted to their various denominational modes of worship.

To effect this analysis we need only take the standard edition of the Church of England, and rearrange its offices in more normal relations on liturgical principles, that is to say, with a careful reference to their original structure, design, and use; making only such editorial changes in the rubrics as will render the reconstructed services coherent and intelligible. The result is the reappearance of two distinct sets of devotional offices, the one Catholic and the other Protestant.

Applying the term *Catholic* to those offices and parts of offices which date before the Reformation, and the term *Protestant* to those which came after that epoch, the editor has endeavored to trace them both to the original formularies from which they were severally compiled and to disentangle them from their present combination in the Prayer-book, restoring the Catholic forms to their primitive integrity and purity, and retaining the Protestant forms in their unmixed state as they first appeared in their original simplicity. Difficult as this task may seem at first sight, it becomes easy enough to a student of the Prayer-book, who approaches it with no other aim than the one here proposed. Those who have been long accustomed to that compilation in its present state may look upon it as fixed and final, or as susceptible merely of greater flexibility and enrichment, and would scarcely think of anything so seemingly radical as the reconstruction of a compilation which has lasted three hundred years. This might occur only to one who can go back of vested rights and prescriptive usages and study the sources of the book afresh, without constraint or prejudice, yet with that reverential feeling which these venerable forms are fitted to inspire.

It is only necessary to take such a position in order to see how incongruous are the two classes of forms which have become mixed together in the Prayer-book. Their diversity will at once appear in their separate origin and use, and it will require no great amount of critical skill to detect it in their very form and structure; the Catholic portions having been designed for a monastic and choral ritual as sung by priest and choir in the Latin tongue, whilst the Protestant portions were composed in English, and plainly adapted to a service that is didactic and popular, to be said by minister and people. This will appear as we proceed in a careful analysis of the several offices.

COMPOSITION OF THE DAILY OFFICES.

"The Order for Daily Morning and Evening Prayer," when traced to its sources, will be found to have been simply a modified translation of the Catholic ritual for matins and vespers with a Protestant preface and supplement. The preface includes the Sentences, the Exhortation, the General Confession and the Absolution or Remission of Sins; and the supplement comprises the Prayers for Rulers, for the Clergy, and for All Conditions of Men, with the General Thanksgiving. Take away the Protestant additions and there will remain the Lord's Prayer, the Versicles, Daily Psalter, Canticles,

Creed, and two Daily Collects; forms well adapted to the musical rendering which they received in the old ritual, and together making a devotional office complete in itself without the preface or supplement. It is so presented in this essay, precisely as it appeared in King Edward's first Prayer-book of 1549, and with the same descriptive title, *The Order of Matins and Evensong Throughout the Year.*

Returning now to the Protestant portions of the office, we meet with a set of forms which are of entirely different origin and structure. The prefatory part which was not prefixed to the English Matins and Evensong until the revision in 1552, was then taken, both as to form and purport, from Calvinistic liturgies where it served as a penitential introduction to divine service on the Lord's Day; the Sentences inciting to repentance, the Exhortation explaining the duties of public worship, and the General Confession and Absolution taking the place of the discarded confessional. The supplement also was a gradual accretion, not fully incorporated in the daily office until the last revision in 1661, and at first consisted of special prayers for occasional use, wholly unlike the ancient versicular petitions for king, ministers and people; the General Thanksgiving having been added to meet a felt want in Protestant worship. Even the Old and New Testament Lessons, now found in the body of the office, were originally ordered to be read to the people in English, the one after Matins and the other after Vespers, several years before those Latin services were rendered in the mother tongue. Bringing together these various Protestant forms and re-arranging them in the order in which they were first used and are still used in other Reformed Churches, we have that didactic and homiletic office which appears in this essay under the original title, *The Order for Divine Service on the Lord's Day.*

The Litany, being an English revision of the Catholic original, to be sung as well as said, is fitly attached to the old ritual for use on certain holy days; but its following miscellany of Special Prayers and Thanksgivings which have accumulated since the reign of Elizabeth, owing to their Protestant date and form, are more appropriately classed with the Reformed Sunday service above described. It will be found that the Daily Office, with the exception of the Canticles, Creed and Collects, has been derived from the Scriptures, in Scripture language, and is simply a devotional expression of the great essential truths common to Catholic and Protestant Christianity; whilst the Sunday service is substantially that now practiced by all the Protestant churches in the land, and sets forth in a liturgical form their essential unity in worship amid diversity in doctrine and polity.

Composition of the Communion Office.

"The Order for the Administration of the Lord's Supper, or Holy Communion," when analyzed in like manner, is found to contain the Catholic ritual of the Mass with Protestant ante-communion and post-communion forms incorporated in it, very much as similar additions were made to the Daily office. The Catholic portion embraces The Lord's Prayer, Lesser Litany, The Collect for Purity, The Collect, Epistle and Gospel for the Day, The Nicene Creed, The Offertory, Versicles, Prefaces, Ter Sanctus, Prayer of Consecration, The Lord's Prayer, Thanksgiving, Gloria in Excelsis, Benediction. Re-arranging these beautiful forms strictly in their original order, and restoring one or two others, The Introit and Agnus Dei, as they appear translated in King Edward's first Prayer-book, we have a communion office which is complete in itself without the Protestant additions, and wonderfully adapted to the most artistic as well as to the plainest modes of celebration. As presented in a separate form in this essay, it is entitled *The Order for the Celebration of the Holy Communion.*

The remaining Protestant portion of the office, except The Ten Commandments, originally formed a separate English communion service for the laity, following the Latin Mass as performed by the clergy, and consisting of forms in which the general communicant might participate as distinguished from the celebrant. It was issued at least a year before the Prayer-book, with the title "The Order of the Communion," and when incorporated in that book, still appeared under the double title, "The Supper of the Lord and Holy Communion." It embraces ante-communion services remarkably fitted to induce in expecting communicants the becoming graces of knowledge, charity, penitence, assurance, and humility. The Exhortation instructs them in the meaning and use of the sacrament. The Invitation encourages them to come at peace with God and their neighbors. The Confession expresses their deep and pungent conviction. The Absolution prayerfully assures them of pardon. The Comfortable Words inspire them with faith and hope; and the Prayer of Humble Access, mingles all these feelings in trustful lowliness. The brief post-communion services have a like fitness to worthy communicants; the Sentences of Scripture, reminding them of consequent privileges and duties; the Thanksgivings, declaring their renewed self-consecration and grateful faith; the Hymn or Doxology, their joyful praise; and the Benediction, their dismissal with the Divine approval. Detaching now all these Protestant forms from their present connections, and re-combining them in the exact order in which they were first used, with one or two forms added to complete the office, we have a communion service substantially the same as that known in the Reformed churches, by the title here prefixed to it, *The Order for the Administration of the Lord's Supper*.

It will be seen that the result of the whole analysis is, the re-appearance of two distinct formularies, each almost complete in itself, the one designed for a ritualistic celebration of the sacrament by the priest and choir, and the other for its actual administration to the people. The two might be used consecutively without any repetition or confusion; or the former might be used without the latter, especially on festival occasions; or the latter might be used without the former, by simply adding a consecrating prayer before administering the elements. As the Prayer of Consecration, though founded upon the Catholic ritual, is essentially Protestant in its whole structure and purport, it has been inserted in both formularies. The same is still more true of the Prayer for the Church Militant, which in its Catholic form belonged to the canon or fixed portion of the Mass (where undoubtedly it has its true place), but in its Protestant form has by long usage become practically dissevered from the Sacrament, and has, therefore, been inserted in the Lord's-day service as well as in the Communion office.

As to the Commandments, it should be observed that they are not to be found in any Catholic sacramentary, but were borrowed from Calvinistic liturgies in 1552, and apparently put in place of the Lesser Litany, a commandment before each Kyrie (*Lord have mercy*) with additional responsive petitions of Protestant tenor. They have therefore been restored to the Lord's Day service, where they follow the Old Testament Lesson as a summary of the Law; and could the Beatitudes in like manner follow the New Testament Lesson as a summary of the Gospel, as has been sometimes proposed, it would be a very appropriate amendment. The editor considers himself limited to formulas which have been at different times authorized and actually used in the Prayer-book, and only in this instance has departed from his rule.

The Kyries, thus freed from the Decalogue, have been retained in their original connection, as they appear in King Edward's first Prayer-book, and the Gloria in Excelsis has also been restored to its true position at the beginning of the office, in accordance with the Lutheran office and with all good liturgical usage. "The Collects, Epistles, and Gospels to be used on the Sundays and Holydays throughout the year," though some of them are of Protestant date, belong to the Ordinary or variable portion of the Mass, and have been ommitted as not essential to the purpose of this essay.

It will now be seen that the Communion office, as thus reduced to its component parts, exhibits the essentially Christian substance of the Catholic ritual with a Protestant form of administration, and expresses liturgically that communion of saints at the table of their common Lord and Master, which is actually experienced in all true churches of Christ, amid all their varied doctrines and usages.

COMPOSITION OF THE BAPTISMAL OFFICES.

The analysis of the Baptismal offices, though as easily made as that of the previous offices, will bring into view the Catholic rite of church initiation with sharper Protestant definitions of doctrine, and would require more or less modification in order to adapt it to the belief and practice of some churches and denominations in this country.

"The Ministration of Public Baptism of Infants" is composed of a few Catholic forms interwoven with Protestant Exhortations, Addresses, Prayers, and Thanksgivings, designed to inculcate upon both adults and children the duties and privileges of church membership. If freed from expressions which are supposed to countenance some invariable moral renovation in the action, and made to admit parents for sponsors, as now allowed in both the Anglican and some American churches, it would not be inconsistent with the teaching of leading denominations, Lutheran, Reformed, Presbyterian, Congregational, and Methodist.

"The Ministration of Baptism to such as are of Riper Years," after similar modifications, would express the views of Baptist congregations which require a public personal profession of faith as a condition precedent to this sacrament, and thus in fact fulfil one design of the office, as originally framed to meet the case of those who from disbelief, neglect, or any cause had not been baptized in infancy.

The Catechism, designed for the instruction of baptized children and other candidates for the communion, corresponds to similar forms in nearly all the Protestant churches, and is in full accord with them, though less dogmatic and scholastic in style and more meagre in its teaching.

"The Order of Confirmation or Laying on of Hands upon those that are Baptized and come to Years of Discretion," as it stands, implies the Episcopal polity of the Latin and Anglican Churches, as was shown by the disuse of the rite in the colonial Episcopal churches during the century when they were without resident bishops. But if freed from that implication, it would agree with the practice of the Greek and Lutheran churches and after slight modification would express liturgically the views of Presbyterian churches which hold to parochial in distinction from diocesan episcopacy, and indeed of all churches which have any mode of publicly admitting baptized persons to the Lord's table and full communion.

Of the Baptismal offices in general it may now be remarked that if, as is often alleged, they are charged with doctrinal views not held by most American churches, yet such views are not essentially involved in their liturgical structure and literary expression, as is proved by the existence not only of diverse interpretations, but of different versions based upon different sacramental theories.

Composition of the Occasional Offices.

The remaining offices, as usually distinguished from "The Book of Common Prayer and Administration of the Sacraments," may be included under the added clause of the title, "and other rites and ceremonies of the Church," and will be found to have only an occasional use and importance at the points of contact between Christianity and social life.

"The Form of Solemnization of Matrimony" contains the Catholic rite amended with Protestant addresses and prayers, and freed from all sacramental ceremonies except that of a discretionary administration of the Holy Communion. Some indelicate expressions in the introductory address, though just in themselves, were happily dropt from the Protestant

Episcopal version; but one or two others inculcating the Scriptural view of marriage have been wisely retained at the recent revision.

"The Order for the Visitation of the Sick," is also largely of Catholic origin, with the exception of the Protestant Form of Absolution, the Special and Commendatory Prayers, and the Benediction; and it would need but slight modification in order to be used by any American minister, either as a model or as a form, in ministering sick-room consolations.

"The Order for the Burial of the Dead," retains portions of the Catholic ritual interwoven with the Protestant Lesson and Psalms, Words of Committal, Consolatory Prayers and Benediction,—the whole making an office justly celebrated for its fitness and beauty in all the English-speaking races. Indeed, the Occasional offices as a class have already won their way to common use in churches which have no liturgical forms, and in others have superseded forms felt to be less expressive and appropriate. Add to these offices the Daily Prayers which are largely used by laymen and ministers, the Proper or Festival services which are at least warranted by the popular recognition of such days as Christmas and Easter, and there will remain only the Communion and Baptismal offices as needing to be modified in accordance with denominational views.

We have now sufficiently analyzed the English Prayer-book to test its claims to general acceptance as an American liturgy by such of our churches or congregations as are inclined to formulize their worship. If it is desired to express liturgically the ordinary devotions of a Christian assembly, the meet commemoration of the chief Christian events and doctrines, and the due administration of the Christian rites and ceremonies, there is no collection of forms to be compared with that which for three centuries has proclaimed the devout heart of the English speaking races of Christendom.

In the more general use of this historic liturgy by the historic Churches in our country, there may be a feeling of inheritance and ownership in many of its forms as well as an appreciation of their intrinsic fitness and beauty. The catholic portions having been reformed from the Roman Breviary and Missal by the reformers themselves, Luther, Calvin and Bucer as well as Cranmer, may be regarded as a common heritage of all the Churches. The Protestant portions may be reclaimed by the Lutheran Church through the formularies of Melanchthon and Bucer; by the Reformed Church, through the liturgies of Calvin, Pollanus, and John à Lasco; by the Presbyterian Church, through the emendations of the whole work by the Westminster divines in the Savoy Conference; and by the Protestant Episcopal Church, through their own version, containing not only the original contributions of the English compilers but some Presbyterian emendations which were rejected or neglected at the Savoy Conference in 1661.

In order that the differences between the Catholic and Protestant forms may appear to the eye, some examples have been appended, in which the Catholic portions are exhibited in antique type and the Protestant portions in modern type; the marginal notes giving the date, origin, authorship, and affinity of all the particulars which each office contains.

For more specific references and authorities the reader is referred to the historical and critical treatise, appended to the Author's edition of "The Book of Common Prayer, as amended by the Presbyterian Divines in the Royal Commission of 1661."

The Order for Matins and Evensong throughout the Year.

THE LORD'S PRAYER.

[*The Priest shall begin with a loud voice the Lord's Prayer, called the Pater Noster*].

Our Father, which art in heaven, Hallowed be thy Name. Thy kingdom come. Thy will be done in earth, As it is in heaven. Give us this day our daily bread. And forgive us our trespasses, As we forgive them that trespass against us. And lead us not into temptation; But deliver us from evil: For thine is the kingdom, The power, and the glory, For ever and ever. Amen.[1]

Then likewise shall the Priest say,

O Lord, open thou our lips.
Answer. And our mouth shall shew forth thy praise.[2]
Priest. O God, make speed to save us.
Answer. O Lord, make haste to help us.[3]

Here all standing up, the Priest shall say,

Glory be to the Father, and to the Son: and to the Holy Ghost;
Answer. As it was in the beginning, is now, and ever shall be: world without end. Amen.[4]
Priest. Praise ye the Lord.[5]
Answer. The Lord's Name be praised.[6]

Then shall be said or sung this Psalm following: except on Easter Day, *upon which another Anthem is appointed: and on the Nineteenth Day of every Month it is not to be read here, but in the ordinary course of the Psalms.*

VENITE, EXULTEMUS DOMINO.[7]

O come, let us sing unto the Lord: let us heartily rejoice in the strength of our salvation.

* * * * * * * * * *

---

[1] The Lord's Prayer. Latin Usage, A. D. 1200. Said secretly, until 1st Book of Edward VI; thereafter, with "a loud voice."

[2] Ps. li : 15. Latin Usage, A. D. 600.

[3] Ps. lxx : 1. Saxon Usage, A. D. 800.

[4] Council of Nicæa, A. D. 325. Greek and Latin Usage.

[5] Ps. English Usage, A. D. 1549.

[6] Bp. Laud's Prayer-Book, A. D. 1637. English Usage, A. D. 1661.

[7] Ps. xcv. Ancient Latin Usage.

Then shall follow the Psalms in order as they are appointed.[1] *And at the end of every Psalm throughout the Year, and likewise at the end of* Benedicite, Benedictus, Magnificat, *and* Nunc dimittis, *shall be repeated,*

Glory be to the Father, and to the Son: and to the Holy Ghost; *Answer.* As it was in the beginning, is now, and ever shall be: world without end. Amen.[2]

Then shall be read distinctly with an audible voice the First Lesson, taken out of the Old Testament, as is appointed in the Calendar, except there be proper Lessons assigned for that day.[3] *And after that, shall be said or sung, in* English, *the Hymn called* Te Deum Laudamus, *daily throughout the Year.*

TE DEUM LAUDAMUS.[4]

We praise thee, O God: we acknowledge thee to be the Lord.

* * * * * * * * * * *

Or this Canticle.

BENEDICITE, OMNIA OPERA.[5]

O all ye Works of the Lord, bless ye the Lord: praise him, and magnify him for ever.

* * * * * * * * * *

Then shall be read in like manner the Second Lesson, taken out of the New Testament.[6] *And after that, the Hymn following.*

BENEDICTUS.[7]

Blessed be the Lord God of Israel: for he hath visited, and redeemed his people;

* * * * * * * * * * *

Or this Psalm.

JUBILATE DEO.[8]

O be joyful in the Lord, all ye lands: serve the Lord with gladness, and come before his presence with a song.

* * * * * * * * * *

---

[1] English Usage, A. D. 1549.   [2] English Usage, A. D. 1549.

[3] English Usage, A. D. 1549.

[4] Augustine (?) Ambrose (?) Hilary, A. D. 355. Ancient Latin and English Usage.

[5] "Song of the Three Children," Dan., Chap. iii and Ps. cxlviii. Jewish, Greek, Latin, and English Usage.

[6] English Usage, A. D. 1549.

[7] St. Luke i, 68. "Song of the Prophet Zacharias." Latin and English Usage.

[8] Ps. c., English Usage, A. D. 1552.

Then shall be sung or said the Apostles' Creed by the Priest and the people, standing: [1]

¶ I believe in God the Father Almighty, Maker of heaven and earth:
And in Jesus Christ his only Son our Lord, Who was conceived by the Holy Ghost, Born of the Virgin Mary, Suffered under Pontius Pilate, Was crucified, dead, and buried, He descended into hell; the third day he rose again from the dead, He ascended into heaven, And sitteth on the right hand of God the Father Almighty; From thence he shall come to judge the quick and the dead.
¶ I believe in the Holy Ghost; The holy Catholick Church; The Communion of Saints; The Forgiveness of sins; The Resurrection of the body, And the life everlasting. Amen. [2]

And after that, these Prayers following, all devoutly kneeling.

The Lord be with you.
Answer. And with thy spirit. [3]
Priest. Let us pray.
Lord, have mercy upon us.
Christ, have mercy upon us.
Lord, have mercy upon us. [4]

Then the Priest standing up, shall say,

O Lord, shew thy mercy upon us.
Answer. And grant us thy salvation. [5]
Priest. O Lord, save the Queen. [6]
Answer. And mercifully hear us when we call upon thee. [7]
Priest. Endue thy Ministers with righteousness.
Answer. And make thy chosen people joyful. [8]
Priest. O Lord, save thy people.
Answer. And bless thine inheritance. [9]
Priest. Give peace in our time, O Lord.

---

[1] English Usage, A. D. 1549; By the Priest alone.
[2] Roman Origin. Ruffinus, A. D. 250.
[3] Apostolic Origin, Catholic Usage.
[4] Lesser Litany. Greek Origin, Latin Usage.
[5] Ps. lxxxv. 7.　　[6] " The State : " P. E. Prayer-book.
[7] Ps. xx. 9.　　[8] Ps. cxxxii. 9.　　[9] Ps. xxviii. 9.

Answer. Because there is none other that fighteth for us, but only thou, O God.[1]

Priest. O God, make clean our hearts within us.[2]

Answer. And take not thy Holy Spirit from us.

Then shall follow three Collects; the first of the Day, which shall be the same that is appointed at the Communion; the second for Peace; the third for Grace to live well.[3]

THE SECOND COLLECT, FOR PEACE.

O God, who art the author of peace and lover of concord, in knowledge of whom standeth our eternal life, whose service is perfect freedom; Defend us thy humble servants in all assaults of our enemies; that we, surely trusting in thy defence, may not fear the power of any adversaries; through the might of Jesus Christ our Lord. Amen.[4]

THE THIRD COLLECT, FOR GRACE.

O Lord, our heavenly Father, Almighty and everlasting God, who hast safely brought us to the beginning of this day; Defend us in the same with thy mighty power; and grant that this day we fall into no sin, neither run into any kind of danger; but that all our doings may be ordered by thy governance, to do always that is righteous in thy sight; through Jesus Christ our Lord.[5] Amen.

A PRAYER OF ST. CHRYSOSTOM.

Almighty God, who hast given us grace at this time with one accord to make our common supplications unto thee; and dost promise, that when two or three are gathered together in thy Name thou wilt grant their requests; Fulfil now, O Lord, the desires and petitions of thy servants, as may be most expedient for them; granting us in this world knowledge of thy truth, and in the world to come life everlasting. Amen.

---

[1] Latin Origin. English Usage, A. D. 1549.
[2] Ps. li: 10, 11.
[3] Ancient Origin. Latin and English Usage.
[4] Sacramentary of Gelasius, A. D. 494. English Usage, A. D. 1549.
[5] Sacramentary of Gregory, A. D. 590. Ancient Usage, A. D. 590.

Catholic Formularies.

[*The Order for Evensong is like that for Matins with different Canticles and in place of the Collect for Grace to live Well the following:*]

THE THIRD COLLECT, FOR AID AGAINST ALL PERILS.

Lighten our darkness, we beseech thee, O Lord; and by thy great mercy defend us from all perils and dangers of this night; for the love of thy only Son, our Saviour, Jesus Christ. Amen.[1]

The grace of our Lord Jesus Christ, and the love of God, and the fellowship of the Holy Ghost be with us all evermore. Amen.[2]

---

[1] Sacramentary of Gelasius, A. D. 494. Ancient Usage.
[2] From 2 Cor. xiii. Apostolic. Greek Usage. English, 1661.

The Litany.

A General Supplication, to be sung or said after Morning Prayer upon Sundays, Wednesdays, *and* Fridays, *and at other times when it shall be appointed.*

O God the Father, of heaven: have mercy upon us miserable sinners.[1]
O God the Father, of heaven: have mercy upon us miserable sinners.[2]
O God the Son, Redeemer of the world: have mercy upon us miserable sinners.[3]
O God the Son, Redeemer of the world: have mercy upon us miserable sinners.[4]
O God the Holy Ghost, proceeding from the Father and the Son: have mercy upon us miserable sinners.[5]
O God the Holy Ghost, proceeding from the Father and the Son: have mercy upon us miserable sinners.[6]
O holy, blessed, and glorious Trinity, three Persons and one God: have mercy upon us miserable sinners.[7]
O holy, blessed, and glorious Trinity, three Persons and one God: have mercy upon us miserable sinners.[8]
Remember not, Lord, our offences, nor the offences of our forefathers; neither take thou vengeance of our sins: spare us, good Lord, spare thy people, whom thou hast redeemed with thy most precious blood, and be not angry with us for ever.[9]
Spare us, good Lord.[10]
From all evil and mischief; from sin, from the crafts and assaults of the devil; from thy wrath, and from everlasting damnation,[11]
Good Lord, deliver us.

---

[1] Greek Origin, Latin Usage. Cranmer, A. D. 1544.
[2] The Repetition an English Usage, A. D. 1544.
[3] Greek Origin. Latin Usage. Cranmer, A. D. 1544.
[4] English Usage, A. D. 1544.   [5] Greek Origin. Cranmer, A. D. 1544.
[6] English Usage, A. D. 1544.
[7] Greek Origin. Latin Usage. Cranmer, A. D. 1544.
[8] English Usage, A. D. 1544.
[9] Latin Origin. English Usage, A. D. 1544.
[10] Latin Origin and Usage. Cranmer, 1544.
[11] Latin Origin. Bucer, A. D., 1543. Cranmer, A. D. 1544.

From all blindness of heart; from pride, vain-glory and hypocrisy; from envy, hatred, and malice, and all uncharitableness,[1]
Good Lord, deliver us.

From fornication and all other deadly sin; and from all the deceits of the world, the flesh, and the devil,[2]
Good Lord, deliver us.

From lightning and tempest; from plague, pestilence, and famine; from battle and murder, and from sudden death,[3]
Good Lord, deliver us.

From all sedition, privy conspiracy, and rebellion; from all false doctrine, heresy, and schism; from hardness of heart, and contempt of thy Word and Commandment,[4]
Good Lord, deliver us.

By the mystery of thy holy Incarnation; by thy holy Nativity and Circumcision; by thy Baptism, Fasting and Temptation,[5]
Good Lord, deliver us.

By thine Agony and bloody Sweat; by thy Cross and Passion; by thy precious Death and Burial; by thy glorious Resurrection and Ascension; and by the coming of the Holy Ghost,[6]
Good Lord, deliver us.

In all time of our tribulation; in all time of our wealth; in the hour of death, and in the day of judgement,[7]
Good Lord, deliver us.

We sinners do beseech thee to hear us, O Lord God; and that it may please thee to rule and govern thy holy Church universal in the right way;[8]
We beseech thee to hear us, good Lord.

That it may please thee to illuminate all Bishops, Priests and Deacons with true knowledge and understanding of thy Word;

---

[1] Latin Origin. Cranmer, A. D. 1544.
[2] Latin Origin. Cranmer, A. D. 1544.
[3] Bucer, A. D. 1543. Cranmer, 1544. Latin: a subitanea et improvisa morte.
[4] Bucer, A. D. 1543. Cranmer A. D. 1544.
[5] Latin Origin. Bucer, A. D. 1543.
[6] Latin Origin. Bucer, A. D. 1543.
[7] Latin Origin. Bucer, A. D. 1543.
[8] Latin Origin. Cranmer and Bucer.

and that both by their preaching and living they may set it forth and show it accordingly ; [1]

We beseech thee to bear us, good Lord.

That it may please thee to bless the Magistrates, giving them grace to execute justice, and to maintain truth ; [2]

We beseech thee to bear us, good Lord.

That it may please thee to give to all nations unity, peace, and concord ; [3]

We beseech thee to bear us; good Lord.

That it may please thee to give us an heart to love and dread thee, and diligently to live after thy commandments ; [4]

We beseech thee to bear us, good Lord.

That it may please thee to give to all thy people increase of grace to hear meekly thy Word, and to receive it with pure affection, and to bring forth the fruits of the Spirit ; [5]

We beseech thee to bear us, good Lord.

That it may please thee to bring into the way of truth all such as have erred, and are deceived ; [6]

We beseech thee to bear us, good Lord.

That it may please thee to strengthen such as do stand ; and to comfort and help the weak-hearted ; and to raise up them that fall ; and finally to beat down Satan under our feet ; [7]

We beseech thee to bear us, good Lord.

That it may please thee to succour, help, and comfort, all that are in danger, necessity, and tribulation ; [8]

We beseech thee to bear us, good Lord.

That it may please thee to preserve all that travel by land or by water, all women labouring of child, all sick persons, and young children ; and to shew thy pity upon all prisoners and captives ; [9]

We beseech thee to bear us, good Lord.

---

[1] Bucer and Cranmer, A. D. 1544.
[2] Bucer, A. D. 1543.
[3] English Version. Bucer, A. D. 1543.
[4] Cranmer, A. D. 1544.
[5] Bucer, Cranmer, A. D. 1544.
[6] Bucer, A. D. 1543. Cranmer, A. D. 1544.
[7] Bucer, A. D. 1543.
[8] Bucer, A. D. 1543.
[9] Bucer, A. D. 1543, and Cranmer, A. D. 1544.

That it may please thee to defend, and provide for, the fatherless children, and widows, and all that are desolate and oppressed ; [1]
We beseech thee to hear us, good Lord.
That it may please thee to have mercy upon all men ; [2]
We beseech thee to hear us, good Lord.
That it may please thee to forgive our enemies, persecutors, and slanderers, and to turn their hearts ; [3]
We beseech thee to hear us, good Lord.
That it may please thee to give and preserve to our use the kindly fruits of the earth, so as in due time we may enjoy them ; [4]
We beseech thee to hear us, good Lord.
That it may please thee to give us true repentance ; to forgive us all our sins, negligences, and ignorances ; and to endue us with the grace of thy Holy Spirit to amend our lives according to thy holy Word ; [5]
We beseech thee to hear us, good Lord.
Son of God : we beseech thee to hear us.
Son of God : we beseech thee to hear us.
O Lamb of God : that takest away the sins of the world ;
Grant us thy peace.
O Lamb of God : that takest away the sins of the world ;
Have mercy upon us.
O Christ, hear us.
O Christ, hear us.
Lord, have mercy upon us.
Lord, have mercy upon us.
Christ, have mercy upon us.
Christ, have mercy upon us.
Lord, have mercy upon us.
Lord, have mercy upon us.[6]
Priest. O Lord, deal not with us after our sins.
Answer. Neither reward us after our iniquities.

Let us pray.

O God, merciful Father, that despisest not the sighing of a contrite heart, nor the desire of such as be sorrowful ; Mercifully as-

---

[1] Bucer, A. D. 1543 and Cranmer, A. D. 1544. [2] Bucer, A. D. 1543.
[3] Bucer, A. D. 1543. [4] Latin Origin. Cranmer, A. D. 1544.
[5] Latin Origin. Cranmer, A. D. 1544.
[6] Lesser Litany. Latin Origin. Bucer, A. D. 1543.

sist our prayers that we make before thee in all our troubles and adversities, whensoever they oppress us; and graciously hear us, that those evils, which the craft and subtilty of the devil or man worketh against us, be brought to nought; and by the providence of thy goodness they may be dispersed; that we thy servants, being hurt by no persecutions, may evermore give thanks unto thee in thy Holy Church; through Jesus Christ our Lord.[1]

O Lord, arise, help us, and deliver us for thy Name's sake.

O God, we have heard with our ears, and our fathers have declared unto us, the noble works that thou didst in their days, and in the old time before them.

O Lord, arise, help us, and deliver us for thine honour.

Glory be to the Father, and to the Son: and to the Holy Ghost;

Answer. As it was in the beginning, is now, and ever shall be: world without end. Amen.

From our enemies defend us, O Christ.

Graciously look upon our afflictions.

Pitifully behold the sorrows of our hearts.

Mercifully forgive the sins of thy people.

Favourably with mercy hear our prayers.

O Son of David, have mercy upon us.

Both now and ever vouchsafe to hear us, O Christ.

Graciously hear us, O Christ; graciously hear us, O Lord Christ.

Priest. O Lord, let thy mercy be shewed upon us;

Answer. As we do put our trust in thee.[2]

Let us pray.

We humbly beseech thee, O Father, mercifully to look upon our infirmities; and for the glory of thy Name turn from us all those evils that we most righteously have deserved; and grant, that in all our troubles we may put our whole trust and confidence in thy mercy, and evermore serve thee in holiness and pureness of living, to thy honour and glory; through our only Mediator and Advocate, Jesus Christ our Lord. Amen.[3]

2 Cor. xiii.

The grace of our Lord Jesus Christ, and the love of God, and the fellowship of the Holy Ghost, be with us all evermore. Amen.[4]

---

[1] Modern Usage. Bucer, 1543. [2] Ancient Origin. Cranmer, A. D., 1554.
[3] English Usage. A. D., 1549. [4] English Usage. Since R. Elizabeth.

The Supper of the Lord, Holy Communion commonly called the Mass.

The Table, at the Communion-time having a fair white linen cloth upon it, shall stand in the Body of the Church, or in the Chancel, where Morning and Evening Prayer are appointed to be said. And the Priest shall say the Lord's Prayer, with the Collect following, the people kneeling.

Our Father, which art in heaven, Hallowed be thy Name. Thy kingdom come. Thy will be done in earth, As it is in heaven. Give us this day our daily bread. And forgive us our trespasses, As we forgive them that trespass against us. And lead us not into temptation; But deliver us from evil. Amen.

THE COLLECT.[1]

Almighty God, unto whom all hearts be open, all desires known, and from whom no secrets are hid; Cleanse the thoughts of our hearts by the inspiration of thy Holy Spirit, that we may perfectly love thee, and worthily magnify thy holy Name; through Christ our Lord. Amen.

Then shall be said or sung the Introit or Proper Psalm of the day, together with the Gloria Patri.[2]

I will wash my hands in innocency, O Lord: and so will I go to thine altar;

That I may shew the voice of thanksgiving: and tell of all thy wondrous works.

Lord, I have loved the habitation of thy house: and the place where thine honour dwelleth.

After which shall be said or sung,

Lord, have mercy upon us.[2]
Christ, have mercy upon us.
Lord, have mercy upon us.

And then shall be sung, all standing, Gloria in Excelsis.[3]

Glory be to God on high, and in earth peace, good will towards men. We praise thee, we bless thee, we worship thee, we glorify thee, we give thanks to thee for thy great glory, O Lord God, heavenly King, God the Father Almighty.

---

[1] Ancient: English Usage, 1549.

[2] Catholic and Lutheran usage: Anglican, 1549: omitted by Cranmer, 1552.

[3] Primitive Hymn: Catholic and Lutheran usage: transferred by Cranmer to Post-Communion.

O Lord, the only-begotten Son Jesus Christ; O Lord God, Lamb of God, Son of the Father, that takest away the sins of the world, have mercy upon us. Thou that takest away the sins of the world, have mercy upon us. Thou that takest away the sins of the world, receive our prayer. Thou that sittest at the right hand of God the Father, have mercy upon us.

For thou only art holy; thou only art the Lord: thou only, O Christ, with the Holy Ghost, art most high in the glory of God the Father. Amen.

Then shall be said the Collect of the Day. And immediately after the Collect the Priest shall read the Epistle. And the Epistle ended, then shall he read the Gospel.

Here shall be said or sung,

Glory be to thee, O Lord.[1]

And the Gospel ended, shall be sung or said the Creed following,[2] the people still standing, as before.

¶ I believe in one God the Father Almighty, Maker of heaven and earth, And of all things visible and invisible:

And in one Lord Jesus Christ, the only-begotten Son of God, Begotten of his Father before all worlds, God of God, Light of Light, Very God of very God, Begotten, not made, Being of one substance with the Father; By whom all things were made: Who for us men, and for our salvation came down from heaven, And was incarnate by the Holy Ghost of the Virgin Mary, And was made man, And was crucified also for us under Pontius Pilate. He suffered and was buried, And the third day he rose again according to the Scriptures, And ascended into heaven, And sitteth on the right hand of the Father. And he shall come again with glory to judge both the quick and the dead: Whose kingdom shall have no end.

And I believe in the Holy Ghost, The Lord and Giver of Life, Who proceedeth from the Father and the Son, Who with the Father and the Son together is worshipped and glorified, Who spake by the prophets. And I believe one Catholick and Apostolick Church. ¶ I acknowledge one Baptism for the remission of sins, And I look for the Resurrection of the dead, And the life of the world to come. Amen.

Then the Minister shall declare unto the people what Holy-days, or Fasting-days, are in the Week following to be observed, and then shall follow the Sermon.

---

[1] Primitive Ascription: Catholic usage: omitted by Cranmer, 1552: Adopted in American liturgy, 1789.

[2] Ancient Eucharistic Confession: Alternative with the Apostles' Creed in American liturgy.

Then shall the Priest return to the Lord's Table, and begin the Offertory, saying one or more of these Sentences following, as he thinketh most convenient in his discretion.

Let your light so shine before men, that they may see your good works, and glorify your Father which is in heaven. *St. Matth.* v.

Lay not up for yourselves treasure upon the earth; where the rust and moth doth corrupt, and where thieves break through and steal; but lay up for yourselves treasures in heaven; where neither rust nor moth doth corrupt, and where thieves do not break through and steal. *St. Matth.* vi.

Whatsoever ye would that men should do unto you, even so do unto them; for this is the Law and the Prophets. *St. Matth.* vii.

* * * * * * * * *

While these Sentences are in reading, the Deacons, Church-wardens, or other fit person appointed for that purpose, shall receive the Alms for the Poor, and other devotions of the people.

And the Priest shall then place upon the Table so much Bread and Wine, as he shall think sufficient. After which done, the Priest shall say,

Lift up your hearts.[1]

Answer. **We lift them up unto the Lord.**

Priest. **Let us give thanks unto our Lord God.**[1]

Answer. **It is meet and right so to do.**

Then shall the Priest turn to the Lord's Table, and say,

It is very meet, right, and our bounden duty, that we should at all times, and in all places, give thanks unto thee, O Lord, Holy Father, Almighty, Everlasting God.[1]

Here shall follow the Proper Preface, according to the time, if there be any specially appointed; or else immediately shall follow,

Therefore with Angels and Archangels, and with all the company of heaven, we laud and magnify thy glorious Name; evermore praising thee, and saying, Holy, holy, holy, Lord God of hosts, heaven and earth are full of thy glory: Glory be to thee, O Lord most High. Amen.[1]

PROPER PREFACES.[2]

Upon Christmas Day, and seven days after.

Because thou didst give Jesus Christ thine only Son to be born

---

[1] The Sursum Corda, Versicles and Tersanctus were in all ancient liturgies.

[2] Catholic: except for Christmas day and Whit Sunday, 1849.

as at this time for us; who, by the operation of the Holy Ghost, was made very man of the substance of the Virgin Mary his mother; and that without spot of sin, to make us clean from all sin. Therefore with Angels, etc.

Upon Easter Day, and seven days after.

But chiefly are we bound to praise thee for the glorious Resurrection of thy Son Jesus Christ our Lord; for he is the very Paschal Lamb, which was offered for us, and hath taken away the sin of the world; who by his death hath destroyed death, and by his rising to life again hath restored to us everlasting life. Therefore with Angels, etc.

Upon Ascension Day, and seven days after.

Through thy most dearly beloved Son Jesus Christ our Lord: who after his most glorious Resurrection manifestly appeared to all his Apostles, and in their sight ascended up into heaven to prepare a place for us; that where he is, thither we might also ascend, and reign with him in glory. Therefore with Angels, etc.

Upon Whit Sunday, and six days after.

Through Jesus Christ our Lord; according to whose most true promise, the Holy Ghost came down as at this time from heaven with a sudden great sound, as it had been a mighty wind, in the likeness of fiery tongues, lighting upon the Apostles, to teach them, and to lead them to all truth; giving them both the gift of divers languages, and also boldness with fervent zeal constantly to preach the Gospel unto all nations; whereby we have been brought out of darkness and error into the clear light and true knowledge of thee, and of thy Son Jesus Christ. Therefore with Angels, etc.

Upon the Feast of Trinity only.

Who art one God, one Lord; not one only Person, but three Persons in one Substance. For that which we believe of the glory of the Father, the same we believe of the Son, and of the Holy Ghost, without any difference or inequality. Therefore with Angels, etc.

After each of which Prefaces shall immediately be sung or said,

Therefore with Angels and Archangels, and with all the company of heaven, we laud and magnify thy glorious Name; evermore praising thee, and saying, Holy, holy, holy, Lord God of hosts, heaven and earth are full of thy glory; Glory be to thee, O Lord most high. Amen.

Catholic Formularies.

When the Priest standing before the Table, hath so ordered the Bread and Wine, that he may with the more readiness and decency break the Bread before the people, and take the Cup into his hands, he shall say the Prayer of Consecration, as followeth.[1]

Almighty God, our heavenly Father, who of thy tender mercy didst give thine only Son Jesus Christ to suffer death upon the Cross for our redemption; who made there (by his one oblation of himself once offered) a full, perfect, and sufficient sacrifice, oblation, and satisfaction, for the sins of the whole world; and did institute, and in his holy Gospel command us to continue, a perpetual memory of that his precious death, until his coming again; Hear us, O merciful Father, we most humbly beseech thee; and grant that we receiving these thy creatures of bread and wine, according to thy Son our Saviour Jesus Christ's holy institution, in remembrance of his death and passion, may be partakers of his most blessed Body and Blood, who, in the same night that he was betrayed, took Bread; and, when he had given thanks, he brake it, and gave it to his disciples, saying, Take, eat, this is my Body which is given for you: Do this in remembrance of me. Likewise after supper he took the Cup; and when he had given thanks, he gave it to them, saying, Drink ye all of this; for this is my Blood of the New Testament, which is shed for you and for many for the remission of sins: Do this, as oft as ye shall drink it, in remembrance of me.[2]

Wherefore, O Lord and heavenly Father, we, thy humble servants, do celebrate and make here before thy Divine Majesty, with these thy holy gifts, the memorial thy Son hath commanded us to make; having in remembrance his blessed passion and precious death, his mighty resurrection and glorious ascension; and rendering unto thee most hearty thanks for the innumerable benefits procured unto us by the same. And we entirely desire thy fatherly goodness mercifully to accept this our sacrifice of praise and thanksgiving; most humbly beseeching thee to grant, that by the merits and death of thy Son Jesus Christ, and through faith in his blood, we and all thy whole Church may obtain remission of

---

[1] In 1549, here followed the Prayer for the Church Militant (see p. 249, below), as part of the Canon of Consecration. In 1552, it was placed by Cranmer in the Ante-Communion, where it is still used.

[2] Based upon the Canon by Cranmer: More Protestant than Catholic.

our sins, and all other benefits of his passion. And here we offer and present unto thee, O Lord, ourselves, our souls and bodies, to be a reasonable, holy, and lively sacrifice unto thee; humbly beseeching thee, that all we, who are partakers of this holy Communion, may be fulfilled with thy grace and heavenly benediction. And although we be unworthy, through our manifold sins, to offer unto thee any sacrifice, yet we beseech thee to accept this our bounden duty and service; not weighing our merits, but pardoning our offences, through Jesus Christ our Lord; by whom, and with whom, in the unity of the Holy Ghost, all honour and glory be unto thee, O Father Almighty, world without end. Amen.[1]

Then shall the Priest say the Lord's Prayer, the people repeating after him every Petition.

Then shall the Minister first receive the Communion in both kinds himself, and then proceed to deliver the same to the Bishops, Priests, and Deacons, in like manner (if any be present), and after that to the people also in order, into their hands, all meekly kneeling. And, when he delivereth the Bread to any one, he shall say,

The Body of our Lord Jesus Christ, which was given for thee, preserve thy body and soul unto everlasting life.[2]

Take and eat this in remembrance that Christ died for thee, and feed on him in thy heart by faith with thanksgiving.

And the Minister that delivereth the Cup to any one shall say,

The Blood of our Lord Jesus Christ, which was shed for thee, preserve thy body and soul unto everlasting life.[2]

Drink this in remembrance that Christ's Blood was shed for thee, and be thankful.

When all have communicated, the Minister shall return to the Lord's Table, and reverently place upon it what remaineth of the consecrated Elements, covering the same with a fair linen cloth.

And after a Hymn has been sung shall be said this Thanksgiving.[3]

Almighty and everliving God, we most heartily thank thee, for that thou dost vouchsafe to feed us, who have duly received these holy mysteries, with the spiritual food of the most precious Body and Blood of thy Son our Saviour Jesus Christ; and dost assure us thereby of thy favour and goodness towards us; and that we

---

[1] Amendment of Laud: More Catholic than Protestant: adopted in Scottish and American liturgies.

[2] Catholic forms, with Protestant additions by Cranmer.

[3] By Bucer and Cranmer, 1552.

are very members incorporate in the mystical body of thy Son, and which is the blessed company of all faithful people; and are also heirs through hope of thy everlasting kingdom, by the merits of the most precious death and passion of thy dear Son. And we most humbly beseech thee, O heavenly Father, so to assist us with thy grace, that we may continue in that holy fellowship, and do all such good works as thou hast prepared for us to walk in; through Jesus Christ our Lord, to whom, with thee and the Holy Ghost, be all honour and glory, world without end. *Amen.*

Then the Priest (or Bishop if he be present) shall let them depart with this Blessing. [1]

The peace of God, which passeth all understanding, keep your hearts and minds in the knowledge and love of God, and of his Son Jesus Christ our Lord; and the blessing of God Almighty, the Father, the Son, and the Holy Ghost, be amongst you and remain with you always. *Amen.*

---

[1] By Bucer and Cranmer, 1552.

THE ORDER FOR DIVINE SERVICE ON THE LORD'S DAY.

At the beginning of Divine Service on the Lord's Day[1] *the Minister shall read with a loud voice some one or more of these Sentences of the Scriptures that follow. And then he shall say that which is written after the said Sentences.*

When the wicked man turneth away from his wickedness that he hath committed, and doeth that which is lawful and right, he shall save his soul alive. *Ezek.* xviii. 27.

I acknowledge my transgressions, and my sin is ever before me. *Psal.* li. 3.

Hide thy face from my sins, and blot out all mine iniquities. *Psal.* li. 9.

The sacrifices of God are a broken spirit: a broken and a contrite heart, O God, thou wilt not despise. *Psal.* li. 17.

Rend your heart, and not your garments, and turn unto the Lord your God: for he is gracious and merciful, slow to anger, and of great kindness, and repenteth him of the evil. *Joel.* ii. 13.

To the Lord our God belong mercies and forgivenesses, though we have rebelled against him: neither have we obeyed the voice of the Lord our God, to walk in his laws which he set before us. *Dan.* ix. 9, 10.

O Lord, correct me, but with judgement; not in thine anger, lest thou bring me to nothing. *Jer.* x. 24. *Psal.* vi. 1.

Repent ye; for the Kingdom of Heaven is at hand. *St. Matth.* iii. 2.

I will arise, and go to my father, and will say unto him, Father, I have sinned against heaven, and before thee, and am no more worthy to be called thy son. *St. Luke* xv. 18, 19.

Enter not into judgement with thy servant, O Lord; for in thy sight shall no man living be justified. *Psal.* cxliii. 2.

If we say that we have no sin, we deceive ourselves, and the

---

[1] Calvinistic Usage: Genevan "Form of Common Prayers," printed by Whitechurch, printer of the Prayer-book, June 3, 1550. Pollanus, 1550. English Usage, A. D., 1552.

truth is not in us: but, if we confess our sins, he is faithful and just to forgive us our sins, and to cleanse us from all unrighteousness.   1 *St. John* i. 8, 9.

Dearly beloved brethren, the Scripture moveth us in sundry places to acknowledge and confess our manifold sins and wickedness; and that we should not dissemble nor cloke them before the face of Almighty God our heavenly Father; but confess them with an humble, lowly, penitent, and obedient heart; to the end that we may obtain forgiveness of the same, by his infinite goodness and mercy. And although we ought at all times humbly to acknowledge our sins before God; yet ought we most chiefly so to do, when we assemble and meet together to render thanks for the great benefits that we have received at his hands, to set forth his most worthy praise, to hear his most holy Word, and to ask those things which are requisite and necessary, as well for the body as the soul. Wherefore I pray and beseech you, as many as are here present, to accompany me with a pure heart, and humble voice, unto the throne of the heavenly grace, saying after me;[1]

A General Confession[2] *to be said of the whole Congregation after the Minister, all kneeling.*

Almighty and most merciful Father; We have erred, and strayed from thy ways like lost sheep. We have followed too much the devices and desires of our own hearts. We have offended against thy holy laws. We have left undone those things which we ought to have done; And we have done those things which we ought not to have done; And there is no health in us. But thou, O Lord, have mercy upon us, miserable offenders. Spare thou them, O God, which confess their faults. Restore thou them that are penitent; According to thy promises declared unto mankind in Christ

---

[1] Calvinistic Usage: Calvin's Strasburg Liturgy translated for Church of Refugees in Glastonbury Abbey, with a Brief Apology for this Liturgy by Valerandus Pollanus, February 23, 1551.   English Compilers, A. D., 1552.

[2] Calvinistic Usage at Geneva, A. D., 1541, and Strasburg, A. D., 1538; at Glastonbury, A. D., 1550; and in London, A. D., 1550, according to the " Form of Church Service," modeled upon Calvin's Liturgy by John à Lasco with permission of Edward VI.

Jesus our Lord. And grant, O most merciful Father, for his sake; That we may hereafter live a godly, righteous, and sober life, To the glory of thy holy Name. Amen.[1]

The Absolution,[2] *or Remission of sins, to be pronounced by the Minister alone, standing; the people still kneeling.*

Almighty God, the Father of our Lord Jesus Christ, who desireth not the death of a sinner, but rather that he may turn from his wickedness, and live; and hath given power, and commandment, to his Ministers, to declare and pronounce to his people, being penitent, the Absolution and Remission of their sins: He pardoneth and absolveth all them that truly repent, and unfeignedly believe his holy Gospel. Wherefore let us beseech him to grant us true repentance, and his Holy Spirit, that those things may please him, which we do at this present; and that the rest of our life hereafter may be pure, and holy; so that at the last we may come to his eternal joy; through Jesus Christ our Lord.[3] *Amen.*

Then the Minister shall kneel, and say the Lord's Prayer; the people also kneeling, and repeating it with him.

Our Father, which art in heaven, Hallowed be thy Name. Thy kingdom come. Thy will be done in earth, As it is in heaven. Give us this day our daily bread. And forgive us our trespasses, As we forgive them that trespass against us. And lead us not into temptation; But deliver us from evil: For thine is the kingdom, The power, and the glory, For ever and ever. Amen.

[*Then shall be sung, all standing, a Psalm, as following*].

PSALM CIII. *Benedic, anima mea.*

Praise the Lord, O my soul: and all that is within me praise his holy Name.

Praise the Lord, O my soul: and forget not all his benefits;

Who forgiveth all thy sin: and healeth all thine infirmities;

---

[1] Composed by Cranmer and other Compilers, 1552.

[2] Calvinistic Doctrine; Institutes, Bk. iv, Ch. i, § 22; Bk. iii, Ch. iv, § 14, A. D. 1536. Calvinistic Usage at Strasburg, 1538, Glastonbury and London, 1550.

[3] Compiled from a Form in Calvinistic Liturgy of John à Lasco, by Cranmer and Compilers.

Protestant Formularies. 247

Who saveth thy life from destruction: and crowneth thee with mercy and loving-kindness;

O praise the Lord, ye angels of his, ye that excel in strength: ye that fulfil his commandment, and hearken unto the voice of his words.

O praise the Lord, all ye his hosts: ye servants of his that do his pleasure.

O speak good of the Lord, all ye works of his, in all places of his dominion: praise thou the Lord, O my soul.

Then shall be read a Lesson taken out of the Old Testament. After which the Minister shall rehearse distinctly all the TEN COMMANDMENTS;[1] and the people kneeling shall, after every Commandment, ask God mercy for their transgression thereof for the time past, and grace to keep the same for the time to come, as followeth.

Minister. God spake these words, and said; I am the Lord thy God: Thou shalt have none other gods but me.

People. Lord, have mercy upon us, and incline our hearts to keep this law.[2]

Minister. Thou shalt not make to thyself any graven image, nor the likeness of anything that is in heaven above, or in the earth beneath, or in the water under the earth. Thou shalt not bow down to them, nor worship them: for I the Lord thy God am a jealous God, and visit the sins of the fathers upon the children, unto the third and fourth generation of them that hate me, and shew mercy unto thousands in them that love me, and keep my commandments.

People. Lord, have mercy upon us, and incline our hearts to keep this law.

Minister. Thou shalt not take the Name of the Lord thy God in vain; for the Lord will not hold him guiltless, that taketh his Name in vain.

People. Lord, have mercy upon us, and incline our hearts to keep this law.

Minister. Remember that thou keep holy the Sabbath-day. Six days shalt thou labour, and do all that thou hast to do; but

---

[1] Calvinistic usage at Geneva, Strasburg, Glastonbury and London. Pollanus, 1551.

[2] The Catholic Lesser Litany with Protestant additions, A. D. 1552.

the seventh day is the Sabbath of the Lord thy God. In it thou shalt do no manner of work, thou, and thy son, and thy daughter, thy man-servant, and thy maid-servant, thy cattle, and the stranger that is within thy gates. For in six days the Lord made heaven and earth, the sea, and all that in them is, and rested the seventh day: wherefore the Lord blessed the seventh day, and hallowed it.

People. **Lord, have mercy upon us,** and incline our hearts to keep this law.

Minister. Honour thy father and thy mother; that thy days may be long in the land, which the Lord thy God giveth thee.

People. **Lord, have mercy upon us,** and incline our hearts to keep this law.

Minister. Thou shalt do no murder.

People. **Lord, have mercy upon us,** and incline our hearts to keep this law.

Minister. Thou shalt not commit adultery.

People. **Lord, have mercy upon us,** and incline our hearts to keep this law.

Minister. Thou shalt not steal.

People. **Lord, have mercy upon us,** and incline our hearts to keep this law.

Minister. Thou shalt not bear false witness against thy neighbour.

People. **Lord, have mercy upon us,** and incline our hearts to keep this law.

Minister. Thou shalt not covet thy neighbour's house, thou shalt not covet thy neighbour's wife, nor his servant, nor his maid, nor his ox, nor his ass, nor anything that is his.

People. **Lord, have mercy upon us,** and write all these thy laws in our hearts, we beseech thee.[1]

Then shall be read a Lesson taken out of the New Testament. [After which the Minister shall pronounce the Eight Beatitudes or Blessings of the Gospel, and the People standing shall, after every Blessing, declare the reason given for the same as followeth].[2]

And Jesus opened his mouth and taught his disciples, saying:

---

[1] Summary Petition in Liturgy of Pollanus.

[2] Proposed Prayer-book A. D. 1682. Presbyterian, Unitarian and Episcopal suggestion.

Blessed are the poor in spirit:
People. For theirs is the kingdom of heaven.
Minister. Blessed are they that mourn:
People. For they shall be comforted.
Minister. Blessed are the meek:
People. For they shall inherit the earth.
Minister. Blessed are they which do hunger and thirst after righteousness:
People. For they shall be filled.
Minister. Blessed are the merciful:
People. For they shall obtain mercy.
Minister. Blessed are the pure in heart:
People. For they shall see God.
Minister. Blessed are the peace-makers:
People. For they shall be called the children of God.
Minister. Blessed are they which are persecuted for righteousness' sake:
People. For theirs is the kingdom of heaven.

And then the Minister and People, still standing, shall say the Apostles' Creed.

I Believe in God the Father Almighty, Maker of heaven and earth:

And in Jesus Christ his only Son our Lord; Who was conceived by the Holy Ghost, Born of the Virgin Mary; Suffered under Pontius Pilate, Was crucified, dead and buried; He descended into hell, The third day he rose from the dead; He ascended into heaven, And sitteth on the right hand of God the Father Almighty; From thence he shall come to judge the quick and the dead.

I believe in the Holy Ghost; The Holy Catholic Church; The Communion of Saints; The Forgiveness of sins; The Resurrection of the body; And the Life everlasting. *Amen.*

Then, if the Holy Communion is to follow, shall the Minister say:

Let us pray for the whole state of Christ's Church militant here in earth.[1]

---

[1] Knox's Book of Common Order. Amended according to Bucer's Censura, A. D. 1552.

Almighty and everliving God, who by thy holy Apostle hast taught us to make prayers, and supplications, and to give thanks, for all men; We humbly beseech thee most mercifully to receive these our prayers, which we offer unto thy Divine Majesty; beseeching thee to inspire continually the universal Church with the spirit of truth, unity, and concord: And grant, that all they that do confess thy holy Name may agree in the truth of thy holy Word, and live in unity, and godly love. We beseech thee also to save and defend all Christian Kings, Princes, and Governors; and especially thy Servant [our chief magistrate]; And grant unto all that are put in authority, that they may truly and indifferently minister justice, to the punishment of wickedness and vice, and to the maintenance of thy true religion, and virtue. Give grace, O heavenly Father, to all Bishops and [Ministers], that they may both by their life and doctrine set forth thy true and lively Word, and rightly and duly administer thy holy sacraments: And to all thy people give thy heavenly grace; and especially to this congregation here present: that, with meek heart and due reverence, they may hear, and receive thy holy Word; truly serving thee in holiness and righteousness all the days of their life. And we most humbly beseech thee of thy goodness, O Lord, to comfort and succour all them, who in this transitory life are in trouble, sorrow, need, sickness, or any other adversity. And we also bless thy holy Name for all thy servants departed this life in thy faith and fear; beseeching thee to give us grace so to follow their good examples, that with them we may be partakers of thy heavenly kingdom: Grant this, O Father, for Jesus Christ's sake, our only Mediator and Advocate.[1] *Amen.*

Or else these Prayers following, together with any special Prayers or Thanksgivings upon several occasions which may be requisite and fitting.

A PRAYER FOR ALL CONDITIONS OF MEN.[2]

O God, the Creator and Preserver of all mankind, we humbly

---

[1] Protestant emendation of Catholic Canon of the Mass by Cranmer, in 1st Bk. of Edward.

[2] Bishop Sanderson or Bishop Gunning, A. D., 1661. Due to Presbyterian Revision.

beseech thee for all sorts and conditions of men; that thou wouldest be pleased to make thy ways known unto them, thy saving health unto all nations. More especially we pray for the good estate of the Catholick Church; that it may be so guided and governed by thy good Spirit, that all who profess and call themselves Christians may be led into the way of truth, and hold the faith in unity of spirit, in the bond of peace, and in righteousness of life. Finally, we commend to thy fatherly goodness all those, who are any ways afflicted, or distressed, in mind, body, or estate; [*especially those for whom our prayers are desired,*] that it may please thee to comfort and relieve them, according to their several necessities, giving them patience under their sufferings, and a happy issue out of all their afflictions. And this we beg for Jesus Christ his sake. *Amen.*

A PRAYER FOR THE CHIEF MAGISTRATE AND ALL IN AUTHORITY.[1]

O Lord, our heavenly Father, high and mighty King of kings, Lord of lords, the Blessed and only Potentate, who dost from thy throne behold all the dwellers upon earth; Most heartily we beseech thee with thy favor to behold [thy chosen servant our Chief Magistrate, his counsellors and all others in authority]; and so replenish them with the grace of thy Holy Spirit, that they may always incline to thy will, and walk in thy way. Endue them plenteously with heavenly gifts; grant them in health, [peace, and godliness] to rule; and finally, after this life, to attain everlasting joy and felicity; through Jesus Christ our Lord. *Amen.*

A PRAYER FOR THE CLERGY AND PEOPLE.[2]

Almighty and everlasting God, who alone workest great marvels; Send down upon our Bishops, [and other Ministers], and all Congregations committed to their charge, the healthful Spirit of thy grace; and that they may truly please thee, pour upon them the continual dew of thy blessing. Grant this O Lord, for the honour of our Advocate and Mediator, Jesus Christ. Amen.

---

[1] Early Reformed. English usage till 1661.
[2] Ancient Collect. Amended in 1641 and 1689.

A GENERAL THANKSGIVING.[1]

Almighty God, Father of all mercies, we thine unworthy servants do give thee most humble and hearty thanks for all thy goodness and loving-kindness to us, and to all men; [*particularly to those who desire now to offer up their praises and thanksgivings for thy late mercies vouchsafed unto them.*] We bless thee for our creation, preservation, and all the blessings of this life; but above all, for thine inestimable love in the redemption of the world by our Lord Jesus Christ; for the means of grace, and for the hope of glory. And, we beseech thee, give us that due sense of all thy mercies, that our hearts may be unfeignedly thankful, and that we shew forth thy praise, not only with our lips, but in our lives; by giving up ourselves to thy service, and by walking before thee in holiness and righteousness all our days; through Jesus Christ our Lord, to whom with thee and the Holy Ghost be all honour and glory, world without end. *Amen.*

A PRAYER THAT MAY BE SAID AFTER ANY OF THE FORMER.

Almighty God, who hast promised to hear the petitions of them that ask in thy Son's Name; We beseech thee mercifully to incline thine ears to us that have made now our prayers and supplications unto thee; and grant, that those things, which we have faithfully asked according to thy will, may effectually be obtained, to the relief of our necessity, and to the setting forth of thy glory; through Jesus Christ our Lord.[2] Amen.

And after the Prayers shall follow a Hymn and the Sermon. And the Sermon ended, then shall be said this Collect[3], or some suitable Prayer, with the Benediction.

Grant, we beseech thee, Almighty God, that the words, which we have heard this day with our outward ears, may through thy grace be so grafted inwardly in our hearts, that they may bring forth in us the fruit of good living, to the honour and praise of thy Name; through Jesus Christ our Lord. *Amen.*

---

[1] The Presbyterian Bishop Reynolds. A. D. 1661.
[2] Ancient Collect. English Usage.
[3] English Reformed, 1549.

The peace of God, which passeth all understanding, keep your hearts and minds in the knowledge and love of God, and of his Son Jesus Christ our Lord : And the Blessing of God Almighty, the Father, the Son, and the Holy Ghost, be amongst you, and remain with you always. *Amen.*

THE ORDER OF PREPARATION FOR THE LORD'S SUPPER.

When the Minister giveth warning for the celebration of the holy Communion (which he shall always do upon the Sunday, or some Holy-day, immediately preceding), after the Sermon or Homily ended, he shall read this Exhortation following.[1]

Dearly beloved, on — day next I propose, through God's assistance, to administer to all such as shall be religiously and devoutly disposed the most comfortable Sacrament of the Body and Blood of Christ; to be by them received in remembrance of his meritorious Cross and Passion; whereby alone we obtain remission of our sins, and are made partakers of the kingdom of heaven.

*   *   *   *   *   *   *   *   *

And because it is requisite, that no man should come to the holy Communion, but with a full trust in God's mercy, and with a quiet conscience; therefore if there be any of you, who by this means cannot quiet his own conscience herein, but requireth further comfort or counsel, let him come to me, or to some other discreet and learned Minister of God's Word, and open his grief; that by the ministry of God's holy Word he may receive the benefit of absolution, together with ghostly counsel and advice, to the quieting of his conscience, and avoiding of all scruple and doubtfulness.[2]

Or, in case he shall see the people negligent to come to the holy Communion, instead of the former, he shall use this Exhortation.[3]

Dearly beloved brethren, on ——— I intend, by God's grace, to celebrate the Lord's Supper: unto which, in God's behalf, I bid you all that are present; and beseech you, for the Lord Jesus Christ's sake, that ye will not refuse to come thereto, being so lovingly called and bidden by God himself.

*   *   *   *   *   *   *   *   *

---

[1] Calvinistic Usage. From Cologne Liturgy or Hermann's Consultation, A. D. 1543, "a quasi-Lutheran production of Melanchthon and Bucer." Inserted in English "Order of Communion" in 1548; sent to Calvin for approval. Knox's Book of Common Order.

[2] Calvin's Institutes, Book III, Chapter IV, § 14. Revisions of 1552 and 1661.

[3] Peter Martyr.

At the time of the celebration of the Communion the Minister may say this Exhortation.[1]

Dearly beloved in the Lord, ye that mind to come to the holy Communion of the Body and Blood of our Saviour Christ, must consider how Saint Paul exhorteth all persons diligently to try and examine themselves, before they presume to eat of that Bread, and drink of that Cup.

* * * * * * * * *

Then shall the Minister say to them that come to receive the holy Communion.[2]

Ye that do truly and earnestly repent you of your sins, and are in love and charity with your neighbours, and intend to lead a new life, following the commandments of God, and walking from henceforth in his holy ways; Draw near with faith, and take this holy Sacrament to your comfort; and make your humble confession to Almighty God, meekly kneeling upon your knees.

Then shall this general Confession be made, in the name of all those that are minded to receive the holy Communion, by one of the Ministers.[3]

Almighty God, Father of our Lord Jesus Christ, Maker of all things, Judge of all men; We acknowledge and bewail our manifold sins and wickedness, Which we, from time to time, most grievously have committed, By thought, word, and deed, Against thy Divine Majesty, Provoking most justly thy wrath and indignation against us. We do earnestly repent, And are heartily sorry for these our misdoings; The remembrance of them is grievous unto us; The burden of them is intolerable. Have mercy upon us, Have mercy upon us, most merciful Father; For thy Son our Lord Jesus Christ's sake, Forgive us all that is past; And grant that we may ever hereafter serve and please thee In newness of life, To the honour and glory of thy Name; Through Jesus Christ our Lord. Amen.

Then shall the Minister (or the Bishop, being present,) pronounce this Absolution.[4]

Almighty God, our heavenly Father, who of his great mercy

---

[1] Calvinistic. Composed by Peter Martyr. Suggested by Bucer and Knox. Presbyterian Revision, 1661.

[2] English order of Communion. Lutheran and Calvinistic.

[3] Calvinistic, Pollanus. English Reformed.

[4] Catholic. Protestant amended. Lutheran and Calvinistic.

hath promised forgiveness of sins to all them that with hearty repentance and true faith turn unto him ; Have mercy upon you; pardon and deliver you from all your sins ; confirm and strengthen you in all goodness; and bring you to everlasting life; through Jesus Christ our Lord. *Amen.*

Then shall the Minister say,[1]

Hear what comfortable words our Saviour Christ saith unto all that truly turn to him.

Come unto me all that travail and are heavy laden, and I will refresh you. *St. Matth.* xi. 28.

So God loved the world, that he gave his only-begotten Son, to the end that all that believe in him should not perish, but have everlasting life. *St. John* iii. 16.

Hear also what Saint Paul saith.

This is a true saying, and worthy of all men to be received, that Christ Jesus came into the world to save sinners. 1 *Tim.* i. 15.

Hear also what Saint John saith.

If any man sin, we have an Advocate with the Father, Jesus Christ the righteous; and he is the propitiation for our sins. 1 *St. John* ii. 1.

Then shall the Minister say in the name of all them that shall receive the Communion this Prayer following.[2]

We do not presume to come to this thy Table, O merciful Lord, trusting in our own righteousness, but in thy manifold and great mercies. We are not worthy so much as to gather up the crumbs under thy Table. But thou art the same Lord, whose property is always to have mercy: Grant us therefore, gracious Lord, so to eat the flesh of thy dear Son Jesus Christ, and to drink his blood, that our sinful bodies may be made clean by his body, and our souls washed through his most precious blood, and that we may evermore dwell in him, and he in us. *Amen.*

And then shall follow the Ministration.

---

[1] Calvinistic usage at Geneva. Strasburg Liturgy.

[2] Protestant. English Order of Communion. Bucer and Cranmer.

IX.
THE SOCIOLOGICAL QUESTION OF CHURCH UNITY.

IX.

THE SOCIOLOGICAL QUESTION OF CHURCH UNITY.[1]

"How were Christians employed," said Voltaire, "whilst the Saracens were ravaging the fairest portion of Christendom? Disputing whether Christ had one will or two!" The sneer was shallow enough; but it seems almost deserved when we weigh the forgotten Monothelite controversy against that Christian civilization which was in peril until after the Crusades. Perhaps, too, we may find history repeating itself in our own time.

The situation of the Christian denominations in modern society is not unlike that of a wrangling army among invading foes. It is not a petty quarrel before the onset, but a bitter feud in mid-battle. The contending factions have become so absorbed that they do not even see the hosts mustering around them and the ranks closing in upon them. Worst of all, they have neither organization nor leadership in their hour of peril.

Meanwhile, too, may still be heard the old Voltairian sneer with modern variations: "You Christians are disputing whether the Holy Ghost proceeds from the Father as well as the Son, whilst multitudes have not even heard if there be a Holy Ghost; whether any infants have been elected from

---

[1] This essay appeared in the *Century Magazine* for 1890, as one of the series of Present Day Papers issued under the supervision of a Sociological Group composed of the Right Rev. Henry C. Potter, Prof. Charles W. Shields, Rev. Dr. Theodore T. Munger, Rev. Dr. Wm. Chauncy Langdon, Rev. Dr. Samuel W. Dike, President Seth Low, Prof. Richard T. Ely, Right Rev. Hugh Miller Thompson, Prof. Charles A. Briggs, Rev. Dr. Washington Gladden, Prof. Francis G. Peabody, President William F. Slocum, Jr., The Hon. Edward J. Phelps, Prof. William J. Sloane, and Charles Dudley Warner, Esq.

eternity, whilst myriads of infants are growing up in vice and sin; whether the heathen on the other side of the globe will hereafter be saved, whilst the heathen at your own doors are already lost. You are splitting hairs of theology, with society falling to pieces around you. If this be Christianity, we want none of it. Settle your useless disputes and unite vigorously in improving the world that now is, and then we will listen to your promises of a better world to come."

The writer would be no alarmist in his view of the social necessities for church unity. But surely, if social ills are fast coming to a crisis, it is folly to ignore them; and if organized Christianity is their only perfect remedy, it is madness to withhold that remedy. The Church would simply be a conspicuous failure did not it thus become the light of the world and the salt of the earth. To instruct and preserve society is at least one design, if not the chief design, of the Christian religion as organized in the Church. Whatever other great purposes it may serve as a training-school of individuals for heaven, it has also this high social mission here upon earth. And with this social mission of Christianity we, in our collective capacity, have mainly to do.

It should be remembered that our social troubles are not wholly economic or political in their nature. The problems of marriage, temperance, education, property, involve moral elements. Even the so-called conflict between labor and capital is no mere play of impersonal forces, but also a fierce struggle of human passions and prejudices, and the actors in it cannot be manipulated like so many chessmen in the game of politics. In fact, our wisest statesmanship already stands baffled before these problems. They have passed beyond the control of parties, the machinery of legislation, and the devices of political economy. It is becoming plain that they are not to be solved by divorce statutes, prohibitory amendments, conspiracy laws against strikes and boycotts; much less by improved police systems and new barricade tactics. If solved at all, the solution must be largely moral and even religious, striking at the roots of social corruption in ignorance and vice; imparting integrity to all classes; binding together laborer and capitalist in bonds of charity as well as interest; and ever nobly diffusing culture with wealth, virtue with intelligence, religion with knowledge, Christianity with civilization.

From this high point of view the Christian religion has an imperious claim upon the patriot and the statesman. Even that citizen who does not accept it must recognize it as at least part of our national life and a potent force in public affairs. If he should choose to view it simply as a moralizing agent, aside from all religious doctrines, it would still have an immense political value. Compared with other religions, it would afford the best political morality that the world has ever known. As a matter of fact, however, we are neither an infidel nor a heathen people. Our whole civilization is essentially Christian. Our institutions and laws have their roots in Christian ethics. The very seat of our sovereignty is in a Christian citizenship. The most unscrupulous politician dare not defy the Christian sentiment of the nation. The most philosophic statesman cannot afford to ignore it. And the time may not be far off when the organization of the Christian denominations against menacing social evils—in other words, church unity—shall have become a social as well as an ecclesiastical question, and a question belonging to the domain of practical rather than mere sentimental politics. This will be seen more clearly as we proceed to trace the historical relations of socialism with Christianity to their present critical stage in this country.

EARLY CHRISTIAN SOCIALISM.

Socialism originated in Christianity. It was born in the golden age of the Church, on the day of Pentecost, when "the multitude of them that believed were of one heart and of one soul; neither said any of them that ought of the things which he possessed was his own; but they had all things common.

Neither was there any among them that lacked; for as many as were possessors of lands or houses sold them, and brought the prices of the things that were sold, and laid them down at the apostles' feet; and distribution was made unto every man according as he had need." That brief brilliant dream of social perfection has lingered ever since in the Christian consciousness as an ideal of prayer and effort. Countless attempts have been made to realize it, many of them crude and grotesque, but some of them noble and hopeful. The monastic communities of the early church, both Greek and Roman, the great religious orders of the Middle Ages, the Benedictines, the Dominicans, the Franciscans, with their various branches, were only so many socialistic organizations based upon the renunciation of property, marriage and citizenship. Communistic sects were born of the pentecostal zeal of the Reformation; some of them, like the German Anabaptists and English Fifth Monarchists, assailing both church and state with revolutionary violence, whilst others, like the Shakers and Harmonists, sought an asylum in the New World and founded peaceful retreats of piety and virtue. Besides these imported forms of Christian socialism we have had our own indigenous growth, such as the Unitarian Association of Transcendentalists at Brock Farm and the Orthodox Community of Perfectionists at Oneida. And now, as mild types of the same spirit, we have in some of our churches revived brotherhoods and sisterhoods with voluntary vows of poverty, celibacy and charity.

Not only has socialism prevailed within the Church, but its offshoots have flourished like the wild olive beyond the pale, if not as direct fruits of Christianity, yet as products of a Christian civilization. The various eleemosynary institutions for the relief of social ills—hospitals, asylums, reformatories, penitentiaries—were once managed by the clergy alone, and may all be traced back to the example and doctrine of that divine Philanthropist who taught the parable of the Good Samaritan and wrought miracles of healing upon the bodies as well as souls of men. The numerous friendly and beneficiary societies for mutual help in sickness and misfortune, such as the Free Masons, the Odd Fellows, the Knights of Pythias, etc., are only remote descendants of the Christian guild, and often born of the Christian spirit, even when not baptized with a Christian name. Propagandist orders, like the Sons of Temperance and the Brethren of the White Cross, aim directly at Christian virtues. Many of the modern schemes of social regeneration have simply borrowed the Christian ideas of liberty, equality, fraternity, charity. Saint-Simon styled his socialistic treatise "New Christianity." It is often claimed that industrial fraternities are doing the work of a practical Christianity. To Christianity, indeed, the working classes owe their enfranchisement and their organization. The pagan world knew nothing of the dignity of free labor. In no heathen land has the toiler ceased to be a slave, or a serf, or a mere drudge and outcast. In Christian nations alone, have associations of workingmen for their own improvement and elevation, such as trades unions, and Knights of Labor, become possible. Even the Anarchist owes to a Christian State the free arm with which he is now blindly striking back at the mother which nourished him.

It would be interesting to trace historically the process by which such socialism has become alienated from the church and even from Christianity itself, and to survey its existing forms in different European countries, such as French communism, German social democracy, Russian nihilism, and international anarchism. At present, however, we need only take into view the amalgamated product as we find it in our own country. No easy task will it be to sift the confused materials of American socialism and trace their proper relations to the Christianity coexisting with them. They involve such a mixture of truth and error, right and wrong, good and evil, that it is difficult even to state fairly both sides of the question. At the same time, any overstatement or understatement alike might prove misleading and hurtful. Trusting that the reader will judge the arguments as a whole rather than in detached parts, I venture now to speak of the several kinds and grades of socialism which confront the American churches and with which they must soon come to an understanding.

ANTI-CHRISTIAN SOCIALISM.

The first is a thoroughly antichristian socialism which is loud and forward, but not formidable in numbers or influence. It is found chiefly among the French, German, Russian, Polish, and Hebrew refugees, known as "Internationalists," though it gains some strange recruits on our own soil. It means revolution as it waves the black and red flags, which have become so portentous emblems of violence and bloodshed. Avowedly, through all its organs, it aims to annihilate the Christian institutions of the church, the state, and the family, and to bring in pure anarchy, either as essential to the freedom of the individual or as a condition precedent to some reconstruction of society on industrial principles for the good of the workingman. By whatever subtle reasonings it vindicates to itself such ends, there can be no mistaking its means and methods. These are not arguments or even ballots, but the torch and the bomb as soon as they shall become practicable. Its incendiary journals plainly advocate arson, pillage, assassination, and hail the discovery of dynamite as a timely boon to the anarchist. Through its chief manifesto at Pittsburg it has declared that "the Church seeks to make complete idiots out of the masses by leading them to forego the paradise on earth for a fictitious heaven;" has advised workmen to the policy of "revolutionary conspiracy;" and has warned their oppressors that just before them are dawning "the scarlet and sable colors of the Judgment Day."

At first sight it would seem that Christianity could make no terms with such socialism, but must simply leave it in the grasp of the outraged law as an enemy of civilization no less than religion. Certainly men with arms in their hands are not open to reason, and dynamite cannot be met with argument. Nor will the issue be doubtful should anarchism ever rouse the great law-abiding mass of the people. But this is not precisely the most Christian mood in which to watch the struggle. Rather may such fanatics become the objects of pity and sorrow than of hatred. It should not be forgotten that the French anarchist and the Russian nihilist are the offspring of corrupt hierarchies and despotic governments; that generations of wrong and outrage are rankling in their blood; and that these hereditary strains are not to be checked at once even by an environment of free institutions. In their view the policeman, the capitalist, the clergyman, are only old oppressors in new guises. It is not necessary to persecute them, but only to make their existence unreasonable. If the churches cannot reach them with religious teaching and consolation, they may hope at least to arrest the growth of such madness in a free Christian land.

SPURIOUS CHRISTIAN SOCIALISM.

There is, secondly, a spurious Christian socialism, which falsely claims for itself religious doctrines and motives. It is a more American product than anarchism, though a remarkable form of it has been imported among us in the writings of the Russian Count Tolstoi. It expresses itself variously, not only in communistic associations which plead a scriptural warrant, but in labor fraternities which seek to indoctrinate as well as to organize the working masses. Its assumption is that Christ himself, as a workingman, founded industrial socialism; that he came to abolish poverty and other class distinctions; and that he now sides with the great labor movement in all its aims and efforts. Consistently it speaks of "Jesus the communistic Anarchist," sings hymns to "the Carpenter Christ," and applies the parable of Lazarus and Dives to the impoverished laborer and pampered capitalist.

The charge is sometimes made that this bastard form of Christian socialism has been misbegotten of the church itself, through its own neglect and sin. Workingmen, it is said, having been long treated as social outcasts by the respectable denominations, have learned to discriminate between the church as corrupted with wealth and worldliness and a plain Christianity retained by them as it came from the hands of its Author. Rashly seconding such views, the priest has left the altar and the minister his pulpit to lead a new crusade against the rich and preach another Gospel to the poor. Some self-sacrificing clergymen, under vows of poverty, have openly joined the ranks of the poor as a class to share their hardships and espouse their cause; whilst others from the pulpit and the platform are eloquently denouncing our luxurious, pewed churches as mere religious club-houses, and laying at their doors all the want, crime, and wretchedness which disgrace our civilization.

Such charges ought not to be lightly brought nor lightly tossed aside. If they seem to have little applicability to the rural districts, they can find only too much justification in our large cities, where vast accumulations of wealth, through the fashion and culture which wealth brings, tend to widen the breach between the social extremes and render even their religious intercourse uncongenial, if not impracticable. There is danger of exaggeration on both sides. Without extenuating the faults of wealthy congregations we should not forget their costly missions and personal efforts in the slums and at the frontiers. Without belittling the grievances of laboring men, we must remember that they are not the only class alienated from Christianity, but may be merely sharing in a general worldliness which rages outside of the churches far more fiercely than within them. After all that may be said there will remain the plain duty of distinguishing the true from a false Christian socialism. No one, high or low, rich or poor, can be interested in having evangelical truths caricatured and perverted.

CHRISTIAN DOCTRINE OF SOCIAL DISTINCTIONS.

As to the right Christian estimate of social distinctions, for example, nothing will ever be gained by telling only half the truth because the other half may be unpopular. It is simply a degradation of Holy Scripture, well meant, but thoughtless and mischievous, to dwell upon the incidents that our Saviour was the son of a carpenter, that some of his apostles were fishermen and his disciples taken largely from the common people, and then throw his glorious doctrine into the opposite scale as a mere makeweight for the want of social culture. It is bartering with the world upon its own terms, and no marvel if it be accepted as but the homage of envy. Besides, it is not founded on facts. The authors of such writings as the Gospels and Epistles could not have been wholly illiterate and rude. The truth is, that many of the distinctions of modern society did not exist among the ancient Hebrews. The prejudice against manual labor was little known, and avocations which are now simply respectable were then even honorable, associated with rank and learning. Every well-educated Jewish youth was taught some handicraft, and would have been disgraced without it. If St. Paul plied his trade of tent-making at Corinth, did he not show the culture of a scholar among the philosophers of Athens, the breeding of a gentleman at the court of Festus, and the patrician spirit of a Roman citizen before the magistrates of Philippi? Even that Divine Son of a carpenter himself, as his human genealogy shows, came of a lineage older than the Pharaohs or the Cæsars and purer than Castilian or Norman blood. At least a few high-born women and honorable personages were among his followers and stood by him when the crowd deserted him. Though he was meek and lowly in heart, his life was ever noble and gentle. A man of sorrows, yet at a wedding-feast he converted water into another beverage with exhilarating properties. A Saviour of harlots and lepers, yet in his perfect wisdom he became an honored guest at the banquets of the rich and worldly, while the Pharisees sneered at him as a gluttonous man and a wine-bibber. In the sorrowful moment of parting from his disciples, with infinite graciousness he took that cup which is the pledge of friendship the world over and taught them how to drink it to his memory. All through his insulted anguish, from the garden to the cross, he bore himself with unspeakable dignity, forbearance, and gentleness. At length Jewish austerity, Grecian culture, and Roman valor alike did him homage. And ever since, among his followers, the highest as well as the lowest ranks have been represented—kings and queens, scholars and soldiers, artists, poets, philosophers; not many wise, not many noble, but at least enough to show that Christianity is of no class or condition, and may as little become a boast of ignorance and vulgarity as a haughty claim of rank and culture.

Christian Doctrine of Poverty.

It is important also to discriminate sound Christian teaching as to the respective conditions of poverty and wealth. On this point scarcely can the merest truisms be uttered without danger of misapprehension. If there be sometimes a clerical sycophancy which pays court to the rich as patrons of religion, yet there is also a pulpit demagogism which flatters the poor as favorites of Heaven. To neither abuse do the Scriptures give the least countenance. The man with a gold ring and goodly apparel is not to have the highest place in the synagogue, nor yet are the needy masses to follow Christ merely for the loaves and fishes. On the one hand, no virtue or grace is ever attributed to simple poverty itself. Not the poor in this world, but the poor in spirit, the souls consciously needing truth and goodness, shall inherit the kingdom of heaven. Not mere physical penury, the being cold and hungry and naked, is most to be pitied, but that dire moral destitution which thinks itself rich when it is in need of all spiritual knowledge and grace and virtue. On the other hand, mere wealth is never stigmatized as a sin, or a crime. Not money itself, but the love of money, is the root of all evil. Not riches in themselves, but the making haste to get them and the setting the heart upon them, are to be deprecated. Moreover, neither extreme poverty nor extreme wealth is accounted favorable to piety and virtue. The poor, amid their cares and sorrows, are tenderly entreated to take no thought for food or raiment, but to trust in a heavenly Father, who feeds the birds of the air and clothes the lilies of the field. The rich, amid their luxuries and pleasures, are solemnly admonished that they may fall into temptation and into many foolish and hurtful lusts, which drown men in destruction and perdition. If the poor man, in his wretchedness and despair, is sometimes tempted to curse God and die, yet, the rich man in his glory and pride finds it proverbially hard to enter into the kingdom of God.

CHRISTIAN DOCTRINE OF PROPERTY.

Most of all has it become needful at this time to distinguish and re-assert the true Christian doctrine of property. We seem fast nearing a crisis in the strife between labor and capital. On the one side are the great national leagues of tradesmen and workmen organizing universal strikes and boycotts, and broaching the most revolutionary theories as to the origin and distribution of wealth; while on the other side are the vast, overgrown fortunes, which represent no just earnings of their owners, the oppressive corporations which are pressing wages down to the point of starvation, and the imperial monopolies which are controlling our elections and legislatures. Between these two mustered forces the voice of Divine wisdom speaks with no uncertain sound. For the capitalist it has some timely lessons. It charges them that are rich in this world that they be not high-minded nor trust in uncertain riches, and warns them that by the passion for money-getting some have erred from the faith and pierced themselves through with many sorrows. It teaches the millionaire that his wealth is not absolute property, but a sacred trust from the sovereign Creator for the good of his fellow-creatures, and if that trust be neglected or perverted the unfaithful steward shall lose even that which he seemeth to have. It requires of masters or employers that they use not their neighbor's services without just wages, nor let the sun go down upon his hire unpaid, nor cause him to do any work on the seventh day of rest. It denounces the usurer, who has increased his substance by unjust gain, built his house with unrighteousness, and filled his chambers with the spoil of the poor. By prophet and evangelist it foretells that Jehovah will be a swift witness against all that oppress the hireling in his wages, and calls upon rich men to weep and howl for the miseries that are to come upon them in the day when the cries of laborers, whose hire is kept back by fraud have entered into the ears of the Lord of Sabaoth. For the laborer also it has some needed counsels. It tells the working masses what Christ himself told them, that he came to preach the Gospel to the poor, not that he came to abolish poverty, and urges them to seek first the kingdom of God, and food and raiment and all good things shall be added to them. It exhorts all that are in service or at labor that they be faithful and diligent, treating their masters or employers as brethren, not with eye-service as men-pleasers, but in singleness of heart, fearing God, and having his blessing when they suffer wrongfully. The vagabond and the idler are warned that if any man will not work neither shall he eat, and that he that neglects to provide for his own household is worse than an infidel. The socialist agitator may learn that although Jesus told the rich young ruler to sell all he had and give to the poor, yet he did not tell either him or them that he was depriving the poor of their rights. The communist will find that the disciples at Pentecost did not deny the right of property in lands or goods, but merely offered in charity that which was their own freely to give or to withhold, and afterwards themselves became objects of the same charity in the churches. To the anarchist in his blind mood of vengeance the learned pulpit, the artistic ritual, the cathedral spire, may seem wasteful as the alabaster box with which Mary worshiped her Lord, but only another Judas could murmur that all this might be sold for much and given to the poor. Finally, for both laborer and capitalist there are those great perennial lessons of Christian brotherhood, sympathy, forbearance, charity, which alone can insure the moral concord of capital and labor, and at length reconcile and unite the poor and the rich as members of the one body of Christ and inmates of the temple whose maker is God.

Without adding more instances of such Christian teaching, we now have enough before us to show that the pseudo-Christian socialism consists not so much of positive errors as of partial truths, or truths forced out of their due proportions and relations in the general system of social doctrine. As the churches come in contact with such socialism—and some contact if not conflict is inevitable—they will have the important task of sifting truth from error, in order to throw themselves heartily into sympathy with the toiling masses along the line of their just grievances and sufferings. Of this enlightened sympathy we have already had noble examples in philanthropists, like Howard, Wilberforce, Raikes, Shaftesbury, Peabody, who have cared for prisoners, slaves, outcast women, homeless children, and houseless laborers; in zealous evangelists, like Wesley and Whitefield, who have preached to the neglected poor outside of the established churches; as well as in earnest churchmen, like Chalmers, Maurice, Kingsley, Toynbee, who have conducted industrial reforms not inconsistent with their churchmanship. Of such sympathy, too, we now have cheering expressions in church dignitaries like Cardinal Gibbons, the House of Bishops and other clerical assemblies, who are issuing timely counsels on the mutual rights and duties of laborers and employers; in faithful pastors and devoted laymen, who are maintaining chapels, schools, reading-rooms for employees in their hours of rest and recreation; and above all, in that intelligent body of Christian workingmen who have not thought it necessary to break away from their respective churches because they have joined labor organizations in efforts to relieve and elevate their fellow-laborers.

NON-CHRISTIAN SOCIALISM.

We come lastly to a non-Christian socialism, which is secular in its spirit and wholly economic in its aims. It is sometimes said that the mass of European socialists are secularists or atheists, whose religion consists in worshiping man as God and making our earth their only Heaven. The leaders of the socialistic labor party are monists or materialists. Without bringing such charges against our new nationalistic socialism, we may say that it has at least a lack of Christian elements, and consequently that such moral elements as it retains are somewhat perverted or defective. At the same time we shall find that it has no sympathy with anarchical or revolutionary socialism, since it expects to see society reformed and transformed peacefully and gradually by means of public opinion, and through existing modes of political action at the polls and in the legislature. Its spirit may best be shown by two popular treatises which are now selling by the hundred thousand copies.

The work of Mr. Henry George, entitled "Progress and Poverty," is written in so clear a style, depicts so boldly the wrongs and sufferings of laboring people, and is so full of humane sentiments and pathetic appeals in their behalf, that it would be much pleasanter to dwell upon its truths, than upon its errors. It is to be hoped that the latter will not neutralize the former. As we have left far behind us the age when obnoxious books were ordered to be burned by the hangman, every fair-minded citizen must approve a recent judicial decision legalizing the circulation of this volume. But many will not adopt one of the opinions upon which that decision was based, that there can be no immoral tendency in a work which teaches that it would be morally right for the people to seize all landed estates without paying anything for them or for the cost of maintaining them. Had Mr. George presented his scheme of nationalizing land or confiscating rent simply as an economic measure, to be effected with due regard to acquired rights and existing interests, it would have been at least debatable, and perhaps something might have been said in favor of it. But, unhappily, he has mixed with it ethical teachings which the Christian conscience cannot accept, and suggested popular movements which might prove as revolutionary as the general land-robbery of the dark ages.

In that pleasant social romance styled " Looking Backward," Mr. Edward Bellamy has brought Utopia as near to us as the next century, and thrown over it a color of probability by tracing its growth out of our own industrial system through the process of nationalizing railways, telegraphs, manufactures, all forms of business and modes of life. As we turn the fascinating pages there rises before us the image of our national government as a vast complex automaton, marshaling its millions of puppet-like citizens through their countless pursuits, under self-executing laws, with all the order and grace of the most faultless mechanism. But on looking a little more closely, we are ready to smile as grimly as the genial Dr. Leete himself when we find that somehow our old human depravity has disappeared in the process. Men have been made virtuous and happy by act of Congress; and the preacher of the twentieth century is informing his myriad hearers through the telephone that "the ten Commandments have become well-nigh obsolete," and with them all the crimes and miseries of former ages.

Of the political socialism represented by both of these works it should be said gladly, that its bearing towards Christianity is not unfriendly, though too silent and inappreciative. Mr. George, while he is wiser than some clerical recruits who are citing chapter and verse for his bad ethics, is always reverent in his few religious allusions. Mr. Bellamy even claims his perfect commonwealth to be a Christian ideal, but depicts it as having been achieved under the natural laws of social progress, through mere industrial and political expedients, not only without miraculous or providential agencies, but without the moral and religious means of social regeneration. These grave defects of nationalism are beginning to be felt in minds having no religious or sectarian bias. Mr. Frederic Harrison draws from the London strikes the lesson that "industry must be moralized by education, by morality, by religion—not recast by the State." Prince Bismarck, as the leader of political socialism in Germany, has been endeavoring to effect an alliance with Catholic socialism in favor of his scheme of national insurance for the laboring classes. As yet such measures have not become practical or practicable in our own politics. But it is safe to say that the genius of a Christian people will never allow its Christianity to be wholly divorced from its social reforms. And the emerging problem now is how to effect this coöperation consistently with our traditional theory of an absolute separation of church and state.

Church and State Socialism.

On the first view it would seem that our state-socialism and church-socialism, if such terms may be used, might come to a cordial understanding, at least as to their common aims, and largely as to their methods of attaining them. Since the church includes while it transcends the state in its scope, their spheres become coincident in respect to the whole physical and moral improvement of society. Such improvement, from the most religious point of view, is good as far as it goes; comes first in the order of nature, of opportunity, and of urgency; and is only part of the Christian conception of a more general improvement, embracing the spiritual with the material interests of humanity. In this common sphere have gradually arisen many practical questions in which all philanthropic citizens, both in and out of the churches, are interested, such as the relief of the poor and unemployed, the sanitary safety of their dwellings and workshops, the security of their Sundays, holidays, and daily hours of rest from labor; the rescue of young children from premature toil and vicious training; their education, physical, intellectual, moral, and industrial; the repression of the social vices of licentiousness, intemperance, gambling, and vagrancy; reform of the primary meeting, the caucus, the ballot, and suppression of bribery in elections and legislatures; civil service reforms; scientific legislation on social questions. As to all these and many other like objects the religious and the political socialist are already substantially agreed; but as to the best methods of reaching these objects they do not proceed far together before they begin to diverge along opposite lines of action. The Christian socialist of the old-fashioned school looks upon the State as a wholly worldly institution; limits its educational functions to such schools as may qualify the citizen for voting; cares little even for the Bible as obligatory in such schools; would not legislate beyond the public conscience on moral questions; and, in a word, would reserve for the churches all the higher education and humane effort, as likely to be spurious if not surcharged with evangelical doctrines and motives. On the other hand, the Christian socialist of the new nationalistic school looks upon the State as itself an educational and moral agency; claims for it the right to give the people the highest schools that they may desire for industrial and even professional training; advocates prohibitory laws against social vices; would nationalize all industries as fast as they become monopolistic; and in the end would render the government as humane and even Christian as the churches can make it. Fortunately, these differences as yet are more theoretical than practical, and the church-socialist and state-socialist may find large common ground where they can work together without collision or conflict.

It is important, however, to clear this common ground of some popular fallacies which are found in many forms of socialism of the non-Christian or secular type. Some of these fallacies have been inherited or imported from European states of society, but others are due to crude notions in economic science or to an abuse of our democratic institutions. They should be clearly and fearlessly exposed, in order to distinguish social grievances which are slight and imaginary from those which are real and urgent and the only proper object of a true Christian philanthropy.

The Masses and the Classes.

One very common fallacy is the false issue of the "masses against the classes." The phrase has more rhyme than reason. In one view the masses simply compose the classes. Even the so-called working masses have the class element in their trades unions, and express it in the very title of their "Noble Order of the Knights of Labor." Their most intelligent champions, such as Hendrik Ibsen and Powderly, have urged that they may oppose a genuine aristocracy of character and moral worth to the old aristocracies of birth, of wealth, and of learning. The more of such a class spirit we can get the better will it be for all classes. The fact would seem to be that our socialistic friends often use the word "class" when they mean "caste." In aristocratic countries, like England and Germany, where classes have long since hardened into castes with impassable barriers between them, the most radical socialism might have a plea and a mission; but not in a democratic country like ours, where the prizes of life are open to all classes, the lowest as well as the highest. With no law of primogeniture to keep wealth and power in the same families, every other generation is likely to be at the bottom of the wheel of fortune. Our millionaires with few exceptions, were laboring men, who did not inherit but made their money; and their menacing accumulations will soon become divided and squandered among their descendants, or perpetuated only in great beneficiary bequests; the ambition to found a college or library having taken the place of the old ambition to found a family and gain a title. In our politics, too, laboring men become the idols and rulers of the people, whilst trained statesmen take second places in their cabinets. One of our Presidents was a rail-splitter, another a tailor, another a boatman; and bootblacks, shoemakers, and blacksmiths have become potent in our highest legislatures. Our science and literature, also, are largely recruited from the ranks of toil, or pursued by men who can work with their brains only because their kindred before them have worked with their hands. Even in the most conspicuous circles of fashion the children or grand-children of workingmen are seen gracefully entertaining aristocratic visitors from the Old World, whilst descendants of our colonial gentry may be found living in poverty and obscurity. Good breeding thus becomes diffused with the wealth which fostered it, and workmen and tradesmen inherit the instincts of gentlemen. How absurd to talk of class tyranny in such a state of society? How futile any war against such classes. And how dismal would life be without them? Let us not confound political equality with social equality. We have abolished castes with all hereditary powers and privileges, but we can never abolish those classes which are rooted in the original diversities of human nature. Nor would any of us be quite ready for a socialism that should march through society cutting off every man's head that is an inch higher than his neighbor's.

CAPITALISTIC LABORING CLASSES.

Another fallacy is the false division of society into only the two classes, "the laborers and the capitalists." The classification, as often made, is crude, and easily becomes vague and misleading. There is no capitalistic class as opposed to a laboring class. Not only are the laborer and the capitalist always changing places through the vicissitudes of trade, but they are everywhere combined in the same persons and in the same classes. Many laborers are also capitalists. The workman who toils by the day saves out of his earnings enough capital to be invested in a homestead. The artisan, the engineer, the inventor, whose toil is even congenial, have a capital in their skill which may yield them larger returns than the salaries paid in the learned professions. The tradesman, the merchant, whose toil is almost luxurious, retire with the fortune of a millionaire. In like manner many capitalists are also laborers. The farmer whose capital is in land and implements, works harder and longer than many a mechanic. The lawyer, the doctor, the clergyman, whose capital is in knowledge, often die of sheer exhaustion as brain-workers. The manufacturer or the railway king, whose capital is in machinery or bonds, is sometimes more overworked than any of his employees or dependents. In fact, with the exception of a few idlers at both extremes of the social scale, the great mass of the American people, whether as capitalists or as laborers, are, in one way or another, working for their living. It is, therefore, scarcely possible to take sides either with labor or with capital. Every citizen is interested in their just cohesion, and in any so-called conflict between them might be found fighting against himself as well as against his neighbor.

DERANGEMENT OF SOCIAL CLASSES.

By far the most serious fallacy now current is a false predominance claimed for the laboring class over all other classes. It is a predominance not justified by the importance of any single class in the social system, and a predominance sometimes asserted against the peace and order of whole communities. We have seen the commerce of half a dozen Western States deranged and the traffic of our large cities hindered for days whilst a few workmen, at the call of one master workman, were parleying with their employers for better terms of employment. Such indifference or obliviousness to all other social interests is intelligible and excusable enough in men who for the time are absorbed in their own sufferings and intent only on getting their rights. But it makes a different impression in the formal manifesto and calm treatise. According to its platform the Socialistic Labor Party would exalt the manual laborer as the sole producer and owner of all existing wealth, and hope for some complete inversion or depression of the social classes in his behalf. Mr. Bellamy, in his ideal republic, would force all classes alike through long apprenticeships of manual toil before they can even be admitted to the higher forms of mental labor. This is trying to make the pyramid of society revolve from its apex to its base. Its material interests must ever remain subordinate to its moral and spiritual interests. A legislative rule of the laboring class, if established, could not be long maintained without Christian knowledge and virtue. Nor are we ready in this country to have any class dominant : not the wealthy class ; not the learned class ; not even the clerical class ; still less that laboring class, least fitted for leadership in all the higher spheres of civilization, such as education, science, art, and religion.

Having thus touched upon some of the socialistic fallacies of the day, we can now make them throw into stronger relief the real wrongs and sufferings of our laboring people. These will still assert themselves after all the abatements that have been made. Whilst it may be true, as we have seen, that the avenues to wealth and power are open to the lowest ranks, yet it is also true that only one person in sixty millions can become president; very few will win any of the other prizes for which so many are contending ; and the great mass must remain hewers of wood and drawers of water as effectually as if they were serfs and bondmen, and therefore as truly the objects of Christian kindness and care. Whilst it may be true that capital and labor are not antagonistic, yet labor is not now getting its full share of their joint product, owing to changed industrial conditions. Although spiritual interests are ever superior, yet material wants are still fundamental and first to be satisfied. American laborers, too, acquire more luxurious tastes than the European, and share more largely the average intelligence of the community. Becoming keen-sighted as to their interests, they are raising problems of which political economists had not dreamed, and forcing issues which our statecraft knows not how to meet. Let us remember that the brain-worker and the hand-worker are fellow-laborers and members of the same body politic. To make them also members of the same body of Christ has become the most difficult and momentous task ever laid upon the American churches.

Social Need of Church Unity.

If we now survey the social phenomena which the whole discussion has brought before us, we shall find our introductory statement more than justified. Within the limits of the same political system known as the United States we behold a confused mass of social organizations, detached from one another and from the government which overshadows and protects them. In the midst of them appears a great cluster of churches and denominations, differing endlessly in doctrine, polity, and worship, held apart by hereditary feuds, and inflamed with sectarian jealousy and pride. Around these Christian bodies, like a beleaguering army intrenched upon the very ground once belonging to them as their natural domain, are countless other social bodies without a Christian name or even a Christian spirit. To the right are the secularized charities for the poor, the blind, the deaf, the maimed, the fallen, and the outcast, on whom Christ lavished his miracles of love and power, and whom he bequeathed to the tender care of his followers through all time. To the left are the unchurched fraternities making a religion of masonry, fellowship, insurance, or practicing the Christian virtues of brotherhood, temperance, charity, under heathen names and with pagan rites. In front are the mustering hosts of insurgent labor no longer asking Christian charity but demanding natural justice, gaining recruits from the Christian ministry itself, and already threatening revolution, violence, and anarchy. At the rear are the retreating bands of rationalism, materialism, agnosticism, infidelity, turning Christian liberty into license and recoiling with random fire upon the ranks which they have deserted. Meanwhile the churches themselves, although thus out-flanked on each side, desperately assailed in front and treacherously weakened in the rear, still stand asunder, without union, without discipline, without enthusiasm against their common foes. Add to all this that just now, at the very height of these encompassing perils, they are engaged in fresh disputes over their respective creeds and forms, and we have the actual situation of the Christian denominations in American society at the present time.

Upon this situation I remark in general that mere Christian unity, the so-called unity of the invisible church, does not meet the social exigency of the churches. The simple fact that they are all Christian sects, composed largely of true Christians loyal to Christ, means no more to the point than that they are like so many wrangling masses of patriots before a disciplined army of invaders and traitors. The invisible unity of the denominations must become visible, potent, and aggressive. They can never rout their common foes by sallying among them single-handed or in scattered bands. They can never cope with the social perils around them until they have some outward agreement, some concentrated leadership, some concerted action; in a word, some organic unity.

THE CHURCH A GREAT SOCIAL TEACHER.

In the first place, without organic unity the Church cannot fulfil its mission as the great moral teacher of society. If it is to become the light of the world, it must illuminate the social relations and duties of men as members of the family and of the State no less than of the Church itself. But in order thus to instruct the multitudes still outside the denominations, mere denominational teaching is not needed. Such teaching, in fact, has proved a hindrance and a failure. The missionary abroad sends back to us word that he cannot preach a sectarian gospel to the heathen; and the missionary at home tells us the same tale. The untaught masses think they do not want a sectarian Christianity, and they are right. How can the denominations teach them Christian brotherhood when they do not themselves treat one another as brethren? How can they teach Christian spirituality when they are scrambling together for worldly place and power? How can they teach the plainest Christian doctrines and duties when they are ever visibly subordinating them to sectarian dogmas and sectarian aggrandizement? If each of the fifty sects could accomplish its aim and plant an endowed church in every frontier village and in every city mission, what a babel of religious teaching they would make, and how the objects of such teaching would laugh them to scorn. Yet something like this is passing before their eyes. Moreover, at a time when the wildest notions are abroad in respect to the social problems of the day, it becomes imperative that the denominations as one Church should utter forth one accordant voice in the name of their common Head and Lord.

The Church the Conservator of Society.

In the second place, without organic unity the Church cannot perform its whole duty as the conservator of society. That it may act as the salt of the earth it must purge the divine institutions of the family and state as well as the church itself, from the corrupting influences and revolutionary assaults to which they are now exposed. But in thus concentrating its purifying agencies upon the social masses mere denominational evangelism will not alone suffice. It does not reach the physical and moral degradation which prevent them from even appreciating spiritual truths and influences. To attempt first to indoctrinate them, or even to evangelize them, is to begin at the end. They feel that they do not want church or gospel so much as fire, food, raiment, and shelter; and they cannot get the former until they have the latter. If the American Evangelical Alliance should accomplish its noble work, and by systematic visitation gather back all the scattered sheep of Christ into their proper folds, it will not have touched directly a single one of the social problems now pressing for solution. Not the mere indoctrination of the toiling masses, were it possible, is first and most needed; not alone their evangelization as now attempted; but their moralization, the practical application of Christian ethics among them, as Christ himself practiced them, in care for their bodies as well as their souls, in eleemosynary, sanitary, and educational reforms. And for such works of charity how wasteful, as well as absurd, are denominational divisions and sectarian efforts. It seems but a truism to say that in order to preserve the family in safe dwellings and pure homes among all classes, in order to preserve the State by means of honest politics at the polls and in legislatures, in order to preserve the Church itself amid the manifold perils which now menace it,—the denominations cannot act apart, but if possible must act together as one united Church.

The Church the Social Regenerator.

In the third place, without organic unity the Church cannot accomplish its destiny as the regenerator of society. Being itself a new social organism with new organizing forces, it must yet include and transform the organisms of the family and the State, as but smaller spheres within its own grander sphere, which is as wide as humanity itself. But in approaching this promised ideal a mere coöperation or confederation of denominations falls far short of the mark. Such a league may be a first step, but it cannot be the last. It would not exhibit the Church to the world as in itself a regenerate society, and it would not embrace surrounding society in its regenerative influence. It would be a cluster of class churches, not one church of all classes. It would still subordinate church unity to mere denominationalism, not denominationalism to true church unity. And it would soon prove to have been a mere makeshift of worldly expediency rather than the perfect bond of Christian charity. Like the Confederate States, which could not exist long either before or after the United States, such confederate churches could only suggest and require some more perfect union of denominations as one catholic Church.

CHURCH UNITY BECOMING PRACTICABLE.

In the fourth place, such a true church unity is becoming intelligible and practicable in American society. While the Christian denominations, as they appear in the Old World, still exist as established churches and dissenting bodies incapable of unification, the same denominations as transferred to the New World, and brought under democratic influences, have been sifted together for a hundred years and assimilated until now they differ less in things than in names. Such differences are fast disappearing from public view. The long lost ideal of one catholic Church is seizing the popular mind like a passion and melting away all prejudices before it. Already it is emerging from the utopian stage in which great social movements often first appear to the generation originating them. It may have been utopian to look for a dogmatic agreement of different denominations, or even for a dogmatic agreement in any one denomination. This never existed in the church of the apostles, and could only exist in the church of the millennium, if it ever exist at all. But it is no longer utopian to look for an ecclesiastical unity which shall embrace dogmatic differences and allow them due scope and action. Such a unity once prevailed. In the New Testament church there were no Episcopalian, Presbyterian, and Congregationalist denominations, but only congregational, presbyterial, and episcopal principles and institutions as duly combined in one organization. That Catholic and Apostolic Church might now return if our congregations would associate in free presbyteries, our presbyteries commit their episcopal functions to bishops, and our bishops become conjoined in the same historic succession, whatever views might be held as to the need or value of that succession. The most extreme degrees of churchmanship, as well as the most varied forms of denominationalism, would be retained and satisfied in such an ecclesiastical system. If this be utopian, then is Christianity itself utopian. Can that unity be impracticable in religious society which has already become actual in political society? We have lived to see the most diverse climates, north, south, east, and west; the most diverse races, European, African, American, Asiatic; the most diverse institutions, social, civil, political, religious; the most varied nationalities, English, French, German, with the most embittered factions, all merged in the United States; and are we never to see the so-called Christian denominations combining as united churches in one American Catholic Church?

Finally, a true church unity is becoming urgent, if not imminent. That we are on the eve of great social changes is a growing feeling. Our democratic institutions are passing under a strain such as they have never before known. According to historical analogy, one sign of revolution is the very blindness and recklessness of those who should be the first to perceive and avert it. Among the polemic divines now mustering to fight their battles over again this appeal for unity may sound like a shepherd's flute amid the din of arms. But communities, like individuals, are sometimes driven by their very passions and interests into the paths of truth and righteousness. The pressure of surrounding perils may soon hasten the tardy impulses of Christian duty. The churches may yet be melted together in the furnace of affliction. When the events so often threatened begin to happen; when our railways and telegraphs have been paralyzed by national strikes; when workmen and soldiers are fighting or fraternizing in the streets of our cities; when our hoarded capital is outvoted by leagued labor; when our servile legislatures are discussing the very measures first broached in the Assembly of the French Revolution; when science and literature and art are at the mercy of ignorance and rudeness, and virtue and piety have been scared back to our homes and altars—then, at least, will it have become plain that the problems of American society, if solved at all, can only be solved by one United Church of the United States.

www.ingramcontent.com/pod-product-compliance
Lightning Source LLC
Chambersburg PA
CBHW032048230426
43672CB00009B/1512